Barbara Steiner: The Captured Museum

Barbara Steiner

THE CAPTURED MUSEUM

On CARTE BLANCHE:
A Research Project by the
Museum of Contemporary Art
Leipzig

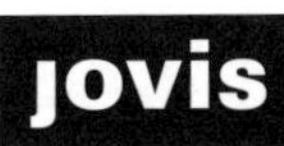

Preface

In 2008 and 2009, the Galerie für Zeitgenössische Kunst/Museum of Contemporary Art Leipzig (GfZK) invited eleven private individuals and enterprises, including one circle of friends and two commercial galleries, to illustrate their commitment to art in the form of exhibitions, thereby drawing it to the attention of the public. They agreed to pay the expenses of their own exhibition and also contributed towards advertising, communication and the running costs of the institution. In addition, they provided funding for a joint opening exhibition. The GfZK put its infrastructure at their disposal, along with the services of its curators.

This book, entitled *The Captured Museum*, analyses the individual contributions of the private partners and defines their position as regards art and art history in greater detail. This also applies to the definition of the museum's position. Who (still) needs it, and what for? Whose interests does it serve? Who are its supporters, in an ideational as well as in a material sense? The title of the book, *The Captured Museum*, indicates a conflict within this context. At the same time, however, it should be understood as an invitation to become involved in debates surrounding the museum and its orientation and, if need be, to win back the museum one desires.

I would like to thank all the private collectors, enterprises, galleries and the Hans Brosch Circle of Friends for having the courage to take part in the project, my colleagues for joining me in exposing themselves to the discussions surrounding a controversial project, and the GfZK librarian, Brigitte Schöppner, for her support in literary research. Special thanks to the designers Kay Bachmann, Markus Dreßen and Philipp Paulsen for a convincing graphic interpretation of a complex project.

The Captured Museum is financed mainly from public funds. In this way, it is possible to (again) link private commitment with public agendas. Not least however it allows us to carry out a fundamental part of the project; after two years of working on the realisation of the series of exhibitions, we can return to a conceptual level, not only to evaluate the social and discursive results of *Carte Blanche*, but also to document them. At this point I would like to thank the Ministry for Science and Arts in Saxony for generously supporting the *Captured Museum*.

Barbara Steiner

Corruption, Corruptibility and Complicity

Corruption, Corruptibility and Complicity [1]

1. From Critique to Complicity

Held at the Pat Hearn Gallery in New York in 1986, the panel discussion *From Criticism to Complicity* between Sherrie Levine, Ashley Bickerton, Jeff Koons, Heim Steinbach, Philip Taaffe and Peter Halley, dealt with how art and the artist interrelate with consumerism and the desires that this generates.[2] The debate was based on the premise that the artist is necessarily involved in capitalist structures, and works were cited that address this issue. It was also in 1986 that Brian O'Doherty, author of *Inside the White Cube: The Ideology of the Gallery Space*, noted that the 1980s elicited 'the ironic turn of history', as 'everything that had been subject to critical analysis earlier on, was now subject to intense affirmation. Commodities and consumerism had become fashionable again [...].' The book ends with the conclusion that 'the elusive and precarious art from the period between 1964–1976, as well as its messages, have disappeared.'[3]

Considering the scope of exhibitions and projects available to the public at the time – such as *documenta VII* in Kassel and the *Zeitgeist* exhibition in Berlin, both in 1982, and the exhibition titled *An International Survey of Recent Painting and Sculpture* on the occasion of the MoMA's reopening in 1984 – it seems that a revision of critical artistic positions was taking place, fostering a more corroborative view of art.[4] With respect to these developments, American art theoretician and critic Douglas Crimp noted that '[...] there has been a concerted effort to suppress this fact [of an intensification of the critique of art's institutionalization, a deepening of the rupture with modernism] and to re-establish the traditional fine art categories by all conservative forces of society, from cultural bureaucracies to museum institutions, from corporate boardrooms to the marketplace for art.'[5] Above all, he focuses on the willingness of artists and art institutions to collude, stating that 'this has been accomplished with the complicity of a new breed of entrepreneurial artists, utterly cynical in their disregard of both recent art history and present political reality.'[6] Crimp views the inaugural exhibition on the occasion of the MoMA's reopening and the financial support offered by the AT&T Corporation as prime examples of this paradigmatic shift. In his text, he quotes the inaugural speech by the director of MoMA: 'AT&T clearly recognizes that experiment and innovation, so highly prized in business and industry, must be equally valued and supported in the arts.'[7] Not only does the museum, in this case one of the world's most prominent museums, open itself up toward the economy, but rather, corporations and the museum seek to cooperate so as to create a mutual space of 'experimentation' and 'innovation'. This at least suggests that both parties engage in comparable activities. In *Postmodernism, or, the Cultural Logic of Late Capitalism* (1991), Fredric Jameson described this as a significant

[1] The text with the same title was published in a reader on the work of Liam Gillick in 2009. Barbara Steiner, 'Corruption, Corruptibility and Complicity', in: Monika Szewczyk (ed.), *Meaning Liam Gillick*, Massachusetts/London 2009. Written back then and intended for publication in the present book, the original text has been partly adapted and substantially extended.

[2] 'From Criticism to Complicity', in: *Flash Art*, no. 129, 1986, pp. 46–9. Art was already considered as commercialised from the very outset – in contrast to Andy Warhol, who first infused the world of commerce into the field of art and high culture.

[3] Brian O'Doherty, Afterword, in: Wolfgang Kemp (ed.), *Inside the White Cube* [1976], Berlin 1996, p. 136 ff.

[4] This development can also be seen parallel to an increasing political conservatism in the United States and in the majority of countries in Western Europe.

[5] Douglas Crimp, 'The Art of Exhibition' [1984], in: *On the Museum's Ruins*, Cambridge/London 1997, p. 272

[6] Of course that doesn't mean that before there were never any 'corruptible' artists. But they were discussed and critiqued as individual cases. However, by insisting on artistic autonomy it was possible to define and maintain idealised boundaries, which de facto did not necessarily exist.

[7] Crimp, op. cit., p. 272

phenomenon of late capitalism: '[...] the *cultural* and the *economic*, thereby collapse back into one another and say the same thing [...] it seems to obligate you in advance to talk about cultural phenomena at least in business terms if not in those of political economy.' [8]

[8] Fredric Jameson, *Postmodernism, or, The Cultural Logic of Late Capitalism*, Durham/NC 1991. Jameson's book was predicated on an essay, which he wrote in 1984 for publication in the *New Left Review*.

When Thomas Krens became the director of the Solomon R. Guggenheim Foundation in 1988, he basically adapted the economic model of franchising, applying it to the museum. Subsequently, 'The Guggenheim' expanded from New York to Venice, Bilbao, Berlin and Las Vegas. [9]

[9] Today, there are a total of four Guggenheim Museums in New York, Venice, Bilbao and Berlin, with a fifth Guggenheim being planned in Abu Dhabi. Inaugurated in 1992, the Guggenheim SoHo in the New York suburb of SoHo became a Prada flagship store after it closed down in 2002. The Guggenheim Hermitage in Las Vegas, which cooperated with the Hermitage in St. Petersburg, was inaugurated in 2000 and shut down in 2008. A series of projects in other cities was unsuccessful or was put on ice in the meantime. Towards the end of his career, Krens's most important project was the Guggenheim Museum in Abu Dhabi, which is reported to be inaugurated in 2013. Again, the architect is Frank O. Gehry. However, the real estate/financial crisis has stifled these ambitious objectives.

[10] To name just two famous architects, the Guggenheim Museum Bilbao and the Guggenheim Hermitage Museum at The Hotel Venetian in Las Vegas were designed by Frank O. Gehry and Rem Koolhaas respectively. Concerning museum architecture Krens says, 'It's important to impress. For a long time I looked for a symbol for the "contemporary museum". When we began planning the museum in Bilbao, our architect, Frank Gehry, asked me if there was anything particular I wanted the building to be. I said, basically I want Chartres Cathedral [...].' Ulrike von Knöfel, Ariane von Dewitz, 'Atemberaubend, riesig, pharaonisch' (Breathtaking, gigantic, pharaonic), in: *Der Spiegel*. www.spiegel.de/spiegel/print/d-56299164.html, 22.3.2008. Designed by architect Richard Gluckman and situated on Unter den Linden in Berlin, the converted building accommodating the Deutsche Bank capital city headquarters and the Deutsche Guggenheim gallery is comparatively unspectacular.

[11] However, Krens's expansion policy was highly disputable, and led to Peter B. Lewis, head of the Guggenheim Foundation's supervisory board, issuing an admonishment in 2005. Although Krens at first prevailed, he suddenly withdrew from office in 2008. He had come under too much pressure. Carol Vogel, 'Guggenheim's Provocative Director Steps Down', in: *The New York Times*. www.nytimes.com/2008/02/28/arts/design/28muse.html?_r=1, 20.2.2008

[12] Charles Esche, 'Eine Erziehungseinrichtung, eine computerisierte Datenbank der Kulturgeschichte, ein Träger für Aktionen' (An educational centre, a computerised database of cultural history, a means of action), in: Barbara Steiner & Charles Esche (eds.), *Mögliche Museen* (Possible museums), Cologne 2007, p. 28

Commissioning internationally celebrated architects guaranteed enormous instant publicity, and also helped coin the term 'Bilbao effect' to describe the enhancement of a particular location by means of spectacular buildings designed by star architects. [10] Furthermore, redefining the Guggenheim and developing it as a global 'brand' enabled Krens, amongst other things, to settle longer term contracts with Deutsche Telekom, the clothing corporation Boss and the Deutsche Bank, as well as consolidate its connections to influential, affluent collectors. [11] In so doing, he intentionally capitalised on art's aura and uniqueness, an approach about which Charles Esche, director of the Van Abbe Museum in Eindhoven, remarked some twenty years later, '[...] the Guggenheim [stands] for the attempt to transfer art's status of autonomy onto other matter, by accumulating the pious aloofness and perfection emanating from such rare and unique commodities.' [12] Here, Esche is referring to exhibitions at the Guggenheim of Harley Davidson motorcycles and Armani dresses. Incidentally, Crimp also identified that the inaugural exhibition marking the MoMA's reopening sought to capitalise on the autonomous aesthetic object. He, clairvoyantly, saw a simple correspondence between attempts at decontextualising art and prioritising aesthetic experience in terms of a specific set of interests, which are not only obscured by the demand for an autonomous aesthetic, but which also seek to selectively exploit the myth of artistic creativity as occurring independently of preconditions, history or context. [13→]

2. Unintentional Complicity

Above all during the 1960s and 70s, the structural authorities of the art world were key areas of artistic investigation. Daniel Buren, an artist whose work explicitly deals with the structural frameworks of art and the formats via which art is shown and seen, accused painting of 'shroud[ing] its own method' as well as 'the field of reference (location) within which it stands (museum/gallery)'.[14] By concealing their field of social reference consequently led to the museum and the gallery taking their isolation for granted, thus becoming 'a mythical and deforming frame for everything presented within its bounds'.[15] To avoid this from happening, one would have to 'examine both the formal as well as the cultural framework (and not merely the one or the other)'.[16] Buren's theoretical and practical designs sought to attack naturalised concepts of art and space. These denied any bias toward special interests and suppressed social and historical contexts in order to strengthen the 'predominant ideology' whereby 'the artist is responsible for leisure and distraction'.

In 1970, Buren stated that 'freedom in art' is 'the luxury and prerogative of a repressive society'.[17] Applied both inside and outside the museum, Buren's serial coloured stripes cite their origin within everyday contexts, whilst precisely delineating the institutional, historical and social frameworks pertaining to art, which Buren refers to in his writings.[18] At that time, numerous other artists were also critically examining the 'mythical and deforming frame' within which art is produced, presented, distributed and contemplated. The analysis of the exhibition space's physical components extended to issues of political, economic and social space. Conversely, the white exhibition space was transformed into a stage and space in which to articulate issues concerning language, education or politics. In many of their projects and exhibitions, these artists referred to the interconnection of art with other areas of society, as well as to the politics of power – thus raising issues of inclusion and exclusion. In this way, the critical analysis of art institutions progressively extended to also include the institution of art. First and foremost, this continued to involve critiquing museums and galleries, but also other

[13] Crimp obliquely extends the critical stance – prevalent above all in the 1960s and 1970s – which perceived the urge of 'autonomous' art to ignore its immediate exploitability and functionality, as an either deliberate or unintentional, yet de facto always prevalent form of complicity with hegemonic (mostly conservative bourgeois) values and ideals. Herbert Marcuse, 'Über den affirmativen Charakter der Kultur' (The Affirmative Character of Culture), in: *Kultur und Gesellschaft I* (Culture and Society I), Frankfurt am Main 1965, pp. 66 & 67; Jürgen Habermas, *Legitimationsprobleme im Spätkapitalismus* (Legitimation Problems in Late Capitalism), Frankfurt am Main 1973, p. 110; Peter Bürger, *Theorie der Avantgarde*, Frankfurt am Main 1974, p. 63. Crimp extends this critique of the instrumentalisation of art to include interests in economic utilisation. Brian O'Doherty adopts a similar view, when he writes '[...] and this is not the first time that aesthetic idealism and the art market vouch for exactly the same interests.' O'Doherty, op. cit., p. 136

[14] The unabridged version of the quote is as follows: 'In the same way, this type of painting, which shrouds its own method is also obviously deceptive about the field of reference (location) within which it stands (museum/gallery). This type of painting considers this to be a neutral background and undercoat having no influence on the work and its subject matter.' Daniel Buren, 'Limites/Critiques' [1970], in: *Daniel Buren* (exh. cat. Staatsgalerie Stuttgart), Ostfildern 1990, p. 275

[15] Buren: 'If we do not draw into consideration the location (of the museum or gallery) or if we take it to be a natural given, then it becomes a mythical and deforming frame for everything presented within its bounds.' Ibid., p. 277

[16] Ibid., p. 290. The artist's studio is not exempted from this: '[...] the museum and gallery on the one hand and the studio on the other are linked to form the foundation of the same edifice and the same system. To question one while leaving the other intact accomplishes nothing.' Furthermore: '[...] it is the first frame, the first limit, upon which all subsequent frames/limits will depend.' Daniel Buren, 'The Function of the Studio' [1971], in: *October 10*, Autumn 1979, pp. 51–8, p. 51. This is one of three texts dealing with the formative systems of artistic practice. The other two texts were 'The Function of the Museum' [1970] and 'The Function of an Exhibition' [1973].

[17] Buren, op. cit., 1990, p. 290

[18] In the project *Position – Proposition*, which Buren carried out in 1971 at the invitation of the Mönchengladbach Municipal Museum, the artist linked 'formal' and 'cultural' frameworks. His work was based on the Mönchengladbach Municipal Museum and various other interior and exterior spaces in a variety of cities in the Lower Rhine and Ruhr regions. Buren glued strips of white and blue striped paper over the walls of the Municipal Museum – the same stripes as on Mönchengladbach's public buses. The areas where works from the preceding exhibition had hung before were left uncovered. The exhibition extended out over and beyond the museum – a variety of activities were announced and launched in unison in the respective participating cities of the Lower Rhine. Their outcomes differed, depending on the type of project, the weather or the extent of destruction.

contexts, ranging from art periodicals to public spaces, as well as questions of production, reception and discourse. [19]

Almost thirty years later, Andrea Fraser describes precisely this process of expansion as a key shift in the work of artists practicing institutional critique: 'Moving from a substantive understanding of "the institution" as specific places, organizations and individuals to a conception of it as a social field, the question of what is inside and what is outside becomes more complex.'[20] As an institution in its own right, art represented a social and historical product, a discursive convention and a powerful construction promoting the cultural dominance of specific advocacy groups.

Furthermore, art could be understood as a disposition (*dispositif*) in the Foucauldian sense, namely as 'a decidedly heterogeneous ensemble incorporating a range of discourses, institutions, architectural fittings, regulatory decisions, laws, administrative measures, scientific declarations, philosophical, moral or philanthropic theorems, in a word, both the said and the unsaid.' [21] In 1974 Hans Haacke examined the issue of unintentional complicity between artists and their 'supporters': '"Artists" as much as their supporters and their enemies, no matter of what ideological coloration, are unwitting partners in the art syndrome and relate to each other dialectically. They participate jointly in the maintenance and/or development of the ideological make-up of their society. They work within that frame, set the frame and are being framed.'[22] Haacke's artworks publicly relay this frame and its intrinsic power mechanisms, revealing conspiracies involving art, corporations and state organisations as a means to advocate the integrity of the museum and protect it from being absorbed by political and economic interests. On many occasions Haake publicly opposed the system he was critiquing, and often had to endure censorship and disapproval as a result. [23] Thirteen years later, in 1987, the artist Barbara Kruger addressed that she too, as an artist, was necessarily involved in the market structures of capitalism: 'The fact that we survive by exchange means that our lives are encompassed by a market that is erratic, virulent, horrendously pervasive. To ignore this, to argue that there's a way around it, is the privilege of a person with an inheritance or a tenured job. [...] I'm just trying to be in the world. Because if my work is not tested by this reality – by the labor and exchange conditions of the market – then it might be

[**19**] Cf. above all the works by Dan Graham, which investigate the reciprocal relationship between the gallery and the magazine. Magazines are points of reference, defining the work's referential context and 'functioning equally both as art and as art criticism'. Dan Graham, 'Meine Arbeiten für Zeitschriftenseiten – Eine Geschichte der Konzeptkunst' (My Works for Magazine Pages: A History of Conceptual Art), in: Ulrich Wilmes (ed.), *Dan Graham. Ausgewählte Schriften* (Dan Graham. Selected Writings), Stuttgart 1994, p.18. See also Michael Asher's work for the Skulpturenprojekte exhibition in Münster in 1977. His installation *Münster (Caravan)*, which involved parking a caravan in constantly different locations in the city, departed from the idea of an artwork's conceptual and perceptual frames. These frames are decisive in determining the status of the object, for instance whether or not we are dealing with an abandoned caravan or a work of art, which functions as a tool and provides information concerning the relationship of the artwork to its respective location and surroundings. See also: Martha Rosler, 'Lookers, Buyers, Dealers, and Makers: Thoughts on Audience', in: Brian Wallis (ed.), *Art After Modernism: Rethinking Representation*, New York 1999, pp. 311–40

[**20**] Andrea Fraser, 'From the Critique of Institutions to an Institution of Critique', in: *Artforum*, no.1, Sept. 2005, pp. 278–83, p. 281

[**21**] Michel Foucault, *Dispositive der Macht. Über Sexualität, Wissen und Wahrheit* (Dispositifs of Power. On Sexuality, Knowledge and Truth), Berlin 1978, p. 119 ff.

[**22**] Hans Haacke, 'All the Art That's Fit to Show', in: A.A.Bronson & Peggy Gale (eds.), *Museum by Artists*, Toronto 1983, p. 152

[**23**] Fraser on Haacke: 'It may be Haacke, above all, who evokes characterizations of the institutional critic as an heroic challenger, fearlessly speaking truth to power – and justifiably so, as his work has been subject to vandalism, censorship, and parliamentary showdowns.' Fraser, op.cit., p. 283. In 1971, the director of the Solomon R. Guggenheim Museum in New York, Thomas Messer, cancelled Haacke's solo exhibition at the museum six weeks before the opening. The reason for this was Haake's work entitled *Shapolsky et al. Manhattan Real Estate Holdings, A Real Time Social System, as of May 1* (1971), which revolves around real estate ownership and speculation. At that time, members of the Guggenheim Museum board of trustees were allegedly involved in the real estate deals documented by Haacke in his work. The curator of the exhibition, Edward Frey, was dismissed from his job.

The Captured Museum   Corruption, Corruptibility and Complicity

politically correct, but I'd be deluded.' [24] Here, Kruger was defending herself against those who accused her of switching sides and of ignoring her own critical practice of many years. The reason was that she and Sherrie Levine had joined a commercial gallery in New York that was rated as uncritical. The works of both Barbara Kruger and Sherrie Levine deal with mass media imageries, advertising and branding, as well as how these categories apply to art, and therefore mark the narrow divide between the temptations expressed by mass media imagery and their critical analysis. Thus, from the outset, their works are deliberately developed in close proximity to capitalist culture, a fact that, already in 1982, caused Benjamin Buchloh in his essay *Allegorical Procedures: Appropriation and Montage in Contemporary Art* to perceive that these artists were inadvertently involved with an all-absorbing capitalistic market and its gluttonous logic of innovation. [25] Similarly, Hal Foster criticised certain methods of artistic appropriation. He writes: '[...] appropriation becomes problematic not only because it implies a truth beyond ideology and a subject (e.g., a critic or an artist) free of it, but because it is predicated on the logic of the sign, not a critique of it. [...] As they shake the sign, contest the code, they may only manipulate signifiers within it and so replicate rather than dismantle this logic.' [26]

In view of these pivotal debates in the 1980s, James Meyer, in the final chapter of his essay entitled 'What Happened to the Institutional Critique? (1993), posits questions concerning the possibility of critical practice in the 1990s: 'What does the artist base his/her practice on in the age of late capitalism? [...] Which alternative situations are available to cultural practitioners as a result?' He proceeds to describe the dilemmas artists are faced with today. [27] Though viewed by Meyer as plausible alternatives to market-oriented art, activist practices too, are ultimately forced to operate within the coordinates of capitalism. [28] Meyer does, however, justify the role of activism within the 'commodity system' as a strategic necessity in order to achieve specific (political) goals. With reference to ACT UP (AIDS Coalition To Unleash Power) he stresses the fact that 'ACT UP's videos, T-shirts, which were produced by the group, primarily had an effect outside the gallery. If they played a part within the commodity system then they did so only in terms of the fight against AIDS.' [29→] Thus, Meyer draws a distinction between the art market and the activities of cultural politics. However, with reference to Bordowitz, he also describes the fundamental difficulties of the relationship between the artist/activist and the economic regulatory

[24] Barbara Kruger in conversation with Douglas Crimp, Abigail Solomon-Godeau, Krzysztof Wodiczko et al., 'Discussion', in: Hal Foster (ed.), *Discussions in Contemporary Culture*, Seattle 1987, p. 52

[25] On Levine the following has been stated: 'The risk of Levine's position is that it might function ultimately in secret alliance with the static conditions of social life as they are reflected in an art practise that is concerned only with the work's commodity structure and the innovation of its product language.' Benjamin H.D. Buchloh, 'Allegorical Procedures: Appropriation and Montage in Contemporary Art', in: *Artforum*, Sept. 1982, pp. 43–56, p. 48 ff. By re-enacting and photographing them again, Levine appropriated photographs by famous (male) photographers. The titles of her works refer to the appropriated images according to the following pattern: *Sherrie Levine, [title of the original work], After [the respective artist's name, e.g., Walker Evans, Edward Weston, etc.], present date.* Levine's photographic re-enactments/reproductions served to subvert the laws of the market and its objective of fetishising an inherently reproducible medium to the ends of high prices. Furthermore, as the new 'author', Levine overwrote the works of her male colleagues. Kruger made use of a graphically powerful visual vocabulary, quoting advertising's attention-seeking modes of visual communication to convey her message of gender critique and anti-consumerism. A famous example is *I shop therefore I am* from 1987. Today, works by both Kruger and Levine sell at high prices on the art market.

[26] Hal Foster, 'Readings in Cultural Resistance', in: *Recordings. Art, Spectacle, Cultural Politics*, Seattle 1985, p. 173 ff.

[27] Meyer, 'What happended to the Institutional Critique?' [1993], reprinted in: Peter Weibel (ed.), *Kontext Kunst*, Köln 1994, p. 252 & 253

[28] For him 'institutional critique (both in its classical as well as extended form), and activism (with which he combines the former) remain [...] the most convincing strategies for a definition of an art which claims to be political.' Ibid., p. 253

[29] Ibid., p. 252. To distribute its critical message, the activist group *Gran Fury* deliberately deployed graphic support systems and visual languages used in advertising. 'Kissing Doesn't Kill' (1989–1990) referred explicitly to the aesthetic employed by Benetton, however using it to campaign for a non-discriminatory AIDS policy. The group's work could be seen on public billboards and buses. Richard Meyer: 'This Is to Enrage You: Gran Fury and The Graphics of AIDS Activism', in: Nina Felshin (ed.), *But is it Art? The Spirit of Art as Activism*, Seattle 1995, pp. 51–83

[30] 'The intended place of his work's reception is the television broadcast, he often emphasised. But even if he were subsidised by public television channels (considering the "controversial" nature of his work this is unlikely), this support would be anything but pure. Art foundations and museums that depend on a pressurised NEA or affluent patrons are similarly problematic.' James Meyer, op. cit., p. 252

[31] Ibid., p. 252 ff.

framework with which he/she is forced to comply. Although Bordowitz had, in a narrower sense, left the art world to work at GMHC (Gay Men's Health Crisis) and ACT UP, there, he also had to confront questions of financing as well as the occasionally rather contaminated interests upon which these questions are based. [30] Meyer asks: 'Yet what is the power of economic resistance today? Is poverty a guarantee of a given practice's integrity or seriousness? On the other hand, the fact that certain kinds of practice are readily commodified – take, for instance a work from a nineteenth-century *salon* – could indicate a lack of commitment. It is not easy to answer these questions. As [Barbara] Kruger suggests, even something, which "doesn't sell", is potentially marketable. This is demonstrated by Duchamp's *ready-mades*, which ultimately became commodities as well, or by artistic "de-materialising practices" in the 1960s.' [31] The author basically describes how hard it is to critique an infinitely flexible capitalist system, and how readily one becomes the accomplice of such a system, although originally, one intended to achieve precisely the opposite. Moreover, Meyer's insights can be applied retrospectively, to better understand critical practice of the 1960s and 1970s. For the urge to instil new and different functions into the exhibition space ultimately opened it up in terms of potential commercial interests. Essentially, the expansion of the field of art also served to hone an awareness of how to utilise all that, which is related to art – be it the act of selling art or the marketing of characteristic qualities associated with art.

Perhaps one of the severest blows suffered by critical practice was the realisation that capitalism is remarkably resilient and capable of absorbing into a logic of economic utilisation (branding) seemingly oppositional stances, especially by employing these stances as a means of demonstrating an ability to perform institutional critique. [32] In a commentary on Buren's exhibition at the Guggenheim, published in the *New York Times* in 2005, Michael Kimmelmann points out how the artist's former 'counter-establishment ideas', which intended to challenge the commodity status of art and critique the institution of the museum, later gave way to a diluted artistic stance: 'By now, he's also a virtual official artist of France, a role that does not seem to trouble some of his once-radical fans. Nor, apparently, does the fact that his brand of institutional analysis, preaching white-box clichés to a converted audience of insiders, invariably depends on the largesse of institutions like the Guggenheim.' [33→] Buren's critical analysis of the institution gradually forfeited much of its credibility, and was subsequently perceived as a standard recipe by which museums could demonstrate their ability to be (self-)critical.

[32] In the majority of cases, this also means that intrinsically complex works are perceived as reduced to a small number of characteristic traits. This makes it possible to even 'brand' critical practitioners without much difficulty. Moreover, the term 'institutional critique' has also become a brand in its own right. Fraser is self-critical about 'the critically shameful prospect of having played a role in the reduction of certain radical practises to a pithy catchphrase, packaged for co-optation.' Fraser, op. cit., p. 279

3. Strategic Complicity I

However, while negative forms of complicity, such as those described by Crimp in *The Art of Exhibition*, were evolving in the 1980s between artists, corporations and conservative politics, and while controversies and debates concerning the artist's involvement in the art market and other capitalist structures were being carried out, there also evolved a positive form of *strategic* complicity. In this connection, the panel discussion at the Pat Hearn Gallery cited at the beginning of this essay appears pivotal. Artists such as Haim Steinbach, Jeff Koons and Ashley Bickerton sought to position themselves and their works within a – at least potentially – corruptible system, thus putting their own potential corruptibility up for discussion. However, their deliberate propensity for the commercial sphere, implied by Steinbach's notion of 'being complicit with',[34] was often read as their abandoning themselves to the world of consumerism and its products. For example, Stephan Schmidt-Wulffen notes, that 'Koons, Steinbach and like-minded people seek to eradicate all possible distinctions between the fetishisation of the art object and the fetishisation of the consumer commodity.' He continues, 'A work of art fulfils its function if it is marvelled at like a Mercedes-Benz.' [35] Although we should not lump all these artists' works together, one aspect common to all is that none eradicate 'all possible distinctions' between the fetish of the art object and the fetish of the consumer good. Indeed, as we perceive them, these two types of fetishised products seem constantly interchangeable, and it ultimately becomes impossible to clearly classify them as a separate entities. When Steinbach speaks of complicity as 'being complicit with', this implies a state of strategic complicity with, and in terms of, the desire attached to a specific object. The object's appearance, material constitution and style, as well as how it is presented and contextualised, aim to trigger discourse. [36] So essentially, the subject is addressed twice – firstly in terms of his/her desire, indeed, as Schmidt-Wulffen suspects, *consumerist* desires,[37] and secondly, in terms of his/her willingness to partake in discourse. The objects provide and interconnect these two alternatives in order to manifestly complicate both a purely consumerist as well as an analytical or discursive understanding of them. For the works do not only look seductive, there is also something hideous and aggressive about them. They engender proximity and distance at the same time. They represent both tributes to, as well as the monstrous, hypertrophic products of – Capitalism. The objects' alluring appearance may induce joy, but may also arouse apprehension and a sense of guilty defiance. This is because one feels seduced by them or considers them aesthetically pleasing, although – or precisely due to the fact that – the occurrence of such emotional reactions seems inappropriate for the contemplation

[33] 'Sometimes uninvited, he plasters benches and billboards with stripes, concocts various architectural and environmental structures or sculptures, and in general produces works whose site-specific, purposive, unapproachable banality has been interpreted to symbolize the death of the author, a challenge to the traditional commodity status of art, a critique of the institution of the museum – counter-establishment ideas when, like Mr. Buren, they emerged 40 or so years ago.' Michael Kimmelman, *Tall French Visitor Takes Up Residence in the Guggenheim*. www.nytimes.com/2005/03/25/arts/design/25KIMM.html?fta=y, 25.3.2005

[34] 'There is a stronger sense of being complicit with the production of desire, what we traditionally call beautiful seductive objects, than being positioned somewhere outside of it.' Haim Steinbach, 'From Criticism to Complicity', in: *Flash Art*, no. 129, 1986, p. 46–9

[35] Stephan Schmidt-Wulffen, 'Von der Kritik zur Komplizenschaft (und zurück) – Notizen zur Rezeption der *cultural studies* in der amerikanischen Gegenwartskunst' (From Criticism to Complicity [and back]. Notes on the reception of cultural studies within American contemporary art) [1998], in: Stephan Schmidt-Wulffen, *PERFEKT-IMPERFEKT*, Freiburg/Breisgau 2001, p. 154

[36] Steinbach, op. cit., p. 49. This does not involve the discourses taking place before or after the work – the objects themselves are discursive. More on this later.

[37] 'In the talk at Pat Hearn the word "desire" is mentioned early on. As a counter-term of the rationality and analysis of earlier forms of art, "desire" has become the guiding expression of the 1980s. Incidentally, the participants do not apply the term to the theories of desire expounded by Freud, Lacan and Deleuze. To them it simply means consumer desire [...].' Schmidt-Wulffen, op. cit., p. 153

of art. Bickerton takes this idea a step further by pointing out that art can conceivably be taken over by the economy. [38] Precisely because artworks are in themselves contradictory entities, and given that the boundaries between the consumer object, the fetish and the artwork are not clearly definable, the viewer is challenged both emotionally and intellectually. Steinbach's question 'Is there such a thing as a consumer object, a fetish object, an art object, or is it our relation to it that concerns us?' [39] clarifies that, now, the subject plays an important role in determining the status of a given object. [40] In other words, the recipient is responsible for activating or deactivating a given artwork's critical content. [41] And that the viewer might just as well not want to react at all is approvingly accepted, as Jeff Koons corroborates in the following statement: 'I don't set up any kind of requirement. Almost like television, I tell a story that is easy for anyone to enter into and on some level enjoy. [...] The objects and the other images that are interconnected to the body of work have other contexts and, depending on how much the viewer wants to enter it, they can try to get more out of it and start dealing in art vocabulary, and start to deal with abstractions of ideas and of context.' [42] Like Koons, both Bickerton and Steinbach apply the concept of strategic complicity so as to produce a common space and relationship through which the artist and the recipient may correspond. It is intended that, upon actively engaging with the object, the viewer can and ought to be in a position to terminate the ensuing state of complicity at any time. Thus, this approach functions on the one hand to open the door toward the viewer. More importantly however, it poses the serious question concerning the extent to which art is prone to complicity and corruption. And ultimately, this question not only concerns the directive authorities in politics, economics or culture, but also artists and, ultimately, the audience as well.

[38] 'Through tactile choices and presentation, the art object has now been placed in a discursive relationship with the larger scenario of the political and social reality of which it is part. In a self-conscious and ongoing dialogue with the social, political, and intellectual climate of the time and place it will operate in, and with the entire process of its absorption.' Ashley Bickerton, in: *From Criticism to Complicity*, op.cit., p. 46

[39] Steinbach, op.cit., p. 49

[40] Stephan Schmidt-Wulffen mentions the 'paradox of "affirmative criticism"', because 'works of art are accepted as part of the marketing chain'. Schmidt-Wulffen, op.cit., p. 154

[41] This binary effect discloses a certain proximity to the 'pictures generation', exploiting both the seductive power and critique of the image. In 1977, Artists Space in New York showed the group exhibition titled *Pictures*. This title was to be eponymous for a generation of artists who based their work on investigations of the mass media, specifically by means of the technical media provided by film and TV. These artists employed a double strategy aimed at generating seductive images whilst critically reflecting them at the same time. Douglas Eklund (ed.), *The Pictures Generation, 1974–1984* (exh. cat. The Metropolitan Museum of Art) New York/New Haven/London 2009. In contrast to these artists who seek to render critique visible, we are now dealing with the potential aspect of critique, whereby critique can be activated, but does not automatically have to be. This is where the recipient comes in.

[42] *From Criticism to Complicity*, op.cit., pp. 47–8. 'I think that through this procession of contingencies, discourses are being pulled together into the object itself, promoting an awareness of the fact that all meanings are contingent upon other meaning, where meanings are appropriated for their relationship to external forces, the larger social schema in which they're involved.' Ibid.

4. Amalgamation Strategies

Similarly, during the 1980s, the long-established antagonisms between art and economics/politics, and artists and curators/collectors/museums started to crumble. On this phenomenon, artist Liam Gillick writes, 'It has become difficult to identify a true and final barricade.' [43] Thus, the question as to exactly where the boundaries between these groups of people and areas of activity may be drawn does not merely have an impact on whichever kind of – identifiably oppositional – concept of 'otherness', but rather on artistic practice itself. Gillick's oft-repeated interest in forms of social utopia, his art-market success, his projects

[43] Liam Gillick, *Maybe it would be better if we worked in groups of three?* [Hermes Lecture, 2008], Camiel Van Winkel (ed.), 's-Hertogenbosch 2008, p. 11. This is an initiative organised by the Research Group of Visual Art, AKV/St. Joost (Avans University) and the Hermes Business Network.

developed for companies such as Porsche or Lufthansa, and finally his artistic method of combining discourse and the input borne of sensory experience of material objects, often accounted for disapproval for ostensibly lacking a clear stance. This is supported by Gillick's own statements in which he refers to his work as an artist in terms of a 'nebulous' practice. [44] The fact that Gillick also works as a curator, graphic designer, art critic and author, collaborating with changing partners on a wide variety of different projects, is often seen as deliberately distracting the observer's attention from his deficiencies as an artist, while Gillick prefers to define his work as the embodiment of an increasingly variegated artistic practice. Interestingly, although he is viewed as the exponent of an entirely different artistic stance and of critical practice, Mark Dion expresses himself in a similar manner: 'To get a call from the World Wildlife Fund, from the Museum of Contemporary Art in Santa Fe, from a gallery in Tokyo, and a letter from a primatologist in South America: that's where the practice is located for me.' [45] As far as he is concerned, the World Wildlife Fund, the commercial gallery and the exchange of information with a primatologist are equally significant benchmarks in his work as an artist. Thus, critical positions as well as those not perceived as representing a critical practice seem to proceed in a similar fashion. The multiple demands on the artist do not merely form the basis of artistic practice, they are considered as being integral to it, in contrast to the way older-generation artists might distinguish between making art and different, albeit related, activities, such as teaching and publishing. The following generation of artists do not restrict themselves to carrying out that which is generally referred to as cultural practice, but rather seek to immediately interconnect 'a means of securing a livelihood with making art', as demonstrated by the early works of Heger & Dejanov for instance. [46] Dion, Bordowitz and numerous other artists, of their and of the following generation, departed from a more comprehensive notion of artistic practice that seeks to integrate the various facets, as well as the preconditions, of artistic production. This applied first and foremost to artists pursuing an activist art practice, and was of course closely tied to the hope that the work of the artist might attain greater relevance within society. Gregg Bordowitz succinctly expresses this idea: 'I believe that each and every activity constituting a practice has to transcend the established boundaries of cultural labour dividing the art world from the rest of society. Art is no absolute, autonomous entity, and perhaps it never was one.' [47]

At the same time, the working profiles of those described as 'opposing' artistic practice changed and made it increasingly difficult to discern demarcations. In the obituary of Colin de Land, a New York gallery owner who passed away in 2003 at the age of forty-seven, he is described as a person 'whose ambivalence about commercialism was reflected in an art gallery that sometimes resembled an anti-art gallery if not a work of conceptual

[44] Gillick deliberately formulates his projects and reflections as open-sided, avoiding clear statements: 'I am working in a nebulous cloud of ideas, which are somewhat partial or parallel rather than didactic.' His texts are full of expressions like 'nearly', 'might be', 'possible', etc. Liam Gillick, *Renovation Filter, Recent Past and Near Future*, Bristol 2001, p. 20

[45] Mark Dion, quoted in: James Meyer, op.cit., p. 243

[46] Barbara Steiner, 'Plamen Dejanov & Swetlana Heger', in: Barbara Steiner (ed.), *ENTER KünstlerInnen, Publikum, Institution.* Commissioned by the Kunstmuseum in Lucerne, Lucerne 1998, p. 8. 'Heger & Dejanov are artists who developed the concept of their work, they are collectors who know the ways of the international art market, they mediate their own projects when it comes to finding potential collaborators and clients for their rental projects/products, and they repeatedly work in areas of activity that are considered as unlicensed and of low social status. And they go on holidays.' Ibid.

[47] Bordowitz, quoted in James Meyer, op.cit., p. 243 ff. According to James Meyer, around the mid-1990s, Dion and Bordowitz conducted numerous interviews with artists including Thomas Lawson, Dan Graham, Martha Rosler, Yvonne Rainer and Joseph Kosuth who 'seemed to embody the concept of critical practice – a practice whose objective is to dissolve the traditional distinctions between the artwork and its production, or between the "actual" work of the artist as creating an artwork, and other activities such as activism or teaching.' Surprisingly, the interviewees emphasised the fact that distinctions did exist and that they did not consider these activities as being equivalent.

art.' It continues: 'Mr. de Land disdained consistency. He allowed one artist to close the gallery for a month to protest art commercialization, but he also taught a course for art collectors and helped found the New York Armory Show, which fills two piers on the Hudson River every year.' [48] Colin de Land not only expanded our understanding of gallery work, he also embarked on conceptual collaborations with various artists including Richard Prince, among others. It is said that together, they invented a fictitious artist called John Dogg. [49]

[48] Roberta Smith, *Colin de Land, Art Dealer Who Fostered Experimentation, Dies at 47.* www.16beavergroup.org/mtarchive/archives/000018.php, 19.3.2003. Gallery owner Christian Nagel expresses himself similarly: 'Colin de Land was not only a gallerist but also a simulacrum of an artist. His gallery was definitely his studio, and he understood it not only as an exhibition surface but as a social space.' In: Dennis Balk (ed.), *Colin de Land American Fine Arts*, New York 2008, p. 246

[49] Ibid. In the US, works by John Dogg are held by the Rubell Collection in Florida. Works by Dogg were exhibited at the Kunsthalle Zurich in 2008.

In 2009, the commercial gallery Koch Oberhuber Wolff (KOW) opened in Berlin. KOW's guiding concept aims at establishing an institutional model that amalgamates economic concerns with the mediation of contemporary art, social commitment and critical discourse. Departing from the observation that the production of art today, is, to an increasing extent, determined by economic forces, the founders of KOW perceive the model of the commercial gallery as an appropriate context offering the necessary freedom to produce and mediate art, while at the same time critically reflecting on the related (contemporary) mechanisms and conditions pertaining to the art field. [50] The tendencies towards diversification described here are not limited to the activities carried out by the artist or gallery only. The increase in egalitarian forms of collaboration between artists, curators, architects, designers, gallery owners and collectors et cetera, and increasingly multifaceted practices reveal that functions and responsibilities within the contemporary art field are becoming more and more hybridised.

[50] In collaboration with architect Arno Brandlhuber, KOW developed a spatial concept combining maximum adaptability according to use, with maximum pragmatism of functionality. www.kow-berlin.info/about/gallery, retrieved 25.4.2010

As already mentioned in the section on 'unintentional complicity', art's expansion into other domains (even though it may be argued that this is inexorable, both artistically and sociopolitically) necessarily implies opening art up to concerns and intents that sometimes directly oppose particular artistic concepts and ideals. In this connection, I refer again to the exhibition held at the MoMA in 1984 on the occasion of its reopening. By demonstratively emphasising the interest in the 'experimental' and the 'innovative' common to both the museum and the corporation, serves to place the two, at least verbally, on an equal level. In the 1980s, this ostensible common ground was a precondition, allowing the museum and the corporation to be conceptually on a par. Krens had taken this idea a step further by transferring the principles of franchising and branding to the institution of the museum, turning it into a company *as well as* a marketable product. As a result of his combinations of reputed 'highlights' from art and architecture to make the Guggenheim more attractive, Krens was able to embark on so-called joint ventures with other global corporations – using the aura of artistic singularity as *the museum's* most important capital. Opening up the museum towards corporate practices and commercial collaborations not only caused museum tasks to coalesce – as immaterial, material, private and public interests and objectives became inextricably intertwined – but also brought about a multifarious range of fetishes that resembled hybrids between auratically charged artworks and marketable commodities, or marketable artworks and auratically charged commodities.

This strategy of ostensive integration was perfected over time, and is best exemplified by the LVMH Moët Hennessy Louis Vuitton luxury group. Designers and artists including Stephen Sprouse,[51] Takashi Murakami and Richard Prince developed designer handbags for this global leader in luxury. The company commissioned artists such as Vanessa Beecroft, Olafur Eliasson and James Turrell to make artworks for the corporation's headquarters on the Champs Élysées in Paris. Situated on the top floor of the building, the company's own exhibition space, the *Espace Culturel Louis Vuitton*, was inaugurated on 12 January 2006, accompanied by a huge social event.[52] Louis Vuitton's president, Yves Carcelle, emphasises that the company is interested in creative processes, irrespective of discipline: '[...] for us it is exciting and inspiring to partake in the creative processes of people not only working in the world of fashion, but also with those from the world of art and architecture, who collaborate with Louis Vuitton from time to time.'[53] Similar to the collaboration between MoMA and AT&T, which, hinged on the notions of the 'innovative' and the 'experimental', establishes connections between the museum and the company, in the case of LVMH, 'creativity' occurs on a level common to, and, interconnecting the realms of art, the artist and the corporate public. Paradoxically, this renders precisely those elitist definitions of art socially acceptable, which celebrate exclusiveness and snobbism whilst implementing these qualities to effectively promote the company image and increase sales.[54] Meanwhile, the synergism between art and LVMH Moët Hennessy Louis Vuitton continues to grow. In 2006, Bernard Arnault, chief executive of LVMH and also an important art collector, set up the 'Fondation Louis Vuitton pour la Création' art foundation. The museum's current director is Suzanne Pagé, who was formerly the director of the Museum of Modern Art in Paris and, in that capacity, responsible for the exhibition entitled *Passions privées* (private passions), which aimed to show the significant commitment of private collectors and collections in France. Indeed, at the time, this was a somewhat complicated undertaking, as, according to Werner Spies in a speech he held on the occasion of awarding the Art Cologne Prize to Suzanne Pagé, a 'post-revolution fear of confiscation and meddling by the state' was still prevalent in France. 'For this reason, concealment and understatement are still very much the French collector's favourite sport.'[55] Repeatedly, Spies and Pagé voiced their conviction that the aloofness or absence of private collectors would in the long term have a negative impact on French contemporary art. Essentially, both address a traditional conflict between private commitment and a state, in which private zeal and enthusiasm for the arts are faced with bureaucracy and mediocrity. About this, Spies stated: 'The *Passions privées* show objected polemically to the monopoly of the state and to the taste of art adjudicators appointed by the state.'[56→]

[51] This extends as far as to include what is commonly referred to as 'street culture'. Stephen Sprouse designed a strictly limited edition of handbags with graffiti-like elements, sold as the Louis Vuitton graffitis 'Speedy' or 'Keepall'.

[52] 'Joining the architects and artists at the cocktail reception were a host of international celebrities, including Uma Thurman, Sharon Stone, Winona Ryder and Salma Hayek.' In: 'Louis Vuitton celebrates the re-opening of its Champs-Elysees store, www.allbusiness.com/retail-trade/miscellaneous-retail/4438848-1.html, 10.10.2005

[53] Sabine Lange, *Interview with Yves Carcelle*, www.arte.tv/de/mode/1542324,CmC=1544050.html, 18.4.2007. The spectacular building costing over an estimated 120 million euros was designed by Frank Gehry and is situated in the Jardin d'Acclimatation, near the Bois de Boulogne. Sam Lubell, 'Louis Vuittons Luxury Architecture', in: *Business Week*, www.businessweek.com/innovate/content/nov2006/id20061106_483439.htm?campaign_id=rss_daily, 6.11.2006

[54] Louis Vuitton also depends on selling its products in large quantities all over the world to ensure both luxury as well as high sales figures.

[55] Werner Spies, *Laudatio von Prof. Dr. Dr. h. c. mult. Werner Spies auf Suzanne Pagé anlässlich der Verleihung des ART COLOGNE-Preises am 17. April 2008 in Köln* (Speech held on the occasion of the Art Cologne Prize, awarded to Suzanne Pagé on 17 April 2008), Cologne 2008, p. 6. Also available on: www.bvdg.de/pdf/reden/Laudatio_Spies_080417.pdf, retrieved 16.3.2010

[56] Many of the 300 collectors asked were not willing to cooperate. Finally, after negotiations, a total of ninety-two agreed to collaborate, of which two-thirds wished to remain anonymous. *Passions privées* (exh.cat. Musée d'Art moderne de la Ville de Paris), Paris 1995

Apart from the fact that this opposition appears somewhat clichéd today – indeed, why are museum experts bureaucrats, and why does zealousness automatically bring about better results? – the situation has undergone crucial changes in the meantime. With regard to financial resources and competition for public attention, private museums are most certainly at a competitive advantage.[57] Alongside Bernard Arnault's financially powerful initiative, further examples deserving to be mentioned include François Pinault's collections shown at the Palazzo Grassi in Venice and in a bonded warehouse (Punta della Dogana) converted by Tadeo Ando on the island of Santa Maria della Salute, and the Ukrainian billionaire and major collector Victor Pinchuk and his Pinchuk Art Centre in Kiev. Due to overly broad media coverage, these projects forcefully affect the public perception of what contemporary art is, and define to a large extent which artistic concepts, artists and curators are in vogue.

[57] Focusing on these or similar activities, the media have contributed to the rise of this tendency, with reports equally gratifying the demands of the art review, society report and gossip.

In effect, not only do disparate stances and reactions, such as corruption, strategic complicity, sycophantic behaviour, refusal or downright protest seem to move more closely together, they actually merge and interlock. The public and the private spheres intermix, whilst curators and artists also seem to effortlessly switch sides within what used to be seen as an antagonistic polarity. As public art curators, Alison M. Gingeras and Francesco Bonami curated the exhibition *Mapping the Studio* for tycoon and art collector François Pinault.[58]

[58] After being a curator at the Musée national d'art moderne in Paris, Alison M. Gingeras is currently an adjunct curator at the Guggenheim Museum. Francesco Bonami works as a Manilow Senior Curator at the Museum of Contemporary Art in Chicago. He is also artistic director of the Fondazione Sandretto ReRebaudengo per l'Arte in Turin, the Fondazione Pitti Discovery in Florence and the Centro di Arte Contemporanea Villa Manin in Udine. He was the director of the Venice Biennale in 2003.

Upon the initiative of billionaire Viktor Pinchuk, star artists such as Andreas Gursky, Jeff Koons, Damien Hirst and Takashi Murakami figure as active mentors of the 'Future Generation Art Prize' for emerging artists. Members of the jury include Nicolas Serota from Tate and Glenn D. Lowry from the Museum of Modern Art. The director of Pinchuk's centre for the arts, the Pinchuk ArtCentre, is Eckhard Schneider, who was formerly the director of the Kunsthaus Bregenz.[59] The Free State of Bavaria and the collector Uwe Brandhorst joined forces to build and run a private museum located near the Modern Pinakothek in Munich. The director is Armin Zweite, who was formerly the director of the Kunstsammlung Nordrhein-Westfalen (Art Collection of North Rhine-Westphalia). [60] Clearly, in the cases cited here, the public institution functions as a springboard.

[59] futuregenerationartprize.org, retrieved 24.2.2010. See the mentors' statements on video. The prize money is 100,000 euros. See also: www.pinchukartcentre.org/en. Members of the international jury include the collector Eli Broad, rock musician Elton John, fashion designer Miuccia Prada, the Solomon R. Guggenheim Foundation's director Richard Armstrong and Alfred Pacquement, director of the Musée Nationale d'Art Moderne, Centre Georges Pompidou. A short list of artists is nominated by about one hundred art experts from all over the world. www.artmagazine.cc/content44990.html, retrieved 11.12.2009. The jury unites prominent individuals from international museums and the world of fashion, and also includes a superstar from the world of glam rock as an added extra. Such a megalomaniac cluster is ostentatious: big names as mediators and jury members plus considerable financial means.

If the merits of esteemed museum experts are profitably transferable to the respective new foundation – as the direct result of a functioning image policy – then, conversely, these experts are evidently allowed to treasure the (financial) possibilities offered to them by the collectors.

[60] www.museum-brandhorst.de/index.php?id=28, retrieved 24.2.2010. In the cases cited here, no information is given concerning the interests and interrelations behind them. This was criticised, also with reference to the Brandhorst collection. See: *Ich fürchte die Sammler, auch wenn sie Geschenke bringen. Der Trend zum uniformen Museum* (I am afraid of collectors, even if they bring gifts: The trend toward the uniform museum). Feature by Florian Zeyn, Bayerischer Rundfunk/ Bayern 2 (Bavarian Broadcasting Corporation), 26.2.2009, 8.30 p.m., see also the German edition of this book, *Das eroberte Museum*, pp.290 ff.

5. Strategic Complicity II

As the most expensive artwork ever to sell by a living artist, *For the Love of God* (2007) by British artist Damien Hirst topped all the sensational reports on contemporary art sales and the hysteria related to 'the most expensive work of art in the world'. At least according to media reports and Hirst himself, the work, a skull cast in platinum and encrusted with 8,601 diamonds, was sold for 50 million pounds sterling to an unnamed investment group in August 2007. [61]

Then, on 15 September 2008, the day Lehman Brothers filed for bankruptcy, Hirst auctioned off his artistic output of an entire year, titled *Beautiful Inside My Head Forever* at Sotheby's for approximately 110 million pounds sterling. In view of such prices, Hirst's statement, 'It's a very democratic way to sell art and it feels like a natural evolution for contemporary art', [62] may at first appear cynical. But auctions are stock markets in which both the rise and fall of prices are difficult to calculate and control. At auctions, top prices can be attained, but artworks can also be purchased far below the market price, which is one of the reasons gallery owners buy back works by their artists at auctions – above all, in order not to leave the pricing policy over to others. Hirst steered the sale of his year's bulk of work by himself, thus bypassing his galleries: if Hirst's gallery owners wanted to sell a given work by the artist from 2008, they had to buy it first, thus having to face precisely those, partly irrational, market mechanisms over which they themselves usually have control. Armed with the respective public attention – well before it actually took place, Hirst's plan was widely debated in the media – the artist was able to attain an unprecedented sales record. [63] It is not without cause that the main lot of the auction, *Golden Calf* (2008), consisting of a bull preserved in formaldehyde whose head is crowned with a disk of solid gold, is reminiscent of a graven image. Irrefutably, the work can be read as an exegesis of an art market that is dependent on its idols and thus dependent on launching these at regular intervals. [64]

Hirst posits the question as to the value of art in conceptual, symbolic and economic terms by simultaneously inflating and dismounting the fetish of the original and the cult of the artist. Intrinsically mechanical and serial, the *Spot Paintings* were painted by Hirst's assistants and only attain their value through the artist's authorisation. They are compelling conceptually, because they posit questions concerning the artistic worth and economic status

[61] Presumably, the record sale was manipulated by the artist himself, who was involved as one of the buyers. Stefan Koldehoff, *Der Künstler kauft sich selbst* (The artist buys himself), www.sued deutsche.de/kultur/379/417145/bilder/?img=0.0, 25.6.2008

[62] Although Hirst was not paid guaranteed sums by the auction house, conversely he did not have to pay any commission for the works delivered. Holger Liebs, *Ich bin Kunst* (I am art), www.sueddeutsche.de/kultur/85/310018/text/, 12.9.2008. See also the press release by Sotheby's at: www.sothebys.com/app/paddleReg/paddler eg.do?dispatch=eventDetails&event_id=28883, 15.9.2008

[63] The reference to the democratisation of distribution is particularly interesting in view of the fact that some auction houses embark on sensational alliances with other players in the art business, like the gallery Haunch of Venison and Christie's or the Saatchi Gallery and Philipps de Pury. In this way, the art market's price policy is primarily controlled by only a few.

[64] Parallel to activities pertaining to being a highly successful 'art market artist', since the 1980s, Hirst is also active as a curator, producer, publisher and collector, and as such has significant influence on contemporary art discourse. Here are some examples of his current activities and projects: in late October 2008, Hirst opened Other Criteria on New Bond Street in London, a store specialising in prints, editions, multiples and publications by both emerging and established artists, as well as his own. Other Criteria was founded as a publishing house by Damien Hirst, Hugh Allan and Frank Dunphy in 2005. Today, Other Criteria is located on New Bond and Hinde Streets in London, and on Madison Avenue in New York. www.othercriteria.com, 14.1.2009. Working in the commercial field, Other Criteria offers products for only a fraction of the price attained on the art market. However, to describe these products as 'devotional objects', as Holger Liebs did, underestimates Other Criteria's policy of directly correlating price and edition size. For instance, a silkscreen print of *For the Love of God* is available in three editions/price categories. They are priced at £10,000, £5,000 or £900 per print, according to whether they belong to an edition of 250, 750 or 1,700 prints respectively. Moreover, Other Criteria's products are more valuable than those sold at museum shops, and less expensive than those offered by commercial galleries. Its objective is essentially the same as what Hirst wanted his auction at Sotheby's to be: the democratisation of distribution modes and public debate concerning the price and value of the products on offer, regardless of whether they are part of high culture or junk culture.

of the artwork, and are also highly sought after commodities. Aesthetically, they are indistinguishable from the unauthorised pictures. [65] Discussions concerning the price to be paid for an artwork's authenticity culminated in the debate about the disintegration of Hirst's work *The Physical Impossibility of Death in the Mind of Someone Living*. Not only the collector, who had paid a very high price when he bought the work from Charles Saatchi, but also a wider public, was preoccupied with the question of whether we were still dealing with the same icon from 1991, after the original shark had been replaced by a new one. [66] Evidently, anticipating that the debate would be covered by the mass media was a significant part of the concept. In this connection, the author Robert Preece analysed how may hits were commanded on Google search by 'Damien Hirst + skull' and other theme words such as 'diamond + 50 million' to investigate the hype throughout society unleashed by Hirst's famous skull piece. [67]

In a conversation with Preece, the author, curator and artist, Patricia Ellis, supports Preece's theory that Hirst skilfully manipulates the economy of attention: 'The skull piece was most likely anticipated to create a huge interest through a wide variety of media. [...] If you look at how media operates it is very much about temporality, multiplication and the sublime. Hirst is not so dissimilar from Andy Warhol. He is a global brand. I don't think you can separate it. I think it is definitely part of the concept of his work.' [68]

Indeed, Hirst places his art objects in relation to their economic, symbolic and cultural context, or, as is the case here, to the specific framework provided by the media, as well as to the art market and art history. In view of this, the artist's strategy of cunningly appropriating and subverting the mechanisms of the media, whilst also inciting a process whereby the intentions of instrumentalisation are reciprocally played off one against the other, must be seen as vital to Hirst's artistic practice.

Although Olaf Nicolai's approach may at first seem to be no more than the extension of the artistic positions (Steinbach, Koons, Bickerton) presented in 'Strategic Complicity I' above, Nicolai, like Hirst, is interested in ways of intervening in the framing conditions of artistic action, and engaging with the artworks' perception, communication and potential instrumentalisation. Nicolai shifts the artwork, the fetish and the consumer product onto a common level of potential consumability, thus facilitating perceptual shifts from artwork to high-priced commodity or from utilitarian object to product fetish. In *Big Sneaker [The Nineties]* from 1999, a gigantic silver Nike sneaker functions

[65] On this, Hirst recounts, 'I had an argument with an assistant who used to paint my spots [...] When she was leaving, and she was nervous, she said, "Well. I want a spot painting. I've painted loads for you. I've painted these spot paintings for a year, and I want one." A year in the studio, getting paid a fiver, a tenner an hour, whatever it is. So I said, "I'll give you a cheque for seventy thousand quid if you like. Why don't I just do that? Because you know you're going to sell it straight away. You know how to do it. Just make one of your own." And she said, "No I want one of yours." But the only difference between one painted by her and one of mine is money.' Damien Hirst, in: Gordon Burn, *On The Way To Work*, London 2001, p. 82

[66] On the deterioration of Hirst's work *The Physical Impossibility of Death in the Mind of Someone Living*, Rose-Maria Gropp writes, 'if there is an icon of art from the 1990s then it is Damien Hirst's shark preserved in formaldehyde. But now the shark is disintegrating. Are we allowed to replace the shark with a new one, or would that adulterate the authenticity of the artwork?' Rose-Maria Kropp, *Unfrischer Fisch* (Old fish), www.faz.net/s/RubEBED639C476B407798 B1CE808F1F6632/Doc~ECDAD35A7EA8D419F8754E3D10A 0EDEEA~ATpl~Ecommon~Scontent.html, 30.6.2006

[67] Robert Preece, 'Why I Love Damien's Skull', in: *Sculpture*, www.artdesigncafe.com/IMG/pdf/ why-I-love-Damien-Hirst-diamond-skull-Rob ert-Preece-Sculpture.pdf, retrieved 23.5.2010

[68] 'Hype, Buzz, Glamour and Art. A Conversation with Patricia Ellis.' In: *Sculpture*. The analysis of the role of mass media with respect to the perception of art is also a key concern in Robert Preece's text about Tracey Emin. Preece investigates Emin's work with reference to how it is covered by media reports, i.e., to how Emin attempts to gain control by strategically inverting this process. Robert Preece, 'ARTIST over – and in – the BROADSHEETS', in: *Parkett*, no. 63, 2001, pp. 50–4

as an oversized floor cushion, as an archetypal cult object from the 1990s, and as a work of art. Due to its positive status as a cult object, the viewer is captured, both emotionally and in terms of discourse, in a direct relationship to the sneaker as a commodity, which is essentially sustainable for the masses. On the other hand, due to its monstrously exaggerated size it can also be read as a critique of consumerism.[69] This recalls the practices developed during the 1980s by both Steinbach and Koons. However, in contrast to these positions from the 1980s, Nicolai seeks to establish correlations between the respective objects and current systems of economic utilisation and incorporation. He primarily refers to the art market's suggestive practices, but also to the way in which museums and corporations deploy the aura of art to the ends of making a profit. In the present text, these strategies have been described in detail with reference to the Guggenheim and LVMH Moët Hennessy Louis Vuitton. Olaf Nicolai challenges this logic of utilisation and incorporation by selectively violating ownership and utilisation rights. For *Big Sneaker [The Nineties]*, Nicolai did not ask Nike first for permission to copy and enlarge the cult sneaker from the 1990s. Prada and Gieves & Hawkes know nothing of Nicolai's *pirate edition* (2000). And of course the rights managers of Donald Judd, one of the most important American artists of the 20th century, were not asked for permission whether Nicolai was allowed to produce the work from 2000 entitled *o.T. (Instruction for Producing a Work After D. Judd)*, which comprised a set of instructions summoning the visitor to make his/her own 'Donald Judd'. On the one hand, Nicolai investigates the mechanisms of instrumentalisation (who is instrumentalising whom?) and appropriation (who claims what?), and on the other hand, he deliberately oversteps the legal boundaries between producer/originator and consumer/user to trigger critical debate about role allocation, legitimate copyright protection and the monopoly on power serving to enforce capitalist interests.[70] Thus, art and the economy interlock. Nicolai not only inquires into the interests guiding corporations and the art industry, he also directly calls upon the recipient to be out of step with the passivity of consumerism, to scrutinise the relation between producer and consumer, and to consider the possibilities of piracy, self-organisation and other alternative economic models. Nicolai and numerous other artists/artist collectives such as Superflex, Christine Hill, Maria Eichhorn and Marianne Heier deploy a dual strategy: on the one hand to challenge and provoke the economic system, which includes the art market, and on the other hand to specifically utilise and capitalise on precisely that system.

[69] A possible reading of the work as a critique of consumerism was supported by a second work included in the exhibition, which, consisting of a large text on the gallery walls, literally functioned as the shoe's contextual frame. *A Short Catalogue of Things That You Think You Want: A Text by Zadie Smith for the Anniversary Issue of the Face*, 05/2000, 2001, consists of a text by Zadie Smith published in the magazine *Face*, in which the author reflects upon the symbiosis of art and commerce. Nicolai deliberately uses this text as a 'frame' to present thematically interrelated works. Susanne Pfleger & Olaf Nicolai (eds.), *Olaf Nicolai, « rewind » forward* (exh.cat. Städtische Galerie Wolfsburg), Ostfildern-Ruit 2003, p.152

[70] As a rule, the infringement of copyright is subject to severe punishment. Louis Vuitton sued the Deutsches Rote Kreuz (German Red Cross) aid organisation for offering a fake Louis Vuitton handbag in a second-hand clothes store in Marburg. In June 2009, *Spiegel Online* reported: 'Luxury brand files suit against charity organisation. The luxury company Louis Vuitton sues Red Cross charity shop for selling counterfeit handbag. The poor people's store has to pay the French company a fine of 2,600 euros. Politicians are indignant.' *Nobelfirma Louis Vuitton verklagt Rotes Kreuz.* www.spiegel.de/wirtschaft/0,1518,631914,00.html, 22.6.2009

6. Criticality

In section 2, I discussed the problem of how to articulate criticism towards and within an – apparently infinitely – adaptable capitalist system, while not, at the same time, becoming an unintentional accomplice of precisely that system. In their book, *The New Spirit of Capitalism*, Luc Boltanski and Ève Chiapello depart from the assumption that capitalism was able to modify and stabilise itself, *above all* as a result of the criticism it received through art and the social domain. Capitalism thus assimilated certain aspects of that criticism, specifically so as to maintain precisely the necessary degree of criticism to justify and sustain itself.[71] Beyond the assertion that artists – precisely by criticising the system which they saw as questionable – contributed substantially to stabilising the latter, it becomes increasingly difficult to separate artistic and economic interests, especially since art's economic potential has itself become a broader social concern. The exploitation of art and its institutions does not merely extend to art's material products, but also to characteristic traits associated with art, such as creativity, authenticity and open-mindedness, but also criticism. Although significantly inspiring for artists, former opposition to the economic domains and issues of an economy driven by capitalism has given way to highly complex integration processes from which neither artists nor art institutions are exempt. In short, the notion of employing art to conceptualise the idealistic, polar opposite of other social domains deteriorated at an increasingly rapid rate in the course of the 20th century.

However, it seems overhasty to draw the conclusion that the perforation of the established boundaries between art and the economy necessarily leads to art being absorbed *by* the economy, just as a lack of distance does not automatically involve the loss of criticism. Rather, we should assume that the modes of the critical have to change. In my opinion, Irit Rogoff's proposed use of the terms *criticism, critique* and *criticality* marks such gradations of change: 'In the project of "criticism" we are mainly preoccupied with the application of values and judgements, operating from a barely acknowledged humanist index of measure sustained in turn by naturalised beliefs and disavowed interests. [...] Critique, in all of its myriad complexities has allowed us to unveil, uncover, and critically re-examine the convincing logics and operations of such truth claims. However, for all of its mighty critical apparatus and its immense and continuing value, critique has sustained a certain external knowingness, a certain ability to look in from the outside and unravel and examine and expose that which had seemingly lay hidden within the folds of structured knowledge.'[72] Rogoff's redefinition of the term 'criticality' demonstrates that a need for an external and objectively critical viewpoint has given way to an awareness of one's own involvement in – and of the innate contradictions of – a culture determined by capitalism: 'In "criticality" we have that double occupation in which we are both fully armed with the knowledges of critique, able to analyse and unveil while at the same time sharing and living out the very conditions which we are able to see through.'[73] For this reason, artists, curators and everyone else working in this field need to develop a critical stance toward precisely the

[71] Luc Boltanski & Ève Chiapello, *Der neue Geist des Kapitalismus* (The New Spirit of Capitalism), Constance 2003, p. 526 ff.

[72] Irit Rogoff, *What is a Theorist?* www.kein.org/node/62, 8.4.2006

[73] Ibid. and Irit Rogoff, 'Was ist ein Theoretiker?' (What is a theorist?), in: Martin Hellmold et al. (eds.), *Was ist ein Künstler? Das Subjekt der modernen Kunst* (What is an artist? The subject of modern art), Munich 2003, p. 274. Although both essays by Irit Rogoff cited here have the same titles, they are different. In the second text, Rogoff emphasises that 'criticality is a significant component of visual culture and not to be separated from an open-mindedness toward new areas of knowledge and the simultaneous rejection of conventional models of analysis and theoretical allies.', ibid., p. 274

established structures on which they depend, to learn how to work within economic structures whilst questioning them at the same time, and how to be actively involved in the economy as well as the art field whilst equally gauging the dangers of exploitation and the possibilities of opposition.

The resulting rift became a central theme of critical art practice, as demonstrated by Andrea Fraser for instance. Already in *Gallery Talks*, in which she acted as her alter ego Jane Castelton, she ushered the way through various American museums, changing her position as speaker several times during the performance.[74] In 1986, on the occasion of the group exhibition *Damaged Goods: Desire and the Economy of the Object* at the New Museum of Contemporary Art in New York, Brian Wallis invited Fraser to present her performance *Damaged Goods Gallery Talk Starts Here*. This consisted of disparate bits of language culled from the exhibition catalogue, the usual visitor guides, Marxist cultural criticism, as well as fashion magazines. The text fragments included descriptions of famous artworks, pieces of pottery and a trip to China, companies' business reports, advertising pointers and statistical extracts on poverty in the Third World.[75] On the one hand, assuming the role of Jane Castelton, Fraser developed an intense identification with the museum, communicating what the institution expected her to communicate, or rather, communicating what she *presumed* the institution expected her to. She thus turned herself into a strategic accomplice of the museum. On the other hand, she formulated a critique of the institution, its sovereignty of interpretation and defining power. In the first case, Fraser functioned as the extended arm of the museum, in the second as its critic or analyst.[76] In later performances, she not only constantly switched perspectives, but rather also swayed playfully between the characteristic identities of various different protagonists from the field of art. In the performance *Inaugural Speech* (1997), presented on the occasion of the opening of SITE97 in San Diego/Tijuana, Fraser first spoke as an artist, then as a curator/organiser, a public funding body representative, a politician, and, finally, as a corporate sponsor. Each respective speech consisted of assorted fragments used on a variety of similar occasions and supplemented by Fraser.[77] Supported by the Friedrich Petzel Gallery in New York, in *Untitled* (2003) she pushed the theme of complicity as far as possible toward the representation of how the artist, the gallery owner and the collector are inextricably entangled. The artist offered her sexual services to a collector, and 50 per cent of the price of the 'work' was due to be paid to Fraser's gallerist, as is common practice in the art business.[78] In this project, Fraser brought together two fundamentally irreconcilable systems: the art market and prostitution. Here, the role of the artist is equivalent to that of the prostitute, just as the collector and gallery owner correspond to the client and pimp respectively.

[74] In terms of appearance or manner of speech, Castelton/Fraser is indistinguishable from other docents in American museums.

[75] 'Damaged Goods Gallery Talk Starts Here', in: Yilmaz Dziewior (ed.), *Andrea Fraser, Works. 1984 to 2003* (exh. cat. Kunstverein Hamburg), Cologne 2003, p. 108. See also Andrea Fraser, 'Damaged Goods Gallery Talk Starts Here (Excerpt)', ibid., pp. 240–3

[76] In *Welcome to the Wadsworth: A Museum Tour*, a project at the Wadsworth Atheneum in Hartford, Connecticut in 1991, Fraser divested herself of her alter ego. From that time on she would act under her own name.

[77] *Inaugural Speech* was recorded on videotape. It exists as both a single-channel video and as a two-channel video installation. The single-channel video includes recordings of speeches by politicians and the audience's responses at the opening. In the two-channel video installation, the projection showing the artist faces the projection showing the audience opposite. This information is taken from *Andrea Fraser*, op. cit., p. 194. Cf. Fraser's speech and sources cited by herself in: ibid., pp. 271–5

[78] The collector received a copy of the video of the performance, published in an edition of five copies.

The resultant blur of a suchlike practice is also prevalent in the work of Liam Gillick, whom I mentioned earlier on. Although it seems paradoxical, it can be said that this artist creates sharply defined uncertainty relations. Significantly, this is not the outcome of specific insufficiencies, but rather a principle. Gillick's artistic vocabulary also combines different elements – images, texts, object-like manifestations and fragments; the materials, surfaces, associative titles and arrangements bring to mind a multitude of references to architecture, design, Capitalism, Socialism, utopian ideas and action. Derived from both the field of art and the corporate domain, the codes inherent to the typefaces, colours, materials and production methods employed by Gillick are mutually interconnected in his works within specific spatio-temporal contexts, and above all are put in relation to the recipient. [79] Gillick's work posits many questions on the status and social purpose of artistic work and the artist, on the possibilities of expressing criticism and critique, as well as on idealism, pragmatism, complicity and corruptibility: nevertheless, the 'scenarios' referred to remain hypothetical as long as they do not actually take place. Gillick says, 'My work is like the light in the fridge, it only works when there are people there to open the fridge door. Without people, it's not art – it's something else – stuff in a room.' [80]

[79] In his most recent exhibition series, Gillick expands his compiled vocabulary to explicitly include numerous locations, continuously reconfiguring it according to the institutional demands and site-specific collaborations. Responsibility is clearly delegated to the respective cooperation partners, viewers and visitors.

[80] Gillick, *Renovation Filter: Recent Past and Near Future*, Bristol 2000, p. 16

Not only Fraser and Gillick deliberately define the division between critique and affirmation as a very fine line. A number of other artists do the same, irrespective of whether or not they engage in, or represent, critical practice. Now, the status of the work essentially depends on the viewer's willingness to classify it as either critical or affirmative. It is crucial neither whether the artist is able to articulate intelligible and unambiguous criticism, nor whether the curator mediates this in a likewise comprehensible manner. More significantly, critical content is generated in the course of the work's reception, and may subsequently continue to change and metamorphose according to context. The role of the viewer becomes increasingly important, as he/she collaborates with the respective artist and curator to determine the work's status and meaning. The concept of criticality outlined here invalidates the hierarchic, asymmetrical relationship between the artist and the audience, which was still characteristic of the first generation of critical practice artists whose works were often latently didactic. This model does not cater to an expectation that some distant deputised individual is responsible for formulating critique. A given work will stand or fall by the recipient's willingness to engage in critical discourse, assume responsibility and adopt a clear position. This implies that the possibilities of criticism/critique, criticality and potential allegations of complicity and corruption not only affect the artist and curator. They also involve the recipient, who, if she or he does not respond to the offer of engaging in critical analysis or debate, becomes a voluntary or involuntary accomplice of a corrupt – or potentially corruptible – system.

7. From Complicity to Criticality

During recent years, significant shifts have taken place within the field of art. The glamorous art of the international jet set has moved in right next to the academic discourse section. Commercial agendas and alternative economic models converge, overlap or emerge shoulder to shoulder. Cool cynicism and attitudes insisting on art's utopian potential coexist. Collective art projects run parallel to branding strategies intent on celebrating the artist-as-genius. Indeed, shifting positions and areas marked by the transitional and erratic make it increasingly difficult to discern unambiguously clear demarcations. [81] If conflicts do arise, then not necessarily between the customary sets of opposing areas and factions, along the lines of corporate domain versus art and politics, artist versus curator, or artist versus museum administrator. Today, conflicts are much more likely within each of the areas or groups mentioned above, whereas alliances have become conceivable between once opposing parties, if there is the incentive to pursue a common objective. [82] In other words, the art world has, contrarily to traditional forms of group bonding, adjusted according to certain political, economic, social and cultural interests.

With reference to the planned construction of the *Tschlin Library* in the Engadine mountain village of Tschlin, the architect and author Markus Miessen appropriately describes today's often highly complex modes of cooperation and the participating partners' changing functions and tasks as 'delicate'. [83] The project was initiated by Miessen and Swiss super-curator and author Hans Ulrich Obrist. They are presently collaborating with the collector and entrepreneur Rudolph Schürmann and businesswoman Michelle Nicol to build a cultural centre offering permanent access to Obrist's private archive, 'focusing on its possible configuration as an open field of possibilities and knowledge [...] as an open work able to reactivate and to reenact historic events and layers of knowledge in which the transparency of organization allows for a richer and more surprising usage'. In addition, the project serves to 'rethink the significance of the politics of storage, individual selection and archival authorship [...]'. An interest in creating a physical place in which collective knowledge is both produced and rendered accessible, is directly connected with the task of digitising the archive. [84] As a venue offering seminars, exhibitions and artist/research residencies, the planned cultural centre is to be funded through the construction and sale of private real estate in the same village. Thus, it is planned that the non-profit-making part of the project will be financed by private sector revenue. In other words, this is an entrepreneurial venture in which different interlocking interests serve to push its realisation forward, even though this involves unforeseeable risks due to the project's enormous investment volume and its merging of material and immaterial components. This model is no longer based on the notion of the

[81] See also Alexander Koch, 'Kunstfeld 8', in: *Text – L'art pour l'art*, Issue 5, Sept. 2007, p. 3 & 5. Koch distinguishes between eight parallel fields, each with its own protagonists and value systems: the 'representational' field, the 'monetary' field, the 'corporate' field, the 'creative' field, the 'therapeutic' field and the 'emancipatory' field.

[82] Of course that is not to say that in the past there were never such alliances between opposing groups. Yet, they were effectively blanked out as soon as the myth of art as being incorruptible was in jeopardy.

[83] 'Nevertheless one should not underestimate the complexity of such an entrepreneurial framework. Because traditional roles and relationships between architect, client, builder and curator no longer exist; partnerships and modes of production become highly delicate.' Markus Miessen, 'A protest against forgetting: the making of the Tschlin library', in: Markus Miessen (with Hans Ulrich Obrist, Ralf Pflugfelder, Arianna Ricciotti, Michelle Nicole and Rudolph Schürmann), *Save Haven*, vol. 15, 4/08, p. 111. For many years, Obrist's archive was located in his hometown of St. Gallen, then at the University in Lüneburg, and at the moment it is stored in an apartment in Berlin, waiting to be shipped back to Switzerland. In between, the archive toured various countries. It comprises over 20,000 books, 1,400 hours of interview tape recordings and DVDs, hundreds of postcards and assorted other artefacts. Ibid., pp. 111–12

[84] The reason for selecting a remote location is that 'visitors will have to make a deliberate attempt to come and see it. This would hopefully stimulate a serious and rigorous engagement with the archive.' Ibid., p. 114. nOffice (M. Miessen, M. Nilsson, R. Pflugfelder) are currently planning the project's realisation.

altruistic patron, but rather on financially strong cooperation partners seeking agreement between their respective goals and ideas. It is basically a strategic partnership aimed at mutual benefits on both sides. [85]

[85] Another example is the Platform Garanti Contemporary Art Centre in Istanbul, which is run by the Garanti Bank. The director of the art centre, Vasif Kortun, utilises the possibilities offered to him by the bank, but also enforces contractual measures whereby specific rights, such as access to the archive of Turkish art for example, are guaranteed in case of conflict. Conversation with Vasif Kortun, Istanbul, 30.4.2010

Although it is still open how the *Tschlin Library* experiment will evolve, the concepts developed up to now are exceptional insofar as they combine the project's idealism with calculated strategies and tactical considerations. This strategy, which not only banks upon the economic framing conditions, but rather incorporates these as a vital part of the project, is comparable to the initiative of Koch Oberhuber Wolff mentioned earlier in section 4. KOW apply the model of the commercial gallery in order to attain new freedoms relevant not only in the production, but also the mediation of contemporary art: this entails reinvesting accumulated capital in art/curatorial projects that could not be accomplished otherwise. In an interview with the German business newspaper *Handelsblatt*, Koch countered Harald Szeemann's popular demand to shatter the triad of studio, gallery and museum: 'We don't have to shatter the triad. [...] On the contrary, we need to mobilise it! We have to exploit it for the right cause. If our gallery contributes to making sure that art is relevant within society, then not by bypassing the market. [...] Then precisely these positions need to be promoted in the market.' [86] The projects discussed here indicate a shift

[86] Christiane Fricke, 'Zum Dreieck Atelier, Galerie und Museum' (On the triad of studio, gallery and museum), in: *Handelsblatt*, 25./26.6.2010, p.61. See also: Harald Szeemann: *Kunst auf Sendung*, 3sat online, www.3sat.de/page/?source=/ard/60504/index.html, 11.12.2003. See also the way economic ideas and their critical reflection are integral to the institutional concepts and programmes of 16 Beaver in New York, e-flux or the newly founded Contemporary Art Centre in Taipei, and ultimately function to similar ends, namely to create freedoms, i.e., a certain independence, necessary to sustain the institution and carry out art projects. The latter three are artist-run initiatives. 16beavergroup.org/about and www.e-flux.com/pages/about. See also: *Hans Ulrich Obrist interviews Anton Vidokle and Julieta Aranda about the history of e-flux* and: www.tcac.tw, retrieved 23.5.2010

of paradigm: they are all part of an economic system, which is no longer criticised but rather actively utilised by its subscribers to the ends of implementing specific institutional, artistic and curatorial concepts. Moreover, these projects neither aim to merely gratify the – sellable – autonomous aesthetic object, nor to accept that there is no alternative to the current economic modes whereby all areas of life are incorporated and utilised in terms of profit. Rather, they seek to intervene in economic processes, actively shaping these to emancipatory ends. This is also a reaction to the argument forwarded by Luc Boltanski and Ève Chiapello that capitalism could always successfully stabilise itself by incorporating its critics and modifiers to the benefit of capitalist principles. As Don-Quixotian as this may seem, today, there are some very real attempts at being active within what used to be understood as the oppositional field, so as to appropriate economic methods of reinvesting consolidated revenue to emancipatory ends. The utopian objective links up with a highly pragmatic approach, while critical perception becomes aware that it too is implicated in capitalistic cycles of utilisation.

Considering that these distinctions and functions have become indeterminate, and that relationships have become contingent and precarious, today it seems all the more necessary to question who is acting on behalf of whose contract, and which interests are being catered to by whom. Given the current developments, I believe that these are precisely the questions that need to be raised in all areas of activity within the art field. With regard to the exhibition curated by Jeff Koons at the New Museum of Contemporary Art in New York, what seems reprehensible is not that it included works from the collection of

Dakis Joannou, but rather that the web of interests behind the exhibition was never mentioned, neither in the exhibition nor on the part of the museum in any of its statements. On the contrary, it was suggested that the interests of the participating parties – the museum, the collector and the artists – were congruent.[87]

To avoid this from happening, and in order to promote a critical, emancipatory practice, it is crucial that we hone our perception of different interests and hierarchies once again, although we now know that these interests and hierarchies are no longer based on traditional oppositions, and alliances are anything but static. It is necessary to formulate a societal perspective in sync with 'the cultural logic of late capitalism', which is not limited to, but rather challenges, economic questions and demands clear positions of itself and of all participating partners. The question is, whether or not, and if so, precisely which regulatory frameworks and spatial contexts can be created to facilitate public debate about our common demands and differences.

In view of this, the Museum of Contemporary Art Leipzig developed *Carte Blanche*, a project seeking to reveal the variety of different interests kept by private persons in art and the museum. The project was guided by the idea to discuss – and concurrently, to exhibit – the dependencies and interconnections at work within the institutional programme, curatorial practice and the exhibitions themselves. I believe that this fostered a crucial prerequisite in order to exchange ideas about the possibilities offered by art and its institutions. Herein lies the sociopolitical dimension of this approach: namely to create, very much in line with Chantal Mouffe's idea, 'a vitally "agonistic" sphere of public competition' allowing different stances to mutually confront and test each other, in order to debate over matters, and if necessary, to demand or generate alternatives.[88]

It goes without saying that with respect to a project such as *Carte Blanche*, the onus is also on the museum to provide a clear statement on its position and motives. However, a constructive process can only develop if all participating partners as well as the audience are willing to develop their own respective standpoint and get involved in the discussion.

[87] With respect to Koons, Niklas Maak perceives the museum's declaration of bankruptcy and self-disempowerment, 'for the New Museum was founded in 1977 so as to offer an alternative space for art beyond economic interests and established power structures. Its founder, Marcia Tucker, quit her position as curator of painting and sculpture at the Whitney Museum of American Art to invent the New Museum as a means of exhibiting alternative art alternatively. She wanted to exhibit the work by those artists who otherwise would not be exhibited. [...] Thanks to Marcia Tucker, many artists without a lobby or collectors to support them were given their first opportunity to exhibit – among them was a young man whose first exhibition at the New Museum in May 1980 included sculptures comprising brand new vacuum cleaners as "a critique of consumer culture". His name was Jeff Koons.' Niklas Maak, 'Die gekaufte Kunstgeschichte' (The bought history of art), in: *Frankfurter Allgemeine Zeitung*, no. 51, 2.3.2010, p. 31

[88] Chantal Mouffe, *Über das Politische. Wider die kosmopolitische Illusion* (On the Political. Against the Cosmopolitan Illusion), Frankfurt am Main, 2007, p. 10

The Preconditions of Carte Blanche

As a museum and exhibition venue, the GfZK selected and invited eleven people and companies from the private sector, including one patrons and friends association and two commercial galleries, to demonstrate and publicise their commitment to the arts by means of exhibitions. All of the eleven associates – the IT systems company alpha 2000 (Leipzig), the Leipzig publishing company Leipziger Verlags- und Druckereigesellschaft, the gas stock corporation VNG – Verbundnetz Gas AG (Leipzig), the galleries EIGEN+ART (Leipzig/Berlin) and Dogenhaus (Leipzig), the collectors Leon Janucek (Berlin), Brigitte and Arend Oetker (Berlin), Doris and Klaus F.K. Schmidt (Dresden), Vivien and Horst Schmitter (Hamburg), and the Hans Brosch Circle of Friends – stand for distinctive modes of supporting and mediating contemporary art, and respective motivation of their commitment ranges from altruism to utilitarianism. Furthermore, a key reason for us to invite these private sector partners to collaborate was our own inquisitiveness about the scope of organisations, ranging in size from the small business run by two single proprietors to the large-scale stock corporation, and funding modes from sponsoring to patronage, as well as diverse, hybrid forms of support. All collaborators, although operating at a supranational level, have close ties to Leipzig and the GfZK institution.

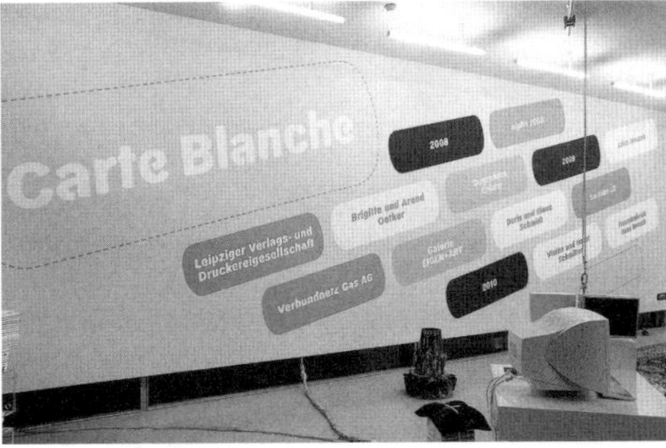

Friendly Enemies. 26.1.–24.3.2008, GfZK-2. Installation view. Design: Kay Bachmann und Philipp Paulsen.

Carte Blanche was not the only project on the GfZK's schedule between 2008 and early 2010. This is a research project parallel to other projects and exhibitions organised by the foundation, and also extends the branch of applied museum research introduced in 2003. [1] The institution's funding body, defined as a public-private partnership (PPP), and related questions concerning how such a model might function given the premises of the present, were the incentive behind *Carte Blanche*. In the early 1990s, the Free State of Saxony, the City of Leipzig and the GfZK's body of private supporters founded a not-for-profit limited company (gGmbH), funded in equal parts by private and public partners. At that time, the PPP was seen as a highly promising model for the cultural sector. However, hopes of private commitment were only scarcely fulfilled, partly because in Leipzig, to complicate matters, there were neither any traditionally West German strands of cultural support, nor remainders from the time of civil commitment prior to the GDR, from where to carry on. With respect to the GfZK, this is reflected by the fact that, since 1996, a third of the utility costs have been paid for by the museum's support group, that is, primarily by one individual – Arend Oetker. [2] Apart from him, the support group has no other significant private members

[1] Essentially, all the research projects deal with the GfZK's specific situation and context. Previous projects include: *Kulturelle Territorien/Cultural Territories*, on the role of art and culture in post-communist societies (2003–2005); *Heimat Moderne*, on the heritage of modernity; *Shrinking Cities* (2003–2005); *dagegen dabei / against within* (2006), on the role of art critique/criticality; and *Sammeln/Collecting* (since 2005).

[2] Without the support of the private sector partner Arend Oetker, the institution's inauguration in September 1996 would never have come about. He and my predecessor, Klaus Werner, were able to persuade the Free State and City of Leipzig that it was of vital importance to establish a contemporary art institution in the new *Länder*. Their efforts led →

to resources of the Cultural Committee of German Business within the Federation of German Industries (BDI) being mobilised in order to finance the construction of GfZK's first exhibition building. Additionally, a substantial number of works were transferred to GfZK on permanent loan from the Cultural Committee of German Business within the BDI in 1992. In 2006, these were donated to the institution with no conditions attached.

wishing to combine non-material and financial support. Today, the City of Leipzig, the Free State of Saxony and Arend Oetker jointly contribute to pay the utility costs due. Up until 2008, primarily national and international foundations financed the GfZK programme, first and foremost the Kulturstiftung des Bundes (German Federal Cultural Foundation), the Cultural Foundation of the Free State of Saxony and the cultural funds of the European Union. However, in contrast to private sector support, public funding often involves an enormous amount of bureaucracy. [3]

[3] Not only does bureaucracy mean a substantial amount of organisational effort for institutions, it involves the deployment of resources reclaimable only after final assessment. This forces institutions to make considerable prepayments, funds that are sometimes returned only years later. The Cultural Foundation of the Free State of Saxony, which promptly assesses the projects it funds, is thus very much an exception to this tendency.

Up to now, sponsoring, in the true sense of the word, played no role in funding GfZK; measured against the annual budget, financial support from the private sector was minor up until the start of *Carte Blanche*, in spite of the fact that the GfZK has been continually supported by Sachsen Bank since 1998, and that the Ostdeutsche Sparkassenstiftung (East German Savings Bank Foundation) and the Leipzig Sparkasse (Leipzig Savings Bank) repeatedly contributed to the funding of projects. Even though a large amount of private capital has, by definition, been poured into the institution since it was founded, the GfZK's funding model cannot be defined as a PPP in a narrower sense, as the idea of motivating private partners by means of economic incentives is comparatively unimportant in this case. Essentially, the GfZK is supported by an old-school type of civil commitment, which is guided by an ambition to serve contemporary society in an exemplary way so as to encourage others to do likewise.

Apart from investigating feasible models through which to financially support the GfZK, *Carte Blanche* also offered the incentive for people to get involved in current debates that pinpoint private commitment – specifically the influence that galleries, corporations and collectors have on museums – as problematical. These debates basically criticise two tendencies: first, that a former patronage system geared to society has been replaced by private individuals, inasmuch as they are even interested in public institutions, seeking to an increasing extent immediate personal benefits. Second – and indeed this should be taken seriously – there seems to be a general loss of interest in public institutions. Developments of the past few years show that more and more private collectors are deciding to build their own private museums. [4] This not only withdraws

[4] Take for instance the Falckenberg Collection in Hamburg, the Boros Collection in Berlin, the Stoschek Collection in Düsseldorf, as well as older establishments such as the Goetz Collection near Munich and the Hoffmann Collection in Berlin.

potential private capital that might otherwise be used to fund public museums, it also hinders important contentual incentives from reaching the museums – vital impulses that public institutions need in order to vividly persist. Arguments supporting this withdrawal generally claim that private individuals are more passionate and uncompromising collectors, while public museum collections tend to be interchangeable as they lack powerful visions and because compromises are the order of the day. In the eyes of the critics advocating this view, the public museum has lost much of its credibility and thus its authority. Despite the large number of, indeed positive, effects kindled by private commitment, it still seems problematical that art is ultimately undergoing privatisation and that public debate over the different, competing forces at work in this process is by no means envisaged. Choices, decisions and alternatives are no longer dependent on public dispute or legitimisation. Even if the majority of private initiatives and collections are publicly accessible, accessibility to them is limited as they remain under the control of private entities and may be revoked at any time. [5] Another key question posited by *Carte Blanche* was the following: if traditional ties to the museum through patronage and community-mindedness are dissolving, how can new forms of partnership be established between private persons and public institutions – notably, beyond egomania and disinterest?

Before *Carte Blanche* was launched, the participating partners were informed about the conditions of the project. A distinction was made between two forms of support: patronage and sponsoring. [6] Upon being invited by the GfZK to take part in *Carte Blanche*, the participating partners were required to pay dues to support the joint project and cover the costs of the exhibition, publicity and communication, as well as a concluding publication and the operating expenses of the exhibition space. Direct payments by the invitees or donations to the GfZK during the course of the project covered the necessary expenditures for the exhibitions. The participants were free to determine the content and co-workers of their exhibitions, on condition that they deliver to the GfZK the exhibition concept and curator's name six months before the show. In return, the GfZK provided them with professional competence and the necessary institutional infrastructure. The domiciliary rights remained with the GfZK. From the outset it was communicated to the public that the tasks and responsibilities related to each exhibition were divided among at least two partners, with the respective curators and institutional contacts being clarified and named in advance. [7] In addition, the associates of *Carte Blanche* committed themselves to take part in the *Carte Blanche Diskursiv* panel talks informing the audience about their respective motivations and ideas. This offered further insight into issues elicited by the project, including questions of patronage, sponsoring and the art market. If a dispute between the project partners was proven irresolvable, the invitee was given carte blanche, i.e., ultimate freedom of action. In this case however, GfZK reserved the right to publicly address and discuss problematical or apparently critical positions and their consequences. These regulations, which were also communicated to the public, clearly distinguish this project from other museums' exhibitions that are supported by collectors or corporations from the private sector. Normally, the conditions of display and essential financial transactions behind such activities are, if not deliberately kept secret, then at least not communicated. [8] The aim of *Carte Blanche* was to find out which partnerships, if applicable, could be feasible in the future, and what impact these would have on art, its institutions and the public sphere. A further objective was to elucidate differing conceptions of art and the participants' respective intents. On the one hand, the GfZK did not attempt to disconnect artistic discourse from economic necessities and constraints. On the other hand, the institution tried not to succumb to these pressures. Rather, it was the project's key aim to encourage the public to join in debates over economic processes in order to shape the latter. [9]

[5] The collections are open to visitors by appointment and during specified hours only, mostly on Saturdays. This serves to raise inhibition thresholds and restrict visitor groups.

[6] The patrons, all of whom were already 'Large Members' of the GfZK Friends Association before the commencement of the project, were not forced to make donations. The participating corporations signed a contract specifying the rental fee.

[7] Thus, the descriptions 'curated by' and 'in collaboration with' designated the respective responsibilities shared: the GfZK's curators either curated the respective exhibition themselves, or, if desired, collaborated as an institutional partner.

[8] The Brandhorst Collection in Munich is a case in point. It was agreed to maintain confidentiality on the contract between the Free State of Bavaria and Udo Brandhorst. See the radio manuscript of Bayrischer Rundfunk in: *Das eroberte Museum*, p. 290 ff.

[9] This applies to other GfZK projects as well, including the *café*, the *garden* and the *hotel*. Economic criteria are also central issues in *Auftrag für die Kunst?/A Contract for Art?*, featured in the 2010/11 programme.

The Realisation of Carte Blanche

As an introduction to the overall project, the exhibition entitled *Freundliche Feinde / Friendly Enemies* marked the beginning of *Carte Blanche*. The exhibition was co-curated by all the curators from GfZK who were also responsible for *Carte Blanche*. The title of the exhibition refers to a book by the Belgian political scientist Chantal Mouffe, describing how 'friendly enemies' share a common symbolic space, yet entertain different ideas as to how this space ought to be organised. [1] The artworks featured in the exhibition either belonged to the eleven participants, or, as in the case of alpha 2000 – who support but deliberately do not buy art – were borrowed from other owners.

The opening exhibition focused on questions concerning the relationship between art and the economy, including, amongst others, Rosemarie Trockel's *Das Capital. Alice im Wunderland* (Capital: Alice in Wonderland) from the Schmidt-Drenhaus Collection and, by Andreas Gursky's *Hauptversammlung (Regierung der Welt durch das Kapital)* (General assembly [using capital to rule the world]) from the Oetker Collection – works that deal with the economic processes shaping society. Other works addressed the economic situation of the artist, such as *Save me, help me* by Jakup Ferri or *Nine Stories, Eleven Dollars* by Kristina Leko, who were both awarded the alpha 2000 'Kunstpreis Europas Zukunft' (Art Prize Future of Europe). The exhibition combined these with the works of artists who have become brands in their own right, and thus integral parts of the economic machine, such as Neo Rauch and Matthias Weischer, as well as with works by artists like Martin Eder or Olaf Nicolai who consciously seek to exploit the mechanisms of the art market. These four artists are represented by Galerie EIGEN+ART.

    At specific locations in the exhibition, the observer was faced with keywords culled from the internet relating to texts on *Carte Blanche*. This structural principle drew together potentially conflicting terms and names like, for instance, 'visibility', 'complicity' and 'public' or 'museum trust' and 'foundations'. The terms 'economisation' and 'economy' figured alongside 'sponsoring', 'promotion', 'patronage' and 'critique'. In addition, large figures showing the costs of each exhibition were posted inside the exhibition space, facing outside. This served to depict the interlocking of the ideational and the material levels of the art exhibition. [2]

    Friendly Enemies was followed by the exhibition *Carte Blanche I* by alpha 2000, marking the start of the two-year project. The show was curated by GfZK curator Ilina Koralova in collaboration with alpha 2000's

[1] Chantal Mouffe, *The Democratic Paradox*, London / New York 2000, p. 13

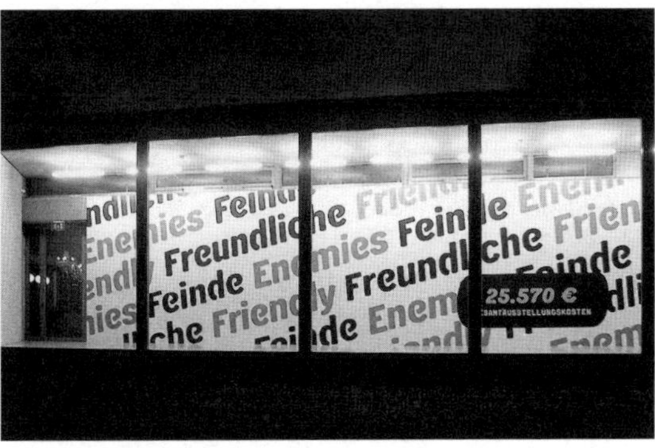

Friendly Enemies. 26.1.–24.3.2008, GfZK-2. Installation view. Design: Kay Bachmann and Philipp Paulsen.

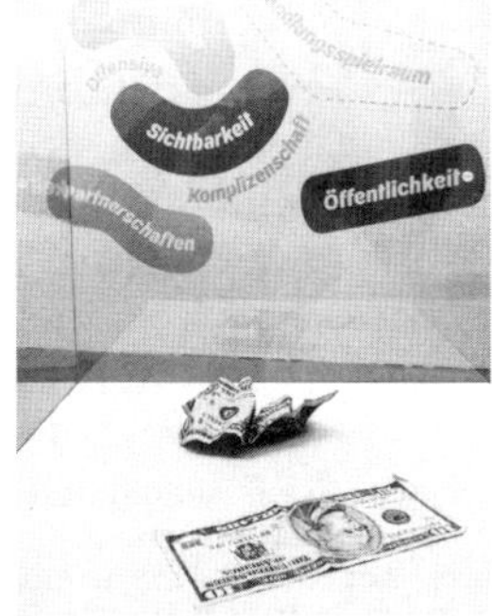

Kristina Leko. *Nine Stories and Eleven Dollars*. Installation view.

[2] Production costs were also specified on all printed matter accompanying the exhibitions.

Matthias Brühl. The works by the five winners of the alpha 2000 'Art Prize Future of Europe' thwarted the fears and expectations that the GfZK was surrendering to the art market, that it was encouraging affluent collectors and corporations to instrumentalise art and the institution as a forum of personal showmanship, and that a greater amount of 'safe art' would be exhibited. The prizewinners confronted economic questions in an uncompromising manner, investigating in various different ways the conditions that determine their lives and work.

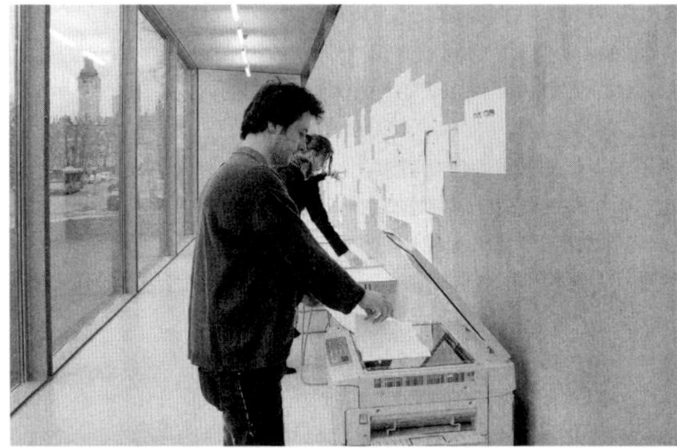

Carte Blanche I: alpha 2000, *Art Prize Future of Europe*. 5.4.–8.6.2008, GfZK-2. Jakup Ferri, winner 2008.

Thematically, their works focused on what it means to be an artist in post-communist societies, on the desire to engage in an art world that is still predominantly western, or indeed on attempts to develop feasible alternatives to this. The exhibited works aimed to parody the fetishisation of art and to play off against each other the original and the reproduction. In this exhibition, one of the gallery's full height windows offered a particularly impactive image, framing a wall pinned with drawings by Jakup Ferri next to which stood a photocopier. Visitors could make complimentary photocopies of Ferri's drawings to take home with them.

The exhibition reflected the aim of the benefactors of the prize, who – because of their experience of the GDR regime and the repressive constraints imposed by it on certain forms of artistic expression – now seek to promote artistic practices that deliberately do not conform to society's prevailing expectations and ideas. Thus, 'Art Prize Future of Europe' is devoted to artists who, at the time of receiving the prize, figure only marginally or not at all in the art market. [3]

[3] The prize is aimed at supporting artists to find a professional path best suited to their needs, which neither necessarily rules out, nor explicitly has to lead to, the art market as a consequence.

alpha 2000's exhibition was followed by *Carte Blanche II* by the Leipziger Druckerei- und Verlagsgesellschaft (LVDG) publishing company. This exhibition again showcased the works of prizewinners, namely the seven winners of the LVZ prize, launched in 1994 to coincide with the newspaper's centenary. In contrast to the exhibition by alpha 2000, this show included works from the LVZ's own collection, accompanied by works on loan from the Leipzig Museum of Art (Museum der bildenden Künste) as well as a selection of works by other artists that the company had acquired over the years. Works by internationally acclaimed artists rooted in the local context, like Neo Rauch and Matthias Weischer account for the importance of the collection. [4] The exhibition was curated by GfZK curator Andreja Hribernik and myself.

[4] The company possesses a significantly smaller number of works by artists who are not from Leipzig or were not educated at the Academy of Visual Arts (Hochschule für Grafik und Buchkunst) in Leipzig. This inspired the curatorial decision, also supported by the LVDG, to borrow for the exhibition a larger work by prizewinner Daniel Roth from the artist's gallery in Karlsruhe.

It was the company's express wish to see the works from the LVDG's collection professionally curated and under essentially very different conditions to those prevailing in the company headquarters. [5→] The exhibition, which was structured according to the curators' enquiries into the status, perception, circulation, distribution, and appropriation of the image, was accompanied by a special supplement in the *Leipziger Volks-*

zeitung newspaper, which dealt with the various different reasons for collecting art advanced by the LVDG as well as the GfZK. The museum's educational and mediatory mandate and the distribution of art via a daily paper were central topics, as were questions concerning possible presentation formats in an exhibition context between household pragmatism and professional criteria. The newspaper supplement was integrated in the exhibition as a huge expanse of wallpaper.

[5] The company's former managing director, Bernd Radestock, is a friend of the arts and also a painter. In other words, he is open towards the idea of supporting the arts: most likely his personal interest in art motivated the decision to take part in *Carte Blanche*.

Carte Blanche III showed part of the private collection of Arend and Brigitte Oetker. The exhibition was curated by Brigitte Oetker and Christine Schneider, and was accompanied by myself on behalf of the GfZK. It focused on the Oetker couple's shared past of some twenty-five years, featuring works the two purchased together and with which they surround themselves to this day. The exhibition included works by Peter Fischli and David Weiss, Isa Genzken, Martin Kippenberger, Hanno Otten, Thomas Struth, Wolfgang Tillmans, Rosemarie Trockel, Franz West, Richard Artschwager, John Baldessari, Alighiero Boetti, Mike Kelley, Louise Lawler, Jorge Pardo, Ellen Gallagher, and Wade Guyton. What is common to the artists selected for the exhibition is their use of simple everyday materials, a tentativeness of expression, and humour as a means to deliberately subvert concepts of representation and repeatedly confront the status and disposition of both the artist and the artwork. The ruminative and occasionally humourously self-reflective quality expressed in their works was transferred to the curatorial concept, which gave short shrift to gestures of gravitas and solemnity. Moreover, the private feel of the exhibition was reflected not only by the selection of specific works and their respective formats, but also by the decision to include additional elements from the Oetkers' private home, ranging from pieces of furniture, carpets and lamps to presentation styles recalling a domestic ambience. [6] The

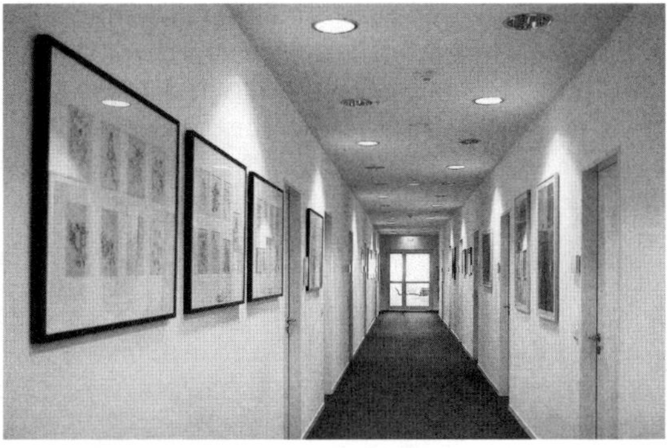

View of a corridor in the Leipziger Verlags- und Druckerei-gesellschaft company headquarters.

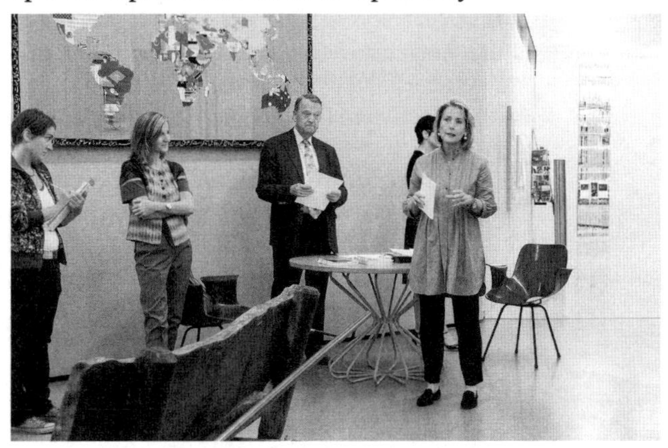

Carte Blanche III: *Poems in View of the Facts – Works from the Arend and Brigitte Oetker Collection.* 30.8.–26.10.2008, GfZK-2. Exhibition opening.

exhibition also featured pieces on loan from museums that had previously received the works as donations to their respective collections. [7→] One of the Oetkers' most important motives to take part in *Carte Blanche* was to subject the artworks with which they surround themselves at home to public appraisal and discussion. Furthermore, the exhibition was an ideal occasion for the Oetkers to embark on the process of systematically

[6] This included a number of artworks such as carpets by Rosemarie Trockel, chairs by Franz West and lamps by Jorge Pardo – all objects whose status oscillates between the artistic and the utilitarian.

[7] This aspect of the exhibition illustrated the principle of donating privately owned works to public museums in order to support their collections. There are no conditions attached to the donation of artworks. The museum director is always asked in advance about his/her specific wishes. After the end of *Carte Blanche III* a total of three additional works by Blinky Palermo, Hanno Otten and Jorge Pardo were given to the GfZK. One work by Mike Kelley was given to the Ludwig Museum in Cologne.

cataloguing and researching their collection. Thus, *Carte Blanche III* was an opportunity combining personal preferences, a passion for art and artists, social commitment, and an interest in kindling public debate.

Carte Blanche IV was anticipated with much excitement for it was an exhibition organised in collaboration with Galerie Dogenhaus, one of the two participating commercial galleries invited by GfZK to take part in the project. Jochen Hempel wanted to present two artistic positions: Mark Lombardi, an artist who is highly esteemed particularly by artists and curators, and the 'emerging' artist Julius Popp. Whereas the Dogenhaus gallery represents Popp, who is also based in Leipzig, Hempel had to ask the Estate of Mark Lombardi in New York to lend him

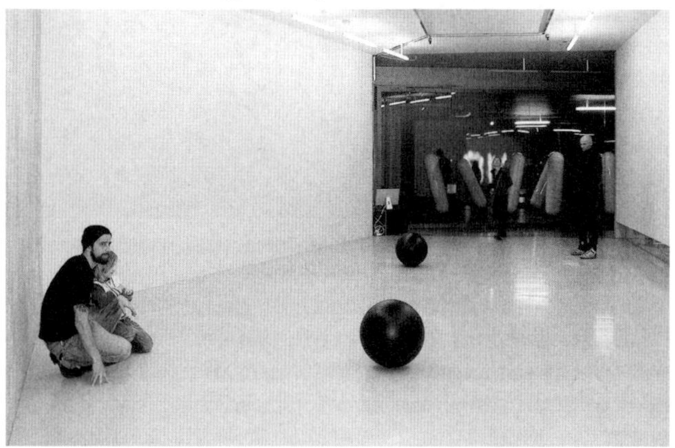

works by the artist, who passed away at a young age. The curatorial concept aimed to elucidate similarities between the two artists, whose works' characteristic complexity is the result of intense research. While Lombardi examines the entanglements genuinely inherent to systems of political and economic power, Popp investigates the flux of information and systems of knowledge production in the context of a highly technological environment. In their works, both artists analyse the mechanisms and processes that control society and impact on human existence. Beside the explicitly contentual and curatorial

Carte Blanche IV: Dogenhaus Gallery, *Mark Lombardi / Julius Popp*. 8.11.2008 – 9.1.2009, GfZK-2. Exhibition opening.

objective to link the work of the two selected artists, the exhibition was also driven by Jochen Hempel's wish to offer Julius Popp a forum for a broader audience – in turn generating greater public exposure and interest. Thus Hempel's choice also obliquely reflects on *Carte Blanche's* intrinsic questions concerning the nature of interest-based entanglements, mutual dependencies, and their consequences. Jochen Hempel chose to curate the exhibition himself, in collaboration with GfZK's Ilina Koralova.

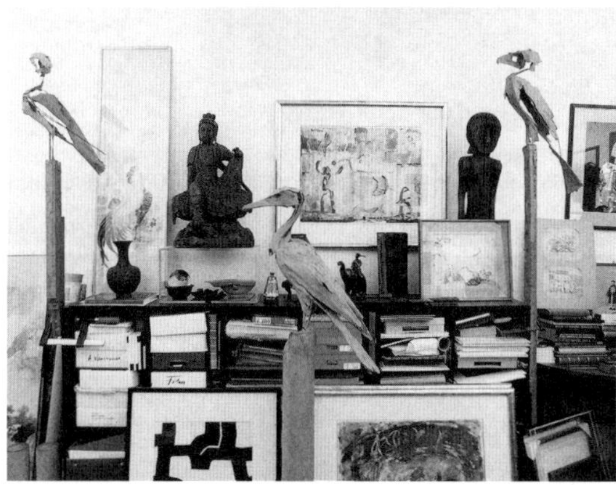

Similarly, *Carte Blanche V* focused on strategies of generating attention. The private collector Leon Janucek decided *not* to showcase his own collection, choosing instead to promote the seventy-year-old artist Dieter Finke, whom he considers underrated, by means of an exhibition and a catalogue raisonné of his œuvre. Leon Janucek asked me to curate the exhibition. Finke has been working in Berlin since the 1950s, with extended stays in New York during the 1970s and 1980s. His works are included in many private collections in Berlin. However, apart from occasional, casual collaborations in the 1980s

Manfred Heckmann's antiques shop with works by Dieter Finke.

and 1990s, Dieter Finke has never been represented by a commercial gallery. His first major solo show was at the Museo Universitario del Chopo (Chopo University Museum) in Mexico City in 2000. *Carte Blanche V* was taken as an incentive to mount an extensive exhibition of work from Finke's formative period up to the present. In close collaboration with the artist, Finke's entire œuvre was catalogued and contextualised art historically and socio-historically for the purpose of the exhibition and the accompanying publication. The works shown

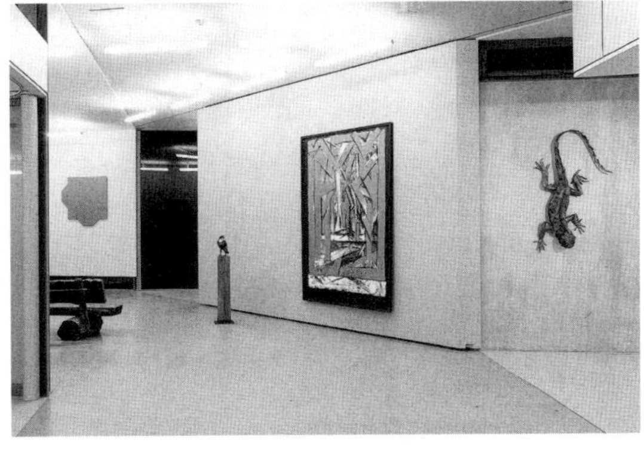

Carte Blanche V: Leon Janucek, *Dieter Finke – Works.* 24.1.–22.3.2009, GfZK-2.

in the exhibition were on loan from other collectors or the artist himself. The only piece in the show belonging to Leon Janucek, a bronze iguana, was produced especially for *Carte Blanche V*. When the exhibition was over, this work was donated to GfZK. [8]

[8] Dieter Finke also donated one artwork to the GfZK consisting of a large landscape painting.

    Carte Blanche V was followed by a presentation of the VNG – Verbundnetz Gas AG collection. In *Carte Blanche VI*, VNG decided to divide the exhibition into two parts, with Frank-Heinrich Müller and Christine Rink curating the photography and painting/drawing parts respectively, in collaboration with GfZK's curator Ilina Koralova. In the exhibition entitled *EAST – for the record*, works from both of the collection's main areas were shown together for the first time. [9] Furthermore, taking part in *Carte Blanche* with *EAST – for the record*, offered VNG an incentive as well as a title for a new building block in its photographic collection, pinpointing the social transformations in Germany between August 1989 and January 1990. This new area of focus concentrates on various different events that were going on at the same time and thus creates a multiperspectival view of this brief, yet historically impactive period. [10] The artworks themselves, which are predominantly from

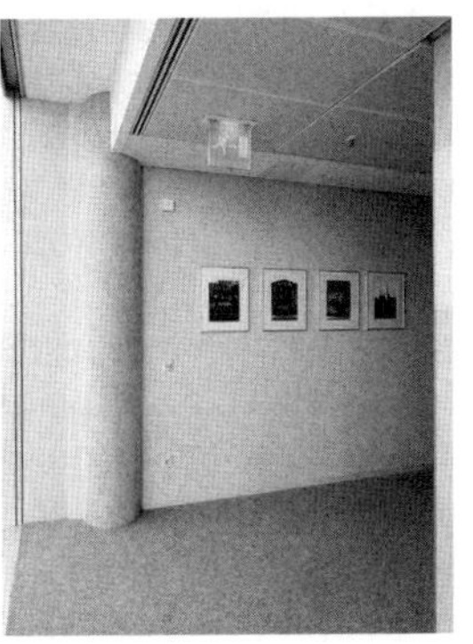

[9] One area of focus, concentrating on the purchase of paintings and drawings by younger artists, offers support during the early stage of their careers.

View of a corridor in the VNG – Verbundnetz Gas AG company headquarters.

Saxony, as well as the collection's contentual emphases, underline the company's high degree of commitment to the local context. *Carte Blanche VI* offered VNG – Verbundnetz Gas AG, who operate at a national/supranational level, the opportunity to effectively publicise and draw attention to their local commitment and fulfilment of responsibility to the regional community. This aspect serves as a significant counterpoint to repeated debates in recent years, often held in and by the mass media, about the shareholdings, shareholders' majorities, and the regional importance of the VNG – Verbundnetz Gas AG, as well as global financial structures.

[10] The majority of the photographs were taken in passing and do not belong to the stock of iconic images documenting the autumn of 1989. Only in retrospect did the photographers select them as a personal testimony to this specific period of history. As an image could not be found for each individual day, the calendric lacunae are integral parts of the project.

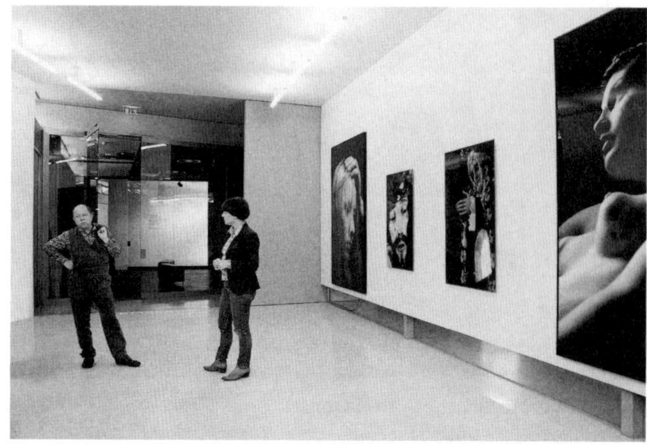

Carte Blanche VII: Gallery EIGEN+ART, *New York – Basel – Berlin – London – Miami*. 20.6. – 6.8.2009, GfZK-2. Exhibition opening.

For *Carte Blanche VII*, the EIGEN+ART gallery chose to make public its art fair curatorial strategies by exhibiting the tactical concepts that underlie the gallery's booths at five major international art fairs. The exhibition was curated by GfZK's curator Julia Schäfer in collaboration with Gerd Harry Lybke and Elke Hannemann from EIGEN+ART. *Carte Blanche VII* consisted of reconstructions of five sections each referencing the gallery's fair booths at Art Basel, Art Forum (Berlin), Frieze Art Fair (London), the Armory Show (New York City), and Art Basel Miami Beach respectively. Art was displayed in all except the last of these zones, as the 'Art Basel Miami Beach' section remained empty at the beginning and end of the exhibition as a reference to the fact that, due to the financial crisis, the gallery did not take part in the art fair. However, Lybke reorganised this decision and adapted it to the Leipzig context by inviting Uwe Kowski, whom his gallery represents and who won the 'Leipziger Jahres-ausstellung' (Leipzig annual exhibition) art award, to present a selection of his works. [11] Lybke's collaboration with Mexican gallery owner Hilario Galguera was a trial run of their joint exhibition later at the art fair in Berlin. Lybke also offered Galguera an independent zone within the exhibition for showing work. Gerd Harry Lybke often emphasised that he was particularly interested in *Carte Blanche* from a cultural-political perspective. His decision to display the economic strategies of the EIGEN+ART gallery is closely related to the project's primary concept, which involves disclosing the conditions determining the exhibition.

[11] Uwe Kowski has been represented by Gallery EIGEN+ART since 1992.

Carte Blanche VIII enabled Doris and Klaus F. K. Schmidt to exhibit part of their collection, combined with examples of their decade-long civic commitment. [12] Centred around photographic works by Eberhard Havekost, Cindy Sherman, Nina Pohl, Beate Gütschow, Thomas Ruff, Lutz Fritsch, and Candida Höfer, Doris and Klaus F. K. Schmidt curated the exhibition themselves in collaboration with curator Johannes Schmidt and myself as the GfZK project partner. Structurally, *Carte Blanche VIII* focused on various artistic themes and genres ranging from landscape/nature, the human body/corporeality, to abstract art. The bodies of work by Rosemarie Trockel, Hermann Glöckner, Blinky Palermo, Thomas Scheibitz, Olaf Holzapfel, and Thomas Schütte reveal the principle by which the Schmidts' collect art, namely by purchasing more than one work by each artist. A primary objective of *Carte Blanche VIII* was to set an example so as to encourage others to similarly support the arts. In this connection, the exhibition also included editions sent by Klaus F. K. Schmidt to his clients since the 1970s with the aim of enthusing them for art. The exhibition

[12] In this connection, the substantial number of works donated to museums located mainly in Dresden, the editions commissioned as gifts for the clients of Klaus F. K. Schmidt's audit and tax consulting companies and the initiation of the Forum for Art in the Present, deserve particular mention. See the interview with Doris and Klaus F. K. Schmidt in: *Das eroberte Museum*, p. 182 ff.

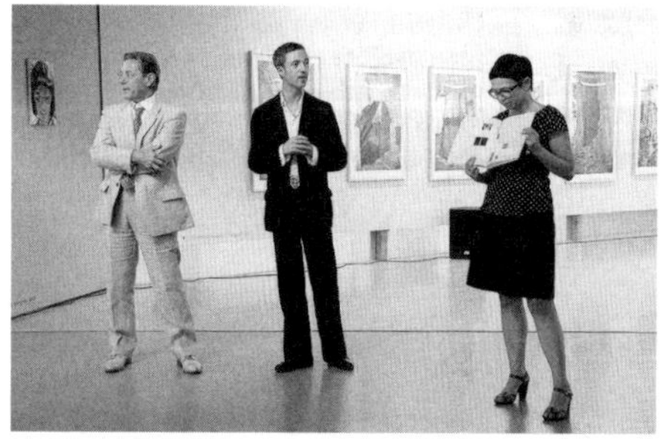

Carte Blanche VIII: *Listen to Your Eyes. Works from the Schmidt-Drenhaus Collection.* Exhibition opening.

also publicised the project *Forum für Kunst in der Gegenwart* (Forum for Art in the Present), co-founded by the Schmidts in Dresden. *Carte Blanche VIII* hosted the 33rd Forum on the following question: do exhibitions curated by private collectors generate a different form or format of display?

Carte Blanche IX presented a selection of works from the Sachsen Bank Collection, with supplementary works from the collection of the regional bank of Baden-Württemberg (LBBW). The exhibition included reconstructions of some of the projects realised during GfZK scholarships funded by Sachsen Bank, as well as collaborative projects from previous years – such as *Schreibstation* (writing station), *Kalender* (calendar) and *Flurstück* (corridor piece). *Schreibstation* and *Kalender* presented images of works from the Sachsen Bank and GfZK collections in the form of postcards and calendar sheets. *Flurstück*, a one-to-one reconstruction in the GfZK of a corridor from the Sachsen Bank, consisted of a three part experimental set-up proposing various hitherto unfamiliar ways of exhibiting art in a bank. [13] Thus, the driving force behind *Carte Blanche IX* was the GfZK's and Sachsen Bank's years of common collaborative experience. The curator of the exhibition, Julia Schäfer, defined the show as a means of physically interconnecting the spatial realms of the bank and art businesses in order to mark out characteristic features of both.

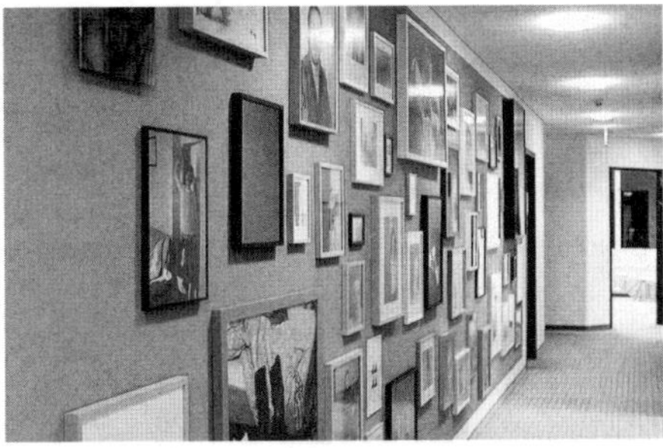

Photographs by students from the class of Prof. Timm Rautert (HGB) at the Sachsen LB (2007).

[13] All the model arrangements were carried out in the bank building proper between late 2007 and mid-2008.

The exhibition included components from the Sachsen Bank/LBBW building, such as the replica corridor mentioned above, office plants, wallpaper, carpets, and pieces of furniture as well as the entire furnishings of the chief executive's conference room, as physical references to their context of origin. Significantly, this fragmentary spatial shift was not limited to material objects. During *Carte Blanche IX*, Sachsen Bank held a number of its official events, including an executive board meeting, at GfZK. Sachsen Bank/LBBW's participation in *Carte Blanche* served a threefold purpose: to render publicly visible ten years of synergism between the bank and the GfZK, to underline the importance of external communication, and to reinforce corporate commitment to local culture, particularly in times of financial crisis.

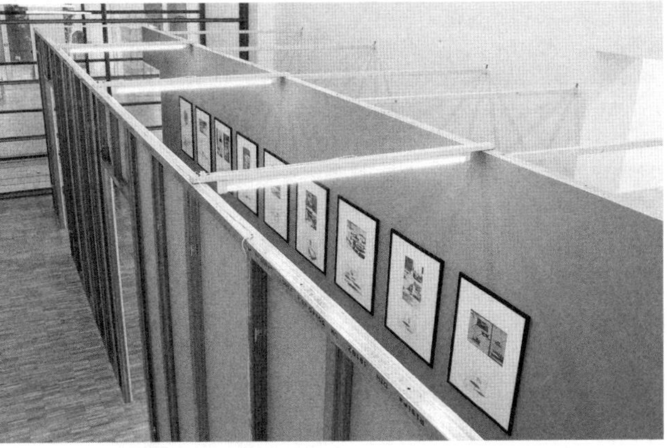

The Corridor as Display: Three Corridor Pieces. Variations of displaying the Sachsen Bank/LBBW Collection, GfZK-1, works by Neo Rauch.

Carte Blanche X aimed to promote and disperse the work of Hans Brosch. [14] Due to his pursuits as an abstract painter and graphic artist, Brosch, who was born in Berlin in 1943, was very much isolated as an artist in the context of the GDR. Encouraged by the interest in his work, Brosch moved to West Berlin in 1978, hence not only relocating but also transferring

[14] As the Schmitters exhibition was not envisaged at first, the Brosch exhibition was originally supposed to take place in the GfZK-2 building designed by as-if berlinwien. Thus, the two final exhibitions, *Carte Blanche X* and *Carte Blanche XI*, were to run concurrently, one in the GfZK-1 villa, the other in the GfZK-2.

to a completely different social system. After his work had been caught in the ideological crossfire of the Cold War, it was now subjected to the friction of the western art market's attention economy. The 'Hans Brosch Circle of Friends', a private initiative with eleven members, was founded in order to, as the name clearly suggests, promote and support the artist and his work. The society employed *Carte Blanche* as a means to mount a retrospective and publish a book about the artist's œuvre. [15] The exhibition was curated by guest curator Carsten Probst together with GfZK's Heidi Stecker. The GfZK owns three works by Hans Brosch, two of which were purchased in 1994 by the institution's founding director, Klaus Werner, the third having been donated by the artist.

[15] The broadcast journalist, author, and curator, Carsten Probst, first came across work by Hans Brosch in an exhibition of pieces from the GfZK Collection in 2007, subsequently initiating that the Hans Brosch Circle of Friends be invited to *Carte Blanche*.

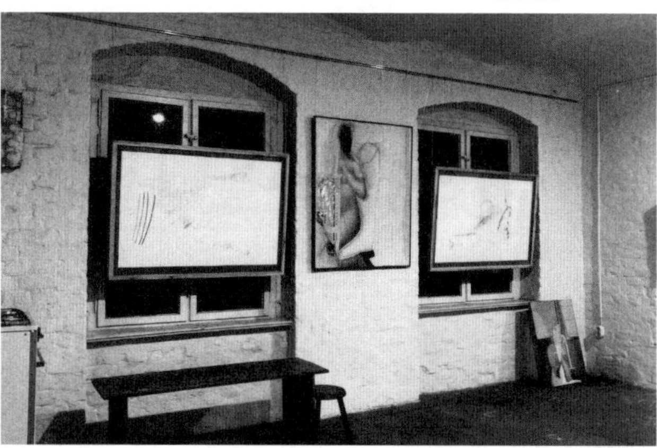

Exhibition of works by Hans Brosch, Klaus Werner's 'Sredzkistraße' gallery, 1989.

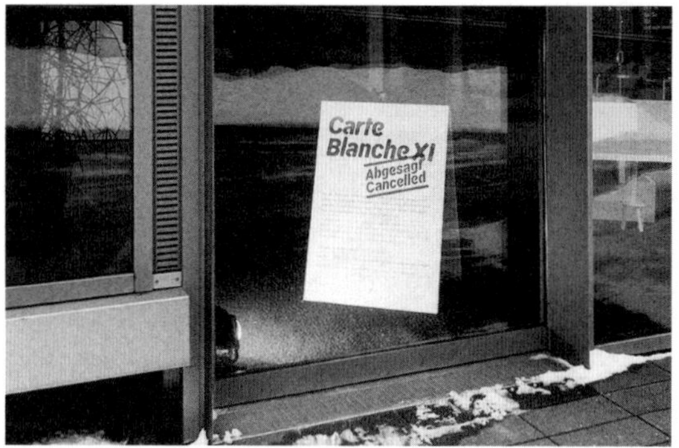

Carte Blanche XI: Vivien and Horst Schmitter, *'Cancelled'*. 23.1.–21.3.2010, GfZK-2, main door.

Whereas the GfZK actively invited these ten partners to take part in *Carte Blanche*, Horst Schmitter, after a dinner held by the 'Friends of the GfZK' association in late 2007, proposed putting on an exhibition combining objects by the American artist Donald Judd and his personal collection of cowboy boots that he had brought together over the years. Even though *Carte Blanche* was originally supposed to be limited to a total of ten positions only, the idea seemed interesting, particularly in view of the Hans Brosch exhibition, which was due to run at the same time. One of the most successful and renowned artists of the western world, Donald Judd, would have exhibited alongside the, at least internationally, largely unknown Hans Brosch from eastern Germany. An exhibition initiated by a private collector would thus have been on a par with those organised by committed art enthusiasts. However, shortly after, Horst and Vivien Schmitter replaced their initial concept for *Carte Blanche XI* with the idea of presenting works by Stephan Balkenhol in an exhibition curated by Jean-Christophe Ammann. One year later, in February 2009, the Schmitters suddenly withdrew from the project altogether for three reasons: the lack of a satisfactory curatorial concept, necessary financial savings during the crisis, and finally, their scepticism and general loss of interest in *Carte Blanche*. [16] As a consequence, *Carte Blanche XI* was called off. Nevertheless, the designated exhibition rooms remained empty for the designated duration of the exhibition. There were regular guided tours through the empty exhibition, informing visitors about the exhibition's unrealised plans and why they were unsuccessful.

[16] Written correspondence between Barbara Steiner and Horst Schmitter dated 26 February and 9 March 2009, the GfZK Archive.

By deciding to conduct *Carte Blanche*, the GfZK opened itself up to a variety of external interests that did not necessarily correlate with those of the institution. Assessments in advance of each respective concept were bound to vary. The GfZK had already collaborated with alpha 2000 and with Sachsen Bank on a continual basis for many years, and it had carried out a project with the VNG corporation as early as 2002. As the chairman of the foundation's board, Arend Oetker's ties to the GfZK are especially close. Previously, the GfZK had not collaborated with any of the other participants of *Carte Blanche*. Yet, in all cases, the sovereignty to define the project's direction was to a certain extent beyond the full control of the institution. For instance, it is probably quite unlikely that GfZK would have hosted exhibitions by Dieter Finke and Hans Brosch, as the institution's discursive focus was on other topics and artistic tendencies before *Carte Blanche* was launched. [17] Furthermore, thanks to the LVDG, VNG, and Sachsen Bank collections, the audience could see works by an unusually large number of painters from Leipzig, who played only a minor role in the GfZK's programme before *Carte Blanche*. [18] On the other hand, due to the occasionally restrictive conditions of loan, high rental fees, and moving expenses, the GfZK could not have afforded to exhibit such a large amount of blue chip works of international art.

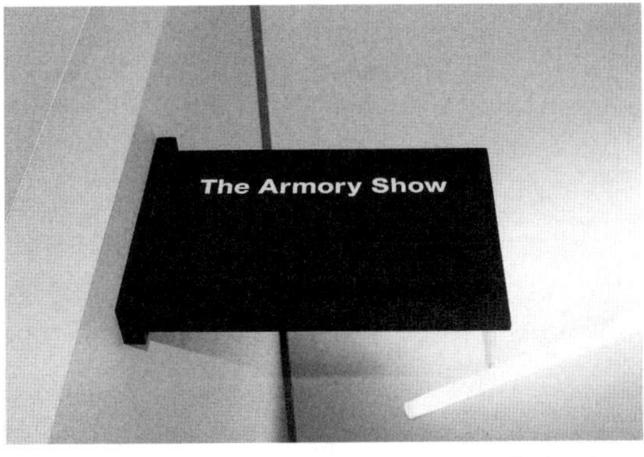

Carte Blanche VII: Gallery EIGEN+ART, *New York – Basel – Berlin – London – Miami*, GfZK-2. Design: Kristina Brusa.

[17] Interestingly, some conjectured that the works of the two artists mentioned here would not have been exhibited due to their lack of artistic quality. More on this in the chapter 'Consequences and Perspectives'.

[18] Numerous works by Matthias Weischer and Neo Rauch were exhibited in a total of four shows.

Apart from selecting the respective artistic positions, the project partners' main challenge was how to respond to different concepts of dealing with art. This applied to both the presentation as well as the specific forms of communicating art. If participants chose to collaborate with a GfZK curator, which was the case in six exhibitions, then GfZK essentially determined the exhibition. If participants curated their respective exhibitions themselves or hired a guest curator, then they were responsible for the show's profile. However, the institution never left the field entirely over to others. As project partners, the GfZK curators and staff represented the interests of the institution. During the preparatory stages that normally lasted several months, exhibition concepts and their spatial or technical feasibility would be discussed, and the specific criteria of presenting art defined – including exhibition signage, framing, and institutional necessities such as visitor services and the applicable mediatory and educational mandates. [19] This process of negotiation also involved setting and enforcing boundaries if participants forwarded unacceptable demands or ideas, for instance if they wanted to work exclusively with their own exhibition personnel, alter in any way the building's architectural substance or change the entrance area without taking into consideration the needs of the visitors. Above all however, *Carte Blanche* enforced a readiness to engage in public discussion. Significantly, the project's conceptual framework allowed for presentation modes and curatorial stances diametrically opposed to those of the GfZK. For instance, the placement of works selected by Galerie EIGEN+ART introduced

[19] The LVDG considered it practical to affix plexiglas signs with information about the artist directly onto the glass in front of the framed pictures, a wholly unsatisfactory form of labelling from the GfZK's point of view. It was also necessary to expressly demand the provision of certain services for visitors, ranging from seating to various art mediation programmes for adults, young people and children. It was decided early on to spend part of the *Carte Blanche* project budget on funding these programmes.

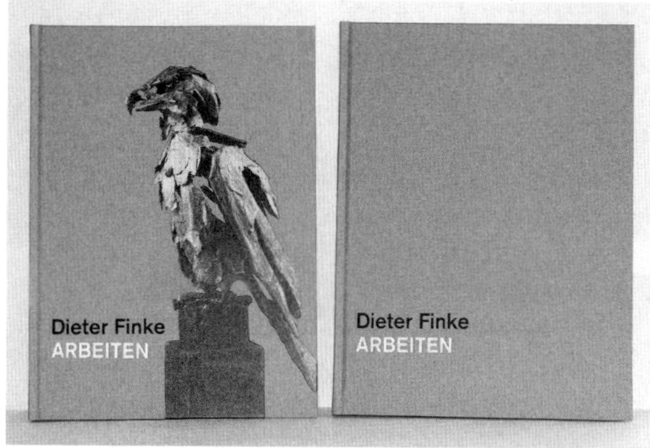

Two cover variations of *Dieter Finke – Works*. Publication in German and English. Design: Nicola Reiter.

into the art institution an economy-oriented, partly spectacular, and speculative exhibition practice. In the case of exhibitions with works from private collections, decisions were made on the grounds of personal motives and points of view, in contrast to the – necessarily more discursive and art historical – curatorial practice maintained by the GfZK. In the case of the two solo exhibitions by Hans Brosch and Dieter Finke, the GfZK not only had to come to an agreement with Leon Janucek or the circle of friends, but also with the artists themselves. Their aims and concepts differed greatly from those of the GfZK curators. Whereas both artists favoured their late works, the curators wanted to view works from all periods from which to draw a selection for the exhibition. The curators were also interested in the works' temporal contextualisation. [20]

In contrast to GfZK's general approach however, common to almost all *Carte Blanche* exhibitions was the idea that additional information on the works and their respective contexts was to be considered as 'external' to the art and was thus rejected. [21] An awareness of specific distinctions and characteristics hones the observer's understanding of different interests and possibilities. For a presentation to be successful at an art fair, it has to generate attention. By contrast, a museum exhibition is allowed to – indeed must be allowed to – offer a forum to less overtly spectacular artistic approaches. A private collector can develop a very personal relationship to art, which is often the strength of private collections. In the context of the museum however, this relationship is defined through discourse and is placed within a broader contentual and artistic time-scope. A private person is able to withdraw from obligations more readily than public or government institutions are, particularly if these obligations – as in Horst Schmitter's case – are not defined by a signed written contract. [22] Several participants, such as Gerd Harry Lybke or the Schmidt couple, responded directly to *Carte Blanche*. Lybke decided to aggressively reveal his own business practices. The Schmidts exhibited their commitment to art as an exemplary, multileveled approach, by means of donations to museums or their discussion forum held in Dresden once a month. The responses of other participants were more indirect. For instance, Jochen Hempel dealt with the contentual issues implied by *Carte Blanche,* such as economic dependencies and special-interest entanglements.

The exhibitions thus made visible the unavoidable process of mutual interaction, although *Carte Blanche* was sometimes criticised for not making the various different interests and conflicts sufficiently clear to the audience. [23→] Perhaps this critique arose from differences being barely distinguishable if one

[20] Whereas it was possible during the exhibition's preparatory stages to persuade Dieter Finke that the show should comprise work across a broad range of artistic media, Hans Brosch refused to show any of his stage designs, and insisted instead on showing only recent paintings. Ideas concerning the design of the two catalogues also differed greatly. The graphic designer who was commissioned to design the Hans Brosch catalogue was ultimately not the one recommended by GfZK. In contrast, Dieter Finke accepted the GfZK's proposal for the book interior, yet prevailed concerning the design of the book's cover. This subsequently involved producing a special edition of 50 copies of the book, in which the motif of the eagle on the cover is replaced by the name of the artist and the title of the book in a purly typographic design. For more information on Hans Brosch, see the interview with Heidi Stecker in: *Das eroberte Museum*, p. 229 ff.

[21] The alpha 2000 and Sachsen Bank / LBBW exhibitions were exceptions, with the two GfZK curators being granted maximum freedom concerning the curation of the shows.

[22] Agreements with the private partners and the companies were sealed with a handshake and in written form respectively.

focused on the individual artworks rather than on how they were presented – the selected configurations, modes of display, and hangs. Alongside the exhibitions themselves, other sources offered background information about the artists and their motivations, for the viewer to compare with the material provided by the GfZK. As by-products of each exhibition, video or audio recordings gave insight into the various different conceptual stances. [24] These documents were posted in the entrance area of the gallery building as well as on the project's official website. [25] In addition, on the website, the visitor could access video recordings of the lecture series *Carte Blanche Diskursiv* and all texts published on *Carte Blanche*. The communication project entitled *GfZK-3* was organised and conducted by GfZK's Andreja Hribernik.

Overall, it was expected that more tangibly real conflicts would arise during the course of *Carte Blanche*, from my point of view an idea fostered by clichéd views and predictable enemy images. [26] Even so, the intent from the very beginning was that *Carte Blanche* provide a surface on which to project a range of different expectations that would subsequently be either partially fulfilled or disappointed by the exhibitions. [27] These offer specific examples encouraging the analysis of existing opinions and judgements. I will elaborate on this objective in the chapter 'Consequences and Perspectives'.

[23] See the interview with Matthias Brühl in: *Das eroberte Museum*, p.123 ff. Presenting works by Dieter Finke, only *Carte Blanche V* was at odds with the GfZK's general curatorial practice, and was perceived as visibly conflicting with the institution.

[24] The Oetkers' wish to recede into the background inspired the decision to produce an audio recording in which the Oetkers' voices, and also that of the museum director, were replaced by actors. The recording is based on an interview published in: Brigitte Oetker, *Aus der Sammlung von Arend und Brigitte Oetker*, Cologne 2008, pp.49–60

[25] Cf. www.gfzk-3.de/index.php?cmd=search&category=1

[26] More on this in the following chapter 'Responses to *Carte Blanche*'.

[27] For example, the corporation alpha 2000 was not interested in the idea that the exhibition might increase the value of the art shown; the Oetkers and Schmidts represent a type of collector whose commitment is explicitly society-oriented; the collector Leon Janucek and Brosch's Circle of Friends support artists that are tangential in terms of the art market and public visibility, and this is unlikely to change after their exhibitions at the GfZK, i.e., their exhibitions will only have a marginal effect on the artists' status and market value.

Responses to Carte Blanche [1]

[1] The press review in the German edition of this book, *Das eroberte Museum*, p.250 ff., provides extensive media responses to *Carte Blanche*.

The exceptional media response to the project already began in January 2006, kindled by my interview in the internet journal *artnet*. One year before the project was due to begin, the press announced: 'Leipzig museum rents out exhibition space to private collectors and companies, including two commercial galleries. Tenants to determine museum programme.' Basically, *Carte Blanche* had been reduced to this journalistic formula before it started, and when it was launched with the exhibition by alpha 2000, the preliminary excitement was already waning. However, negative remarks by Chris Dercon, former director of Haus der Kunst in Munich, provoked a further outcry in the summer of 2008. Although he knew about the project only from hearsay (*The Art Newspaper*'s Jane Morris conducted a telephone survey about *Carte Blanche*), Dercon repeatedly described it as 'insane', 'opportunistic' and 'naive'. [2] In spite of the somewhat facile arguments forwarded in *art*, *Monopol* and *The Art Newspaper* emphasising the project's obvious scandalousness, other publications such as *Boot Print*, *Die Presse*, *Kristiansbladet* and *Artforum* analysed in a far more differentiated manner the relationship between the public and private spheres in the art field. Views of the project parted significantly towards its end, ranging from 'public-private collaboration unsuccessful' to 'one of the most important projects of the recent past'. [3] Surprisingly, in almost none of the talks was there any critical reflection of the changing economic conditions to which art institutions are subject today, and hardly any comparisons were drawn between the differing responses to this situation. While the national and international press focused mainly on the concept of *Carte Blanche*, the viewers of the individual exhibitions were primarily from the vicinities of Leipzig, Dresden and Berlin.

[2] Dercon publicly took back his accusation at the conference, which we both attended, about potential forms of partnerships between private art collections and public museums held at the SIK ISEA, Swiss Institute for Art Research ('PPP – On the Relationship between Public and Private').

[3] Cf. Robert Schimke, ddp: 'Kooperation zwischen öffentlicher Hand und Privaten gescheitert' (public-private cooperation failed), www.news-adhoc.com/kooperation-zwischen-oeffentlicher-hand-und-privaten-gescheitert-idna2010031689173/,16.03.2010 (reprint denied) and 'Laissez Faire. Maria Lind on Carte Blanche', in: *Artforum International*. XLVIII, no.10 2010, pp.147 & 380, cf. *Das eroberte Museum*, p.305

In terms of media coverage, the show by Brigitte and Arend Oetker received the highest, while alpha 2000 received the least response. In all cases, however, the number of articles published reflects the respective level of name recognition and social status of *Carte Blanche*'s participating partners and artists. Thus, the project's press coverage displays a clearly recognisable hierarchical structure of perception. Many journalists (*Sächsische Zeitung*, *Kreuzer*, *Leipziger Volkszeitung*) repeatedly formulated their disgruntlement with the exhibitions, arguing that *Carte Blanche* lacked internal conflict, or that the project failed to express the 'real' conflicts between the participating parties. However, the majority of rumours proliferated about the gallery owners. The remark that Jochen Hempel of Galerie Dogenhaus sold a work by Mark Lombardi from the exhibition, hinted at a potential scandal. Ultimately, it transpired that the work had been sold to Reina Sofia in Madrid prior to the exhibition, and not by Dogenhaus but by Pierogi. For curatorial reasons, the work was exhibited one last time in Leipzig – and not for the entire duration of the exhibition – before it was shipped to Spain. [4→] Furthermore, rumours claimed that Gerd

Harry Lybke deducted from his rental agreement the remaining square metres of exhibition space occupied by his 'Art Miami zone' and that he sublet another area to Hilario Galguera. Both claims were false. [5] Nonetheless, looking at the overall response to this two-year project, at least the *Leipziger Volkszeitung's* reporter Meinhard Michael upheld the idea that the 'individual exhibitions are rewarding' although he considered *Carte Blanche* to be problematical inasmuch as the project 'solicits the intruder (as the crime rate is high anyway).' [6] Other writers viewed *Carte Blanche's* insights into forms of collaboration between private partners and a public museum as comparatively insignificant. Still, the total number of articles about this particular GfZK research project is substantially ly higher than those dealing with any other previous projects.

Visitor numbers marginally increased during *Carte Blanche*. However, this was very much in line with a general, continual increase during 2008 and 2009. Contrary to what might have been expected, the exhibition series accounted for neither a severe rise nor fall in visitor numbers. They remained roughly the same for each exhibition, with Oetkers taking a slight lead in the final count. Visitor feedback indicates that the greatest response was to the Oetker collection, the Dieter Finke exhibition and the LVDG and VNG – Verbundnetz Gas AG collections. [7] The Oetkers were praised particularly for including works by artists who were never or scarcely exhibited in eastern Germany. The Dieter Finke exhibition was marked by a high degree of emotional identification, thus reaching visitors that do not belong to the GfZK's regular audience. This was also true in the case of the show with works from the LVDG collection. [8] The VNG exhibition aroused attention above all because it focused on photographs of events leading up to and taking place around 1989. Visitors' responses to *Carte Blanche* tended to be positive, and the massive fears voiced prior to the project about the sellout of art and the GfZK declined significantly during *Carte Blanche*. The specialist audience's interest in *Carte Blanche* was tremendous from the very outset, beginning as early as 2007. [9] At the Bildmuseet (Museum of Art) in Umea and the Bonniers Kunsthall in Stockholm, Sweden, the project aroused interest first and foremost in the possibilities of collaboration between institutions and private partners; at Bard College in Annandale-on-Hudson, New York, interest was voiced in how private commitment can be effectively exhibited to the public, an aspect that ties in well with ongoing debates in the internet forum *artworldsalon*. [10] At the ICA in Dunaúyváros, Hungary, the Muzeum Sztuki in Lódz, Poland and the Moderna Galerija in Ljubljana, Slovenia, this type of project was seen above all as an opportunity to mobilise individuals/corporations from the private sector to support art institutions. Held at the Swiss Institute of Cultural Sciences SIK ISEA

---

[4] Cf. the conversation with Jochen Hempel, ibid. p.151ff. and the press reports on his exhibition, ibid. p.282ff.

[5] Cf. the conversation with Gerd Harry Lybke, ibid. p.177ff. and the press reports on his exhibition, ibid. p.297ff.

[6] 'This is a tactic originally used by people from Schilda. Burglars are invited into the house (because the crime rate is high in any case) and are politely asked to behave like janitors.' In: Meinhard Michael, 'Von Einbrechern und Hausmeistern. Halbzeit des Projektes Carte Blanche in der Leipziger Galerie für Zeitgenössische Kunst', (On Burglars and Janitors. A Halftime Report on the Project Carte Blanche at the Leipzig Museum of Contemporary Art.), *Leipziger Volkszeitung*, 24.&25.1.2009, cf. *Das eroberte Museum*, p.287ff.

[7] Cf. the interview with members of GfZK's visitor service personnel, ibid. p.237ff.

[8] Strangely, the subjective assessments of the visitor service personnel do not correspond with the visitor statistics, according to which the LVDG exhibition does not rank second place after the Oetkers, as was originally presumed.

[9] During the past two and a half years, numerous art institutions and art colleges invited me to give lectures about *Carte Blanche* or to take part in discussions about the relationship between the public and private sectors, and the economisation of the museum. From late 2007 to early 2008, I also held a lectureship at the University of Applied Arts in Vienna and lectured on art and economics.

[10] Cf. www.artworldsalon.com/blog/, 27.12.2009, see ibid. p.263

in Zurich, the congress entitled *PPP – On the Relationship between Public and Private*, foregrounded the necessity of egalitarian discourse between the collector and the institution, and at the University of Applied Arts in Vienna, discussions focused on the need to render increasingly transparent private sector commitment to the museum. [11] All of these examples were based on the specific situation prevailing in each of these art institutions and museums, exemplifying selective viewpoints based on a variety of different interests. This shows, at least to some extent, the variety of definitions associated with the correlation of the private and the public in different cultural contexts. [12]

[11] Whereas in Sweden there are practically no private initiatives to support the arts, in the United States the majority of museums rely on benefactors from the private sector for financial support. In post-communist countries, there is a general loss of interest in public institutions. Colleagues often reported that while the state is cutting back its financial support for the arts, individuals from the private sector do not feel inclined to compensate this lack. In Switzerland, there is a long tradition of partnerships between the private sector and public museums. In Austria, different groups regularly complain about the fact that collaboration agreements are always made within a small circle of people and are generally not communicated to the public before negotiations have been concluded. This situation was repeatedly addressed in the context of panel discussions at the University of Applied Arts in Vienna.

[12] This section of the analysis is about the personal opinions and observations resulting from the discussions held at the respective locations. It is by no means an exhaustive investigation. However, these views partly correspond with responses to *Carte Blanche* in the foreign press.

Consequences and Perspectives

Visitor numbers and the reactions to *Carte Blanche* indicate that this controversial project was 'profitable', at least in terms of the resulting exhibitions. Thus, as a representation of 'profitability', this demonstrates that involving external parties might potentially improve the GfZK programme. In March 2007, Meinhard Michael, critic of the *Leipziger Volkszeitung*, tried to put his finger on it by rhetorically pondering, 'Will anyone miss the wordy, analytically critical intervention art that lacks artworks, so favoured by the GfZK?', then proceeding to answer the question himself: 'Indeed, its revision is long overdue.' [1]

Three groups of players from the private sector that continue to be powerful are pivotal to the *Carte Blanche* research project. These include corporations, commercial galleries and private collectors who have either decoupled themselves from the public museum to pursue their own parallel projects, or who seek to introduce their own private interests into the museum, thus distancing themselves from the type of society-minded activities described earlier on in the first chapter. Conceived as an experimental forum, *Carte Blanche* revolved around the question of whether or not, and to which extent, the groups mentioned above are still integral to the agendas of society. At the same time, *Carte Blanche* aimed to make this group of protagonists face the opposing expectations that other social groups hold toward the museum. [2] Ultimately, the project addressed not only the relations between the eleven participants and the GfZK, but also focused more generally on the relations between companies, collectors, museum managements, curators, artists, (disparate) audiences, political representatives, and so on. In this connection, potential conflicts arose not only between, but also within, each one of these various factions, a phenomenon that led to specific 'enemy images' no longer being distinctly ascribable to any specific group(s). [3]

In the following, I would like to delineate several areas of conflict. In *'The Realisation of Carte Blanche'* above, I described in detail the differing approaches adopted by *Carte Blanche's* protagonists and the GfZK. The different concepts served to define the objects and objectives of each respective exhibition, and were relevant mainly in terms of curatorial strategies, visitor services, and public relations. However, opposing opinions were also voiced by individuals from the field of professional art, who thought the entire project was questionable or who considered certain artists – especially Finke and Brosch – as artistically inferior or irrelevant in the context of contemporary art, despite their being visibly defended by the GfZK. [4] Moreover, the

[1] Meinhard Michael: 'Gute Idee, sagt der Therapeut. Warum die Waffen ausliefern und das Arsenal dazu? Zu den Plänen der GfZK', (Good idea, says the therapist. Why deliver the weapons as well as the arsenal? On the GfZK's plans.), *Leipziger Volkszeitung*, 29.3.2007, cf. *Das eroberte Museum*, p. 253 f.

[2] This raises questions as to the role of state financing of public institutions and its connection to private commitment. During *Carte Blanche*, negotiations were conducted with the Free State of Saxony and the City of Leipzig concerning the need to increase the annual funds. The negotiations were successful and the municipal council raised their funds in 2010. In 2007, Arend Oetker had already confirmed his willingness to up his financial support. The Free State of Saxony has yet to confirm its position. Resources from the project funds will be used to pay the 2010 balance.

[3] I am convinced that particularly this accounted for the qualms people had about *Carte Blanche*, as the GfZK refused from the outset to perceive the project's protagonists as its enemies, or to play the economic and ideational spheres against each other. Rather, the main goal was to seek, within each respective group, the possibilities and potentially overlapping interests that might foster partnerships.

[4] Providing these artists with a forum seemed only to justify the reservations towards *Carte Blanche* based on the assumption that such a project would be detrimental to artistic quality. These reservations were voiced in private conversations but also on numerous public occasions. Many people were not prepared to buy into the fact that I was genuinely interested in Dieter Finke's stance as an artist. If I hadn't been, I wouldn't have curated the exhibition. Since 1994, the GfZK Collection includes two works by Hans Brosch, which we also recently exhibited.

exclusively local scope of the project was often criticised. Indeed, the GfZK perceives the fact that in the new *Länder* there are no international collections comparable to those in western Germany merely as a reflection of the situation in eastern Germany, and not necessarily as a reflection of the artworks' quality. [5] Furthermore, the views of certain audience strata opposed those of GfZK, and the audience by no means generally agreed on *Carte Blanche*, just as a variety of different opinions were voiced by the press. [6] However, the project was largely welcomed at a municipal, that is to say, state level, because it was understood as fostering potential future forms of bilateral collaboration. Yet there were also voices that were critical, warning that the private sector influence on art institutions could become too great. [7] However, these diverging opinions, expectations, and reactions did not necessarily yield conflicts, and when they did, the conflicts were very different and of varying intensity. At least conflicts were not predetermined: *Carte Blanche* was driven by the desire to achieve a state of productive cooperation and exchange, and also by our successful collaborations with some of the project partners in the past. Still, conflicts did temporarily arise if participants planned exhibits that interfered with the structure of the building, if a participant wanted huge company logos to feature in the presentation, or if the standards of GfZK's visitor and communication services were in danger of being violated. Depending on the collaborative setup, almost all parties involved had to deal with additional frustrations, as the curators from GfZK were allowed to articulate, but not necessarily enforce, their ideas, and conversely, the curators sometimes blocked the participants' proposals. [8] Some conflicts could not be resolved, and subsequently remained in the exhibitions precisely as visible reminders of diverging opinions. [9] Conflicts also endured with members of the professional art field, the audience and the press, although certain expectations, opinions and ideas did evolve during the course of *Carte Blanche*, and this was expressed on various occasions. [10] Within these processes – and I emphasise the project's processual and not just discursive orientation – GfZK did not act as a higher-ranking neutral mediating between the opposing parties, but adopted a clear stance as one of the protagonists. This triggered enormous debate, as shown by the concluding event of *Carte Blanche Diskursiv*, in which I recapitulated and commented on the project. A key question raised by the audience concerned the concurrence of critical ability and involvement. In this connection, members of the audience criticised the description of *Carte Blanche* as a 'research project', and demanded that its evaluation should be conducted by an external entity in order to be objective. [11→]

In view of this, it is no coincidence that the introductory exhibition to *Carte Blanche*, which was conceived and curated by the GfZK, refers in its title

[5] This was an important point in the lecture I held on 21 October 2009 before an audience comprising directors of art institutions from Stuttgart and the collector Rudolf Scharpff.

[6] Some members of the GfZK's core audience were extremely critical, whereas other visitors outside this group were enthusiastic. Cf. the interview with members of GfZK's visitor service personnel, *Das eroberte Museum*, p. 237 ff.

[7] The question of whether GfZK ought to conduct *Carte Blanche* at all was discussed by the GfZK Foundation Board with representatives of the City Council and the Free State. The project was substantially supported by Arend Oetker from the very outset. Cf. the transcripts of meetings of the Foundation Board in the GfZK Archive.

[8] The bureaucratic burdens lessened substantially during *Carte Blanche*, as most of the private sector partners either assumed the administration of costs for the exhibition themselves, or, as in the case of the private collectors, they were not interested in a specification of costs. Due to the permanent negotiations concerning the exhibition conditions, psychological factors became increasingly important.

[9] In the interviews conducted with the project protagonists, it became apparent that this factor was not to be underestimated.

[10] In an interview conducted by me on 3 March 2010, the Leipzig based journalist Robert Schimke said that since he knew that all the texts about *Carte Blanche* would later be published in a book, he felt as if someone was looking over his shoulder while he was writing about it. This shows that the reception of *Carte Blanche* is an integral part of the project.

to Chantal Mouffe's *Friendly Enemies*. While the author initially developed her theses to be applied in the field of political theory, it seems apposite to apply them to *Carte Blanche*. Mouffe perceives conflict as a proactive force and rejects for various reasons the model of social consensus – primarily because this model is controlled by far too optimistic and idealised assumptions, and by the possibility of universal, rational approval. These, she argues, are not compatible with human societality. Mouffe believes that 'an approach geared towards consensus inevitably leads to antagonisms, rather than creating the conditions for a reconciled society', indeed discovering within this correspondence 'a blindness towards antagonism'. [12] Mouffe advocates replacing antagonistic forces with the idea of agonism through 'a vital "agonistic" sphere of public contest to enable various hegemonic projects to confront one another, thus affording conflicts legitimate expression'. [13] This describes the GfZK's position and the model upon which *Carte Blanche* is based. I am primarily interested in where, when and how conflicts arise in the art field, where they can be resolved and where they should or indeed must be maintained. Neither should antagonistic forces ever be fully reconciled, nor should opposing opinions and values feed all-encompassing relativism. Contrarily, *Carte Blanche* lends these competing viewpoints, opinions and stances the necessary spatial and discursive context, so that these can interact through the artworks, the configurations and modes of display. From the outset, the research projects, of which *Carte Blanche* is the most publicly visible, are conceived as offering potential friction surfaces both inside and outside the institution, although the primary focus is on continually challenging the art field's value system. [14] The temporary research projects as well as the changing annual exhibitions of works from the collection and the architectural concepts of the two exhibition buildings express this approach. [15]

Owing to the architectural concept, the GfZK-2 exhibition space provided ideal conditions for *Carte Blanche*, which is indeed why the project was conducted in that building. Whereas GfZK-1, a 'white cube' contained within a converted villa, epitomises the ideal exhibition space, the GfZK-2, designed by as-if berlinwien, is based on a spatial and functional concept that is modifiable and reversible. [16] The concept of the building revolves around constant redefinition, allowing the spaces to be 'charged' with ever changing functions. The glass sections can also function as display windows. The cinema doubles as a gallery or lecture theatre, and the café and exhibition space can be used as a project space or vice versa. A crucial point is that while the facility and fittings sensitise users to the potential changeability of the spaces and their respective functions, the building also imposes specific limitations on concepts of changeability and

[11] *Carte Blanche Diskursiv*, a project overview discussion held at GfZK-2 on 17 March 2010. On the possibilities of simultaneously conducting critique and complicity, see the text 'Corruption, Corruptibility and Complicity' in the present publication, p. 9. For a description of the characteristics of the *Carte Blanche* research project, see the introduction, ibid. p. 31

[12] Chantal Mouffe, *Über das Politische. Wider die kosmopolitische Illusion* (On the Political. Against the Cosmopolitan Illusion), Frankfurt am Main, 2007, pp. 8 & 10

[13] Ibid., p. 10

[14] At this point it already became apparent that GfZK's area of subsequent research, investigating 'A Contract for Art' from commissioned art to the art's social contract, would undoubtedly provide conflict potential once again, as these issues concern the status of the artwork, authorship and the creative myth. Frictions due to differing concepts of art are preprogrammed. This project focuses on committed citizens who, in contrast to the actors of *Carte Blanche*, do not belong to the group of people who usually control the art field. Their ideas and concepts confront those of professionals from the art field, i.e., the visions of individuals who have experience in continually supporting the arts. In each successive research project, the critical surfaces created by the institution open themselves to changing groups of people.

[15] The collection was reorganised in early 2007 based on the changed perception, assessment and evaluation of art after the political changeover of 1989. Specific thematic areas and constellations of works are intended to inspire debate about the heritage of the GDR, as well as discussion concerning the criteria of collecting art and defining artistic quality.

[16] Large sliding and revolving doors, ground-level slits, and curtains provide means to selectively interconnect or (sub)divide the rooms according to the exhibition situation and desired spatial configurations thus allowing for contentual and formal links.

stageability. Not all the walls are moveable, and it is technically impossible to completely remove any of them. Curtains can only be attached in specified locations, and some sections of the space cannot be darkened or screened off. Ground-level slits and incident sunlight function as deliberate 'disruptions' of visibility. Recesses and apertures throughout the building provide views inside and vistas toward the city centre, indicating that the gaze regime is determined by visibility and transparency. Its changeability affords the building a contingent, flowing character. Outside and inside merge, boundaries become blurred. [17]

[17] For an extensive description of the building and the projects conducted within it, see: as-if berlinwien, Barbara Steiner (eds.), *Spaces of Negotiation*, Berlin 2010.

Due to these characteristics, the building was ideally suited for *Carte Blanche*, in which private and public objectives constantly overlapped and different interests and expectations had to be negotiated within the parameters determined by the project.

In conclusion, I would like to mention the difficulties and consequences of an institutional project such as *Carte Blanche*. The institution jeopardised itself by conducting this project. It put itself in a precarious position by opening up to external concepts and ideas, voluntarily forfeiting a part of its institutional power of definig in the process. Nevertheless, such a method requires articulating a clear stance, to formulate programmatic interests and determine subsequent steps and actions if the institution does not want to be eroded by opposing expectations. But how can these processes of negotiation be stipulated? This approach presupposes that all participants are willing to subject themselves to protracted negotiation procedures. As I mentioned earlier, the desire to engage in such a contest, however, naturally tends to diminish. As a result, the institution must not remain passive. It has to be proactive instead, supplying thematic impulses and actively creating friction surfaces by raising – and exhibiting – controversial, artistically relevant issues within a context of public debate. [18]

[18] One might assume that this has become harder in consensus-oriented society. In my experience, the opposite is the case. A sufficient amount of neuralgic topics and issues remain that move against the respective status quo and challenge social trends. However, these no longer inhabit the simplistic, the sensational and the scandalous, presumably because the latter have become formulaic and fully mainstream classifications.

Furthermore, the institution has to actively invite the public to take part in the discussion. In other words, this institutional model is based on the precondition that the institution provides a conceptual, contentual and spatial context for different approaches and views to clash in the first place, and one in which the resulting opinions can be voiced. Indeed, the institution incited this initiative, but the prerequisites defined by the institution necessarily changed during the course of the project by force of external participation. As this book extensively depicts, the approach outlined here is thus partly a reaction to the increasingly precarious conditions prevailing in the art field. This is the point of departure for a method with the aim of defining a new form of institution that no longer has to rely on automatic legitimacy or any predetermined social contract. [19] On the contrary, a given institution's mandate

[19] The premises of the *Carte Blanche* project also reflect a method of action within a specified 'problematised' context. Precisely this approach was repeatedly criticised on the grounds of the assumption that critique is only possible from a position outside of the field to be criticised. The project departs from the opposite of this idea: *Carte Blanche* assumes that all entities involved are inevitably complicit in economic processes, advocating that economic issues be integrated into conceptual ideas in order to define a new scope of institutional action.

and acceptance have to be continually defined and redefined in a process of negotiation, which involves different groups and participants. The aim is to discover what is potentially of common, albeit temporary, interest, and which issues give rise to dissent.

During the past two years, I was repeatedly asked about the outcome of *Carte Blanche*. Essentially, I felt like I was expected to deliver unambiguous statements about collaboration strategies with the private sector in the context of the museum, as if there were a single formula that could, once discovered, be applied indefinitely. However, the pertinence of *Carte Blanche* was clearly that it incited a method of reciprocal convergence. [20] This defined the conceptual distinctions and differences between corporations, private collectors, and art institutions as motivating an extended and initially open-ended process. *Carte Blanche* resulted in the production of discrete exhibitions that disclosed both the discrepancies as well as the consensual elements inherent to this process. Thus, the objective of this method is to address and display – in the institution's programme, curatorial practices, and exhibitions – the field of contesting interests, dependencies, and entanglements. [21] In my opinion, this is a fundamental requirement in order to communicate about art's possibilities and institutions, and to, if necessary, demand and develop alternatives. Essentially, this method can be read as an instrument of activation – to enable the individual to participate in this process and adopt a stance in relation to it.

[20] Apart from the methodology, this naturally gave rise to a series of tangible results, described in the present text.

[21] This marks a clear departure from traditional forms of exhibition that concentrate on displaying the art while maintaining silence about the conditions of its display. In contrast to this approach, exhibition practice has to be understood as a complex field interconnecting artistic, political, economic and social interests.

Let us conceptualise the art field then as having open boundaries towards other fields of social activity, in which various actors interrelate via a more or less pronounced state of antagonism. [22] In a project such as *Carte Blanche*, it was possible to translate antagonism into agonism, creating that which Chantal Mouffe defines as 'a vital "agonistic" sphere of public contest'. In this context, differing opinions and stances could confront each other to the ends of assessment and debate. [23] And in my opinion, therein lies the task and potential of the contemporary art institution.

[22] Here, I refer to Pierre Bourdieu's concept of the field as a social setting in which various protagonists are located. Bordieu examines how groups of protagonists constitute themselves and the way in which networks and dependencies are constructed. He scrutinises the rules determining these relationships. The field is contested, and the protagonists fight for the extension of its boundaries or simply for its continued existence. Cf. Pierre Bourdieu, *The Rules of Art: Genesis and Structure of the Literary Field*, Stanford 1996

[23] Mouffe, op.cit., p.10

Installation Views

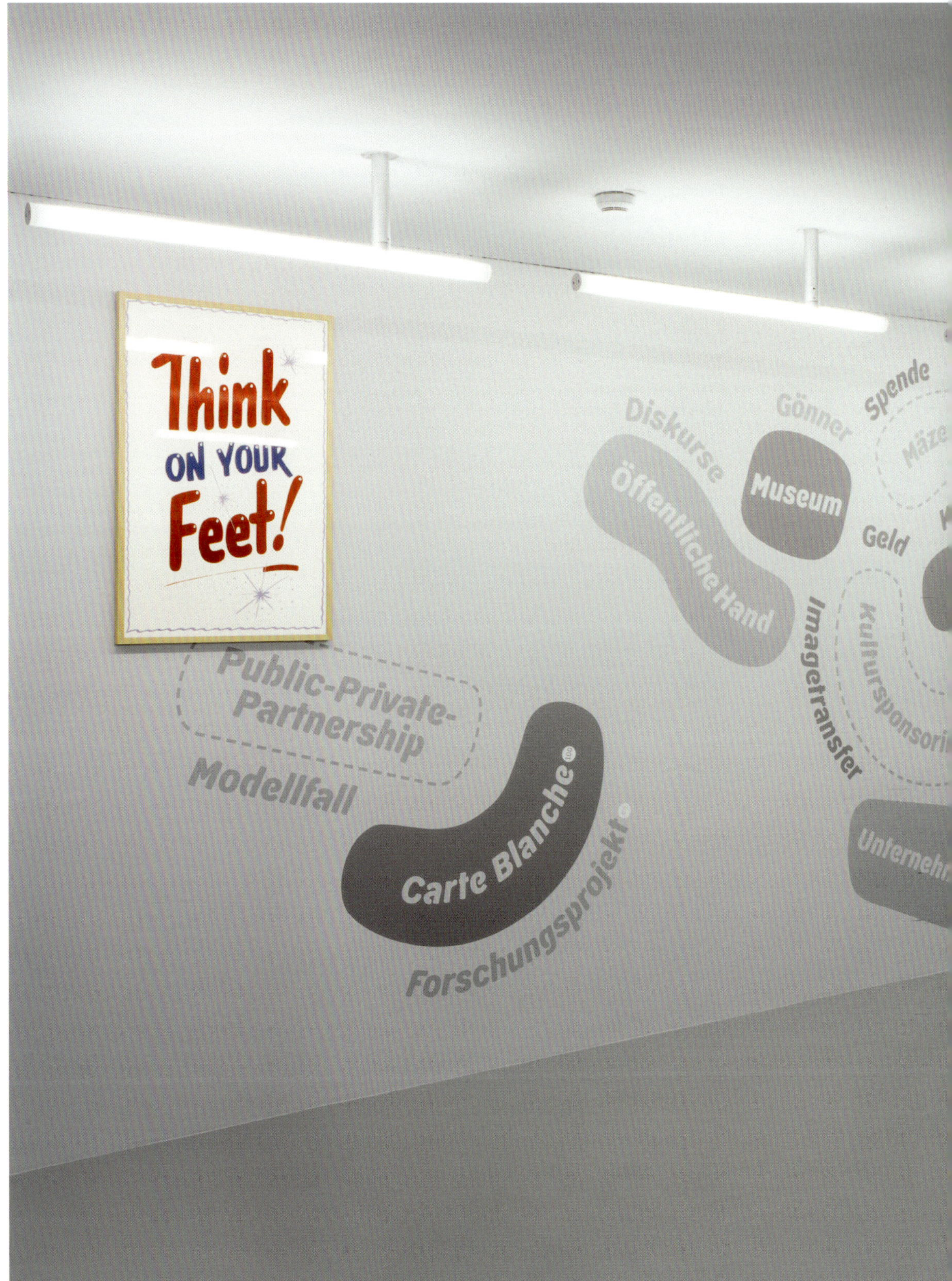

Think
ON YOUR
Feet!
Diskurse
Gönner
Spende
Mäze
Öffentliche Hand
Museum
Geld
Imagetransfer
Kultursponsori
Public-Private-
Partnership
Modellfall
Carte Blanche
Forschungsprojekt
Unterneh

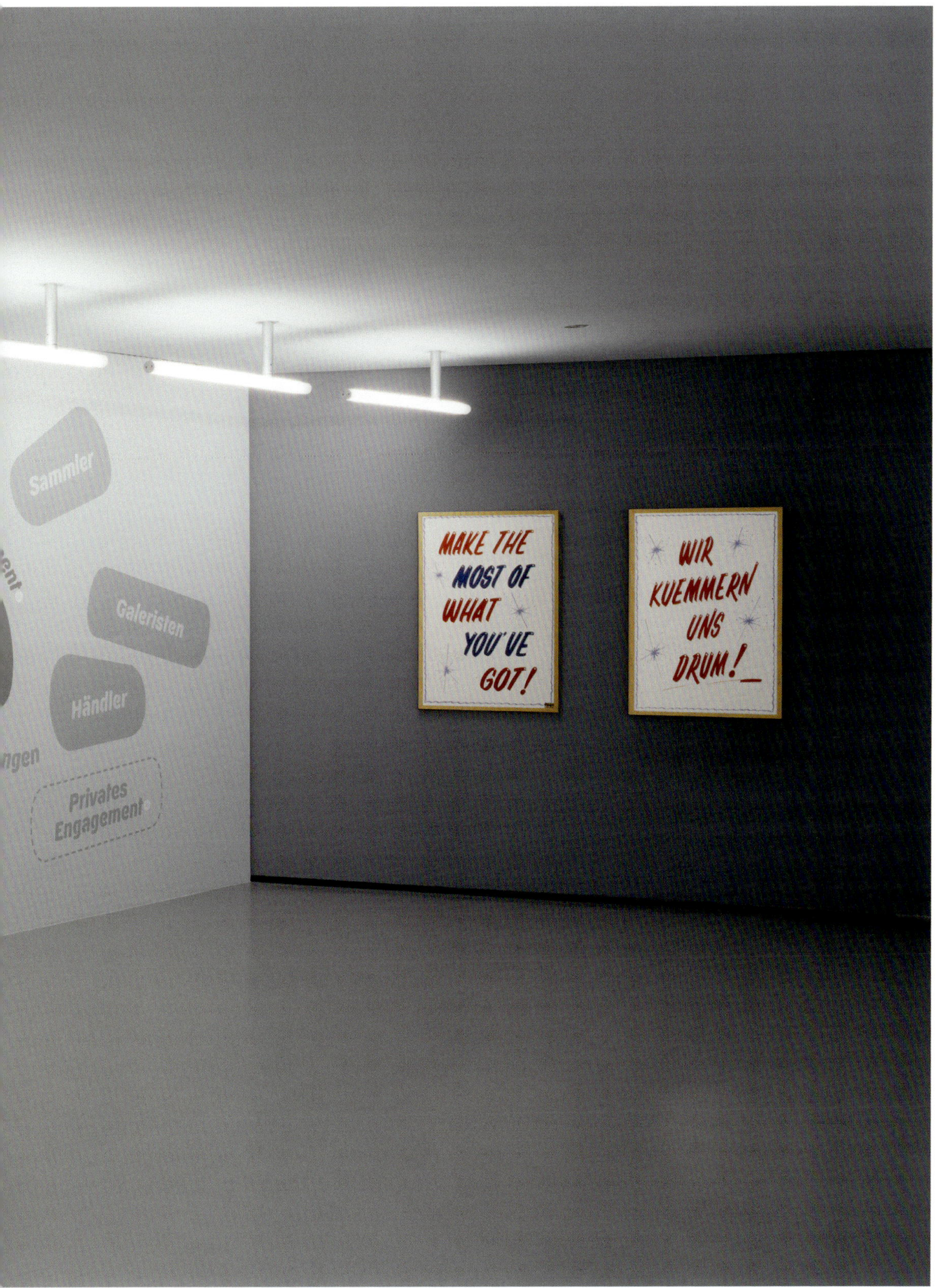
Sammler
Galeristen
Händler
Privates
Engagement
MAKE THE
MOST OF
WHAT
YOU'VE
GOT!
WIR
KUEMMERN
UNS
DRUM!_

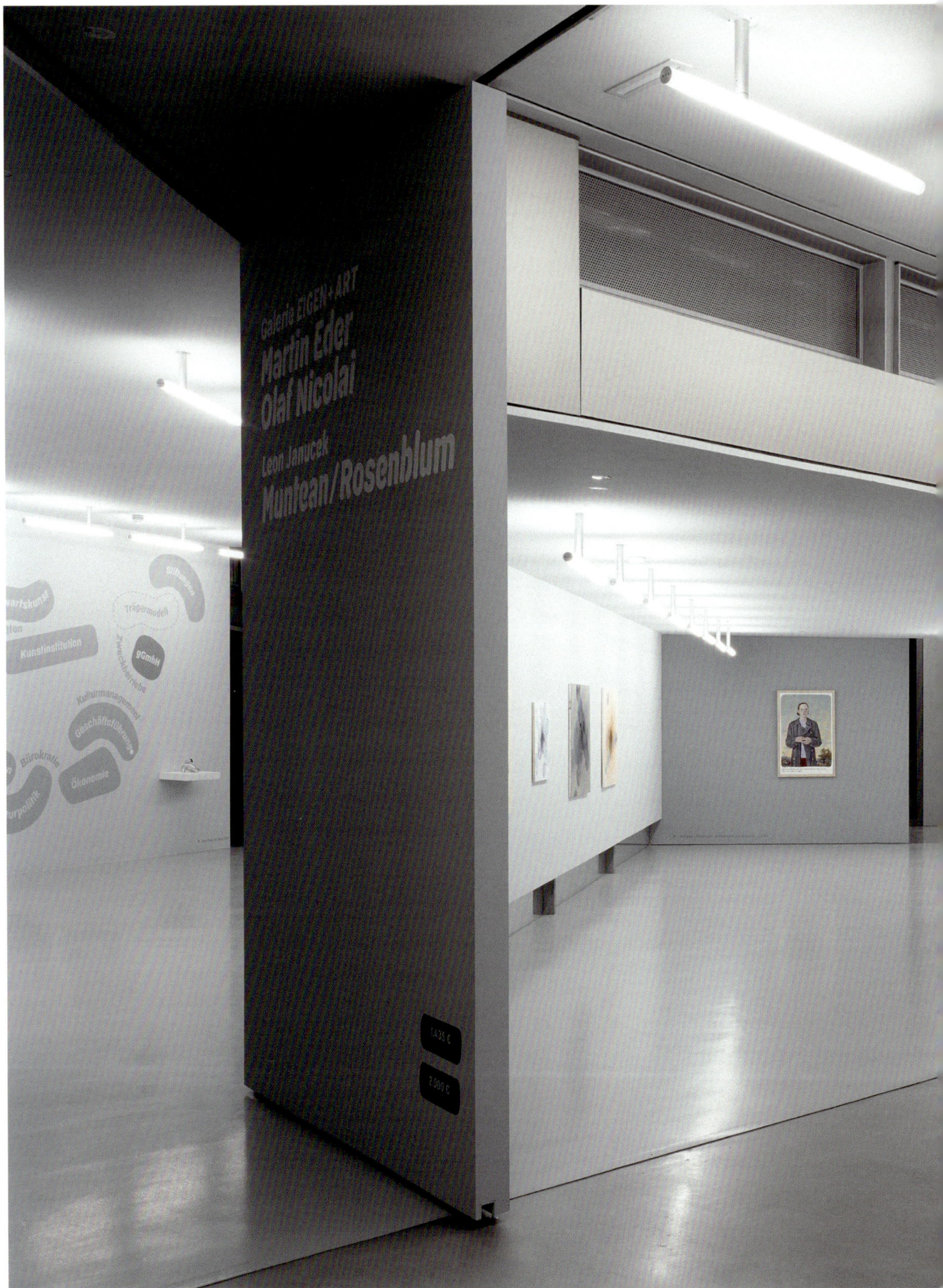
Galerie EIGEN+ART
Martin Eder
Olaf Nicolai
Leon Janucek
Muntean/Rosenblum

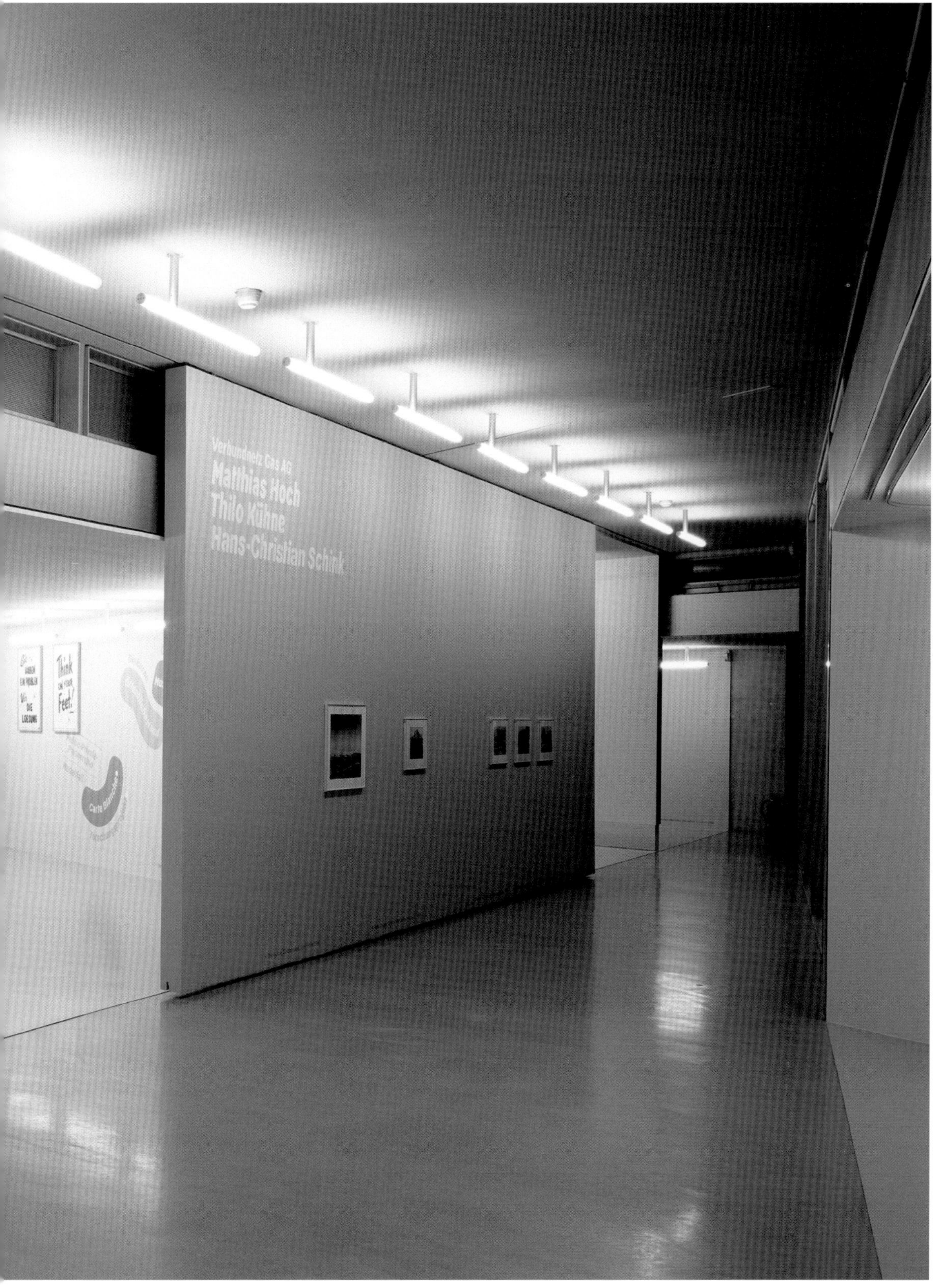

Verbundnetz Gas AG
Matthias Hoch
Thilo Kühne
Hans-Christian Schink
Think
ON YOUR
Feet!

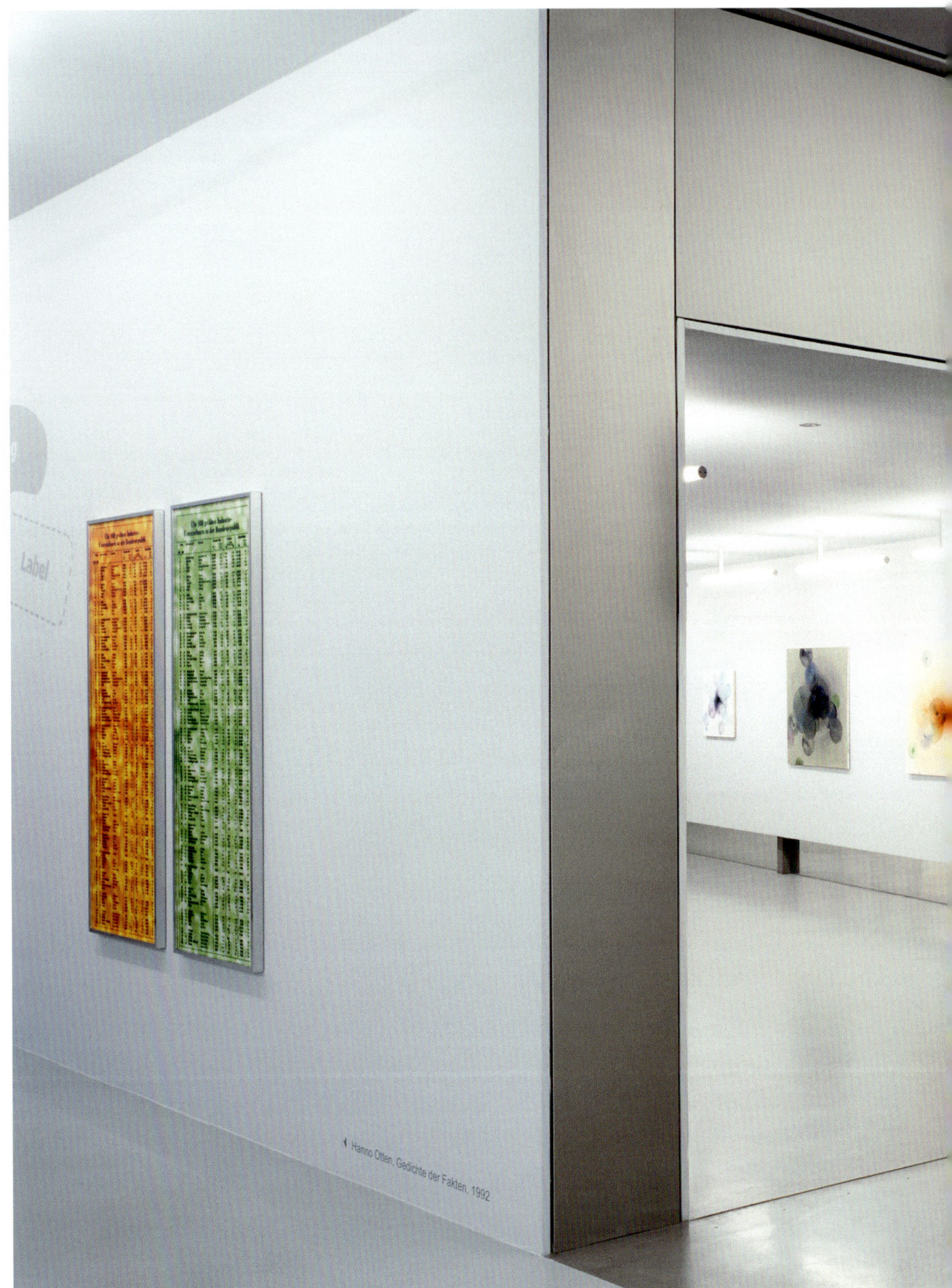

◀ Hanno Otten, Gedichte der Fakten, 1992

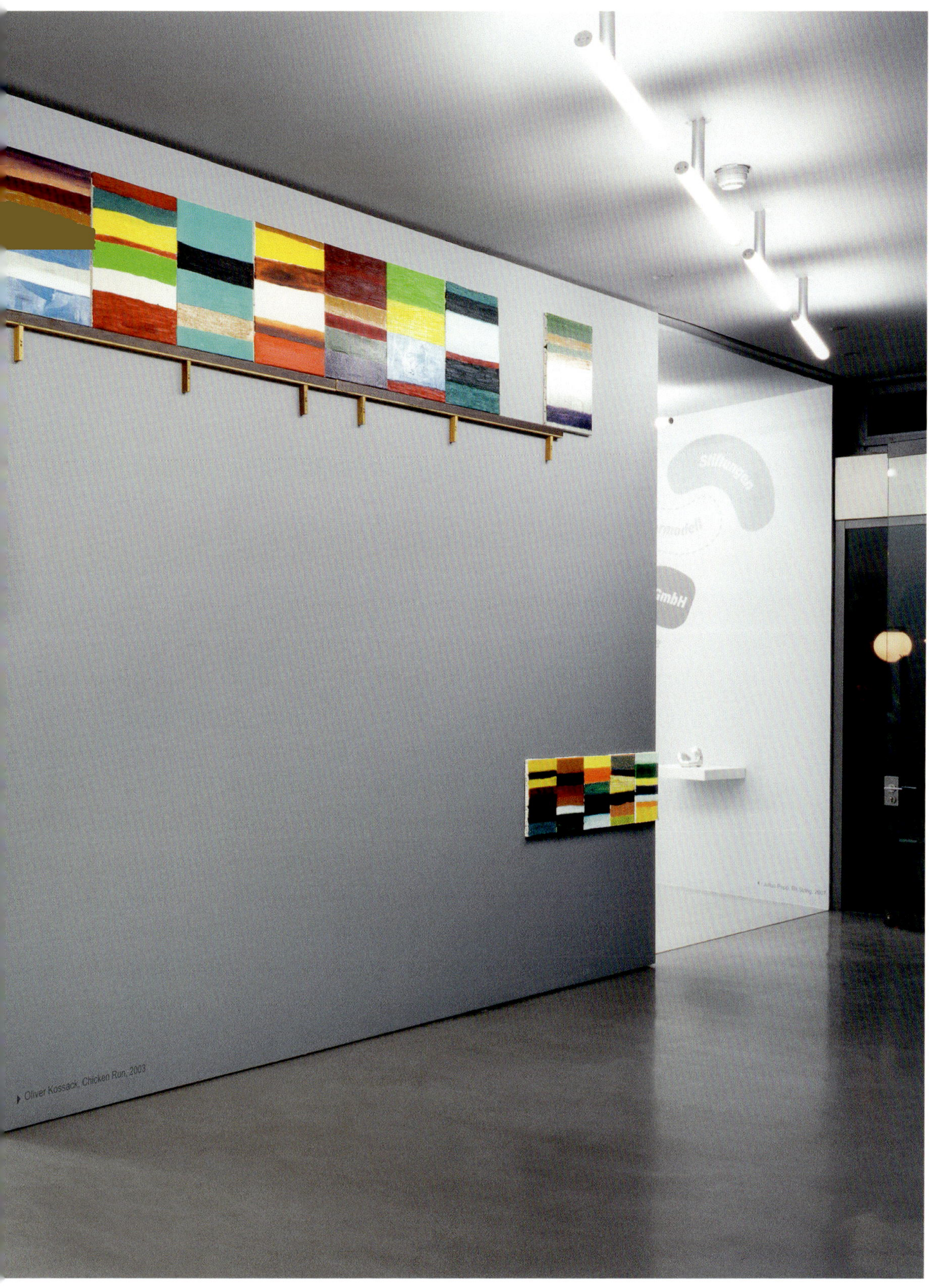

▶ Oliver Kossack, Chicken Run, 2003

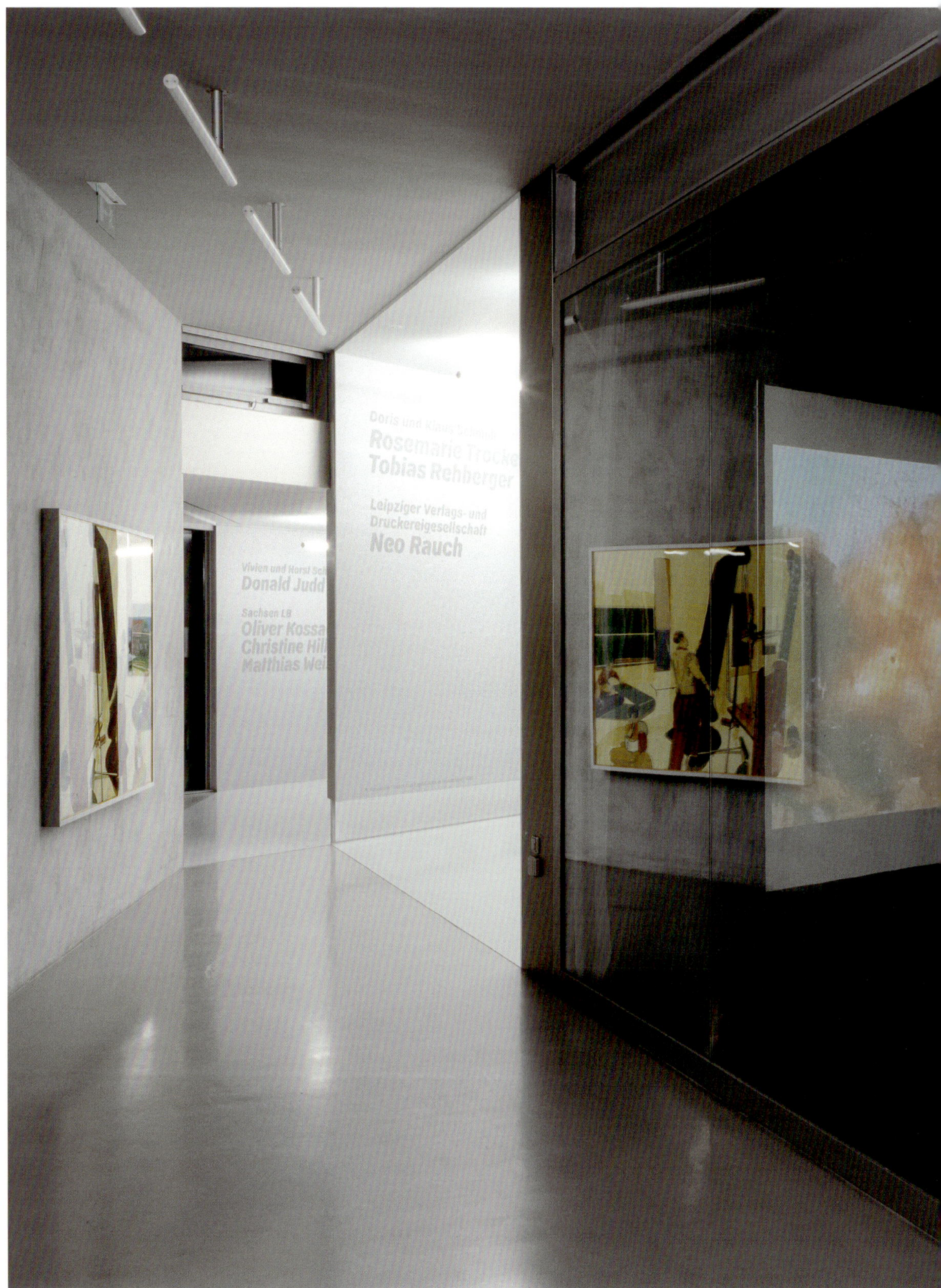
Doris und Klaus Schmitt
Rosemarie Trockel
Tobias Rehberger

Leipziger Verlags- und
Druckereigesellschaft
Neo Rauch

Vivien und Horst Sch
Donald Judd

Sachsen LB
Oliver Kossa
Christine Hill
Matthias Wei

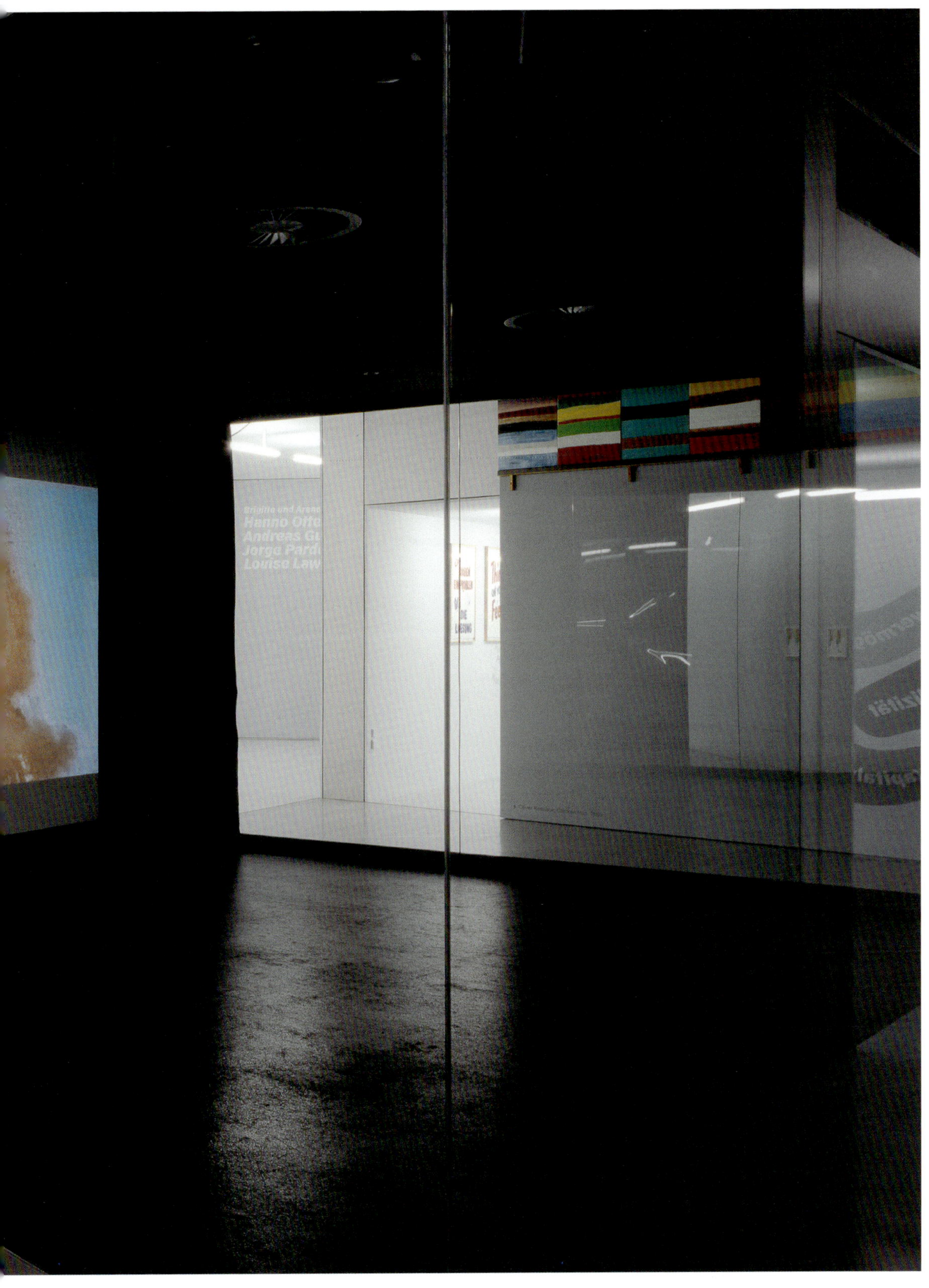

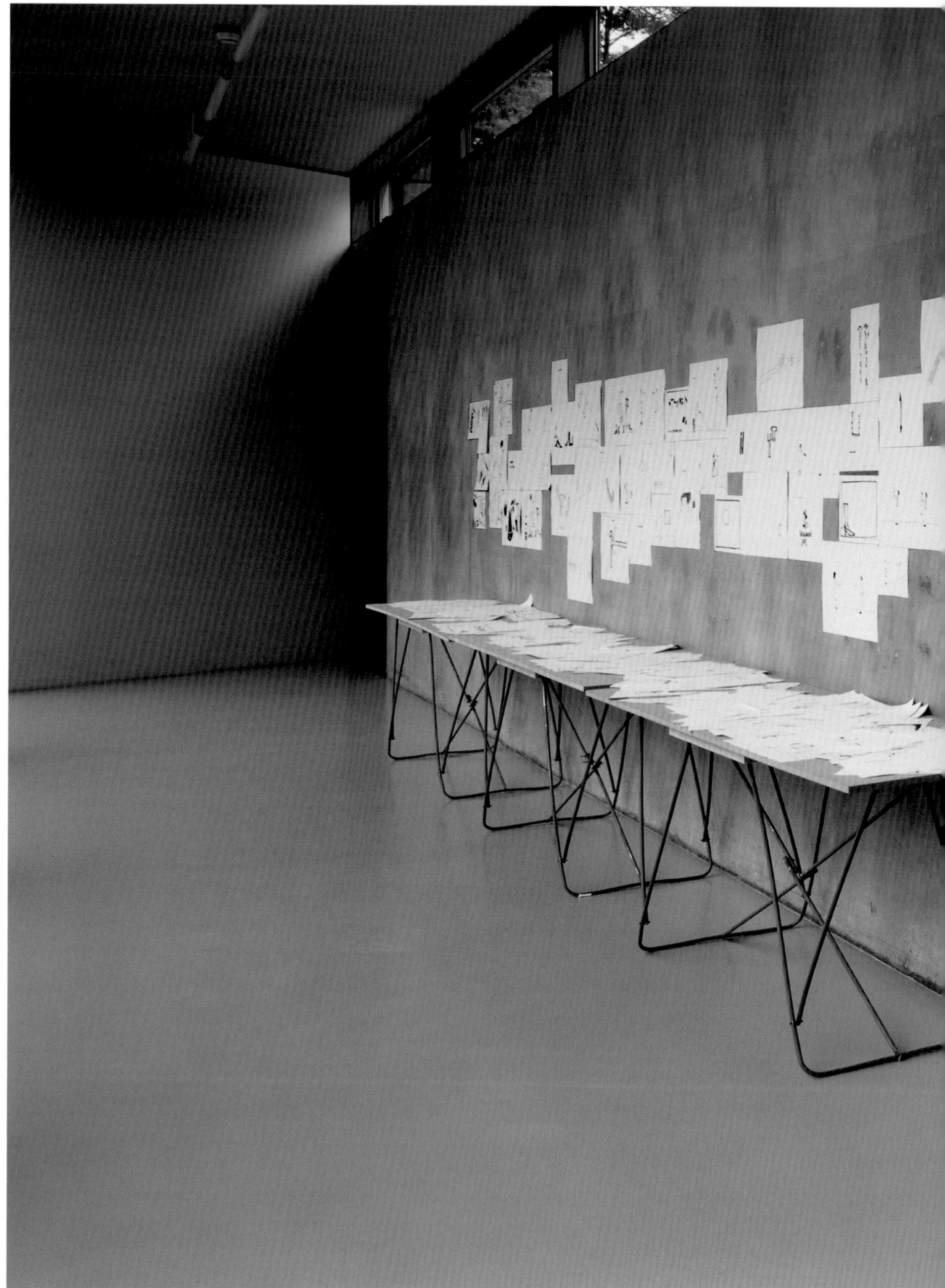

   The Captured Museum   Installation Views

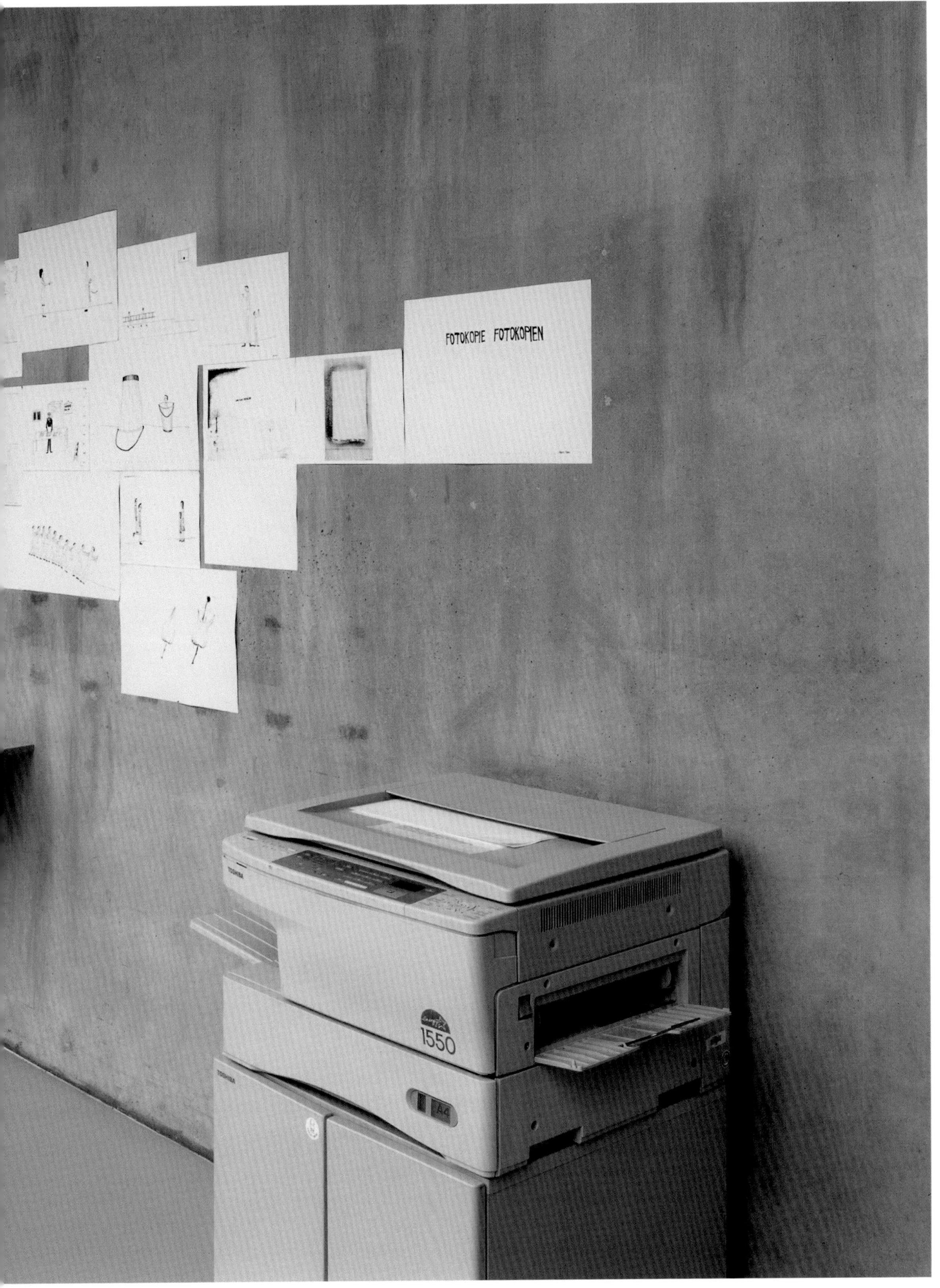

FOTOKOPIE FOTOKOPIEN
1550
A4

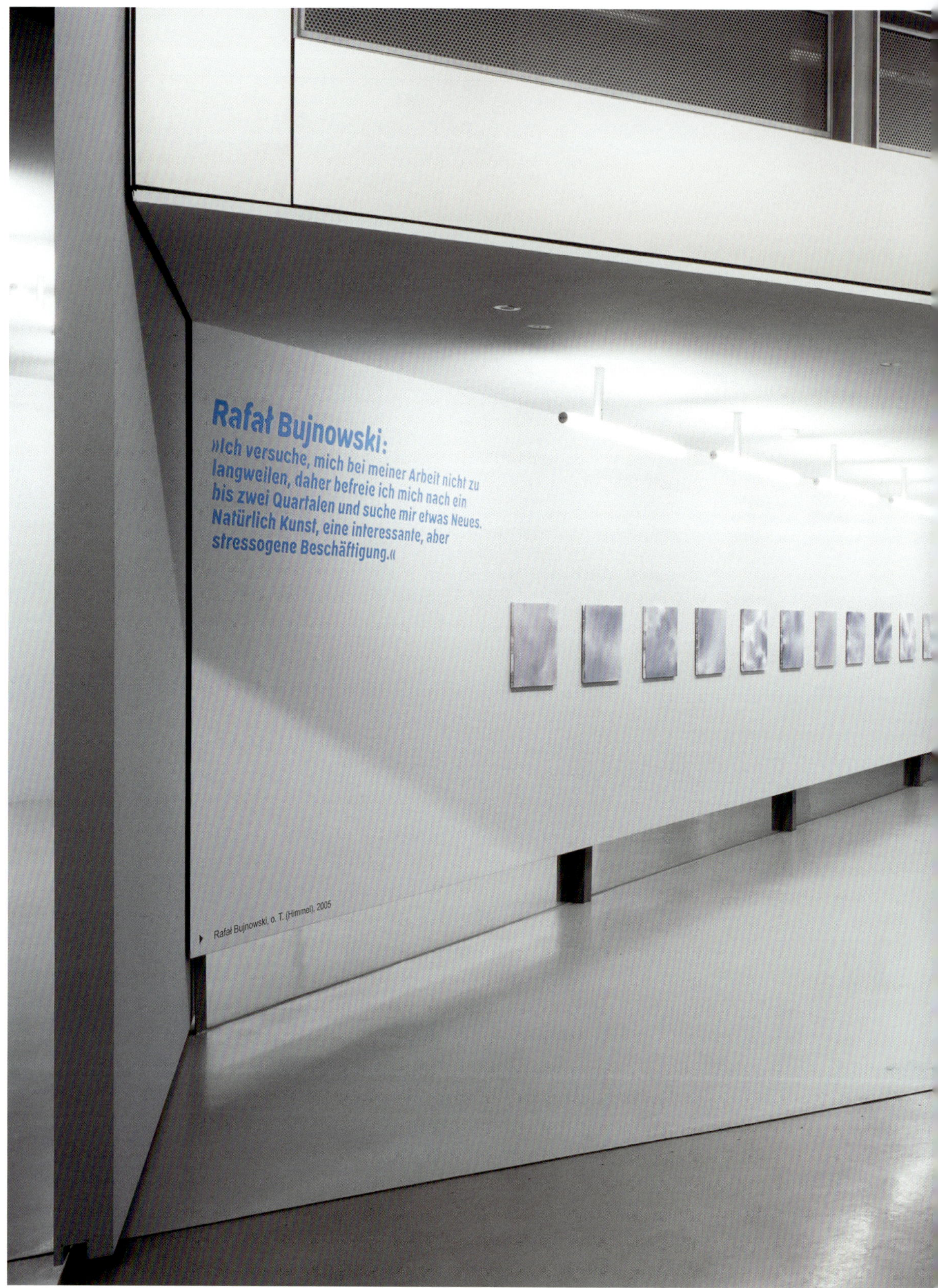

Rafał Bujnowski, o. T. (Himmel), 2005

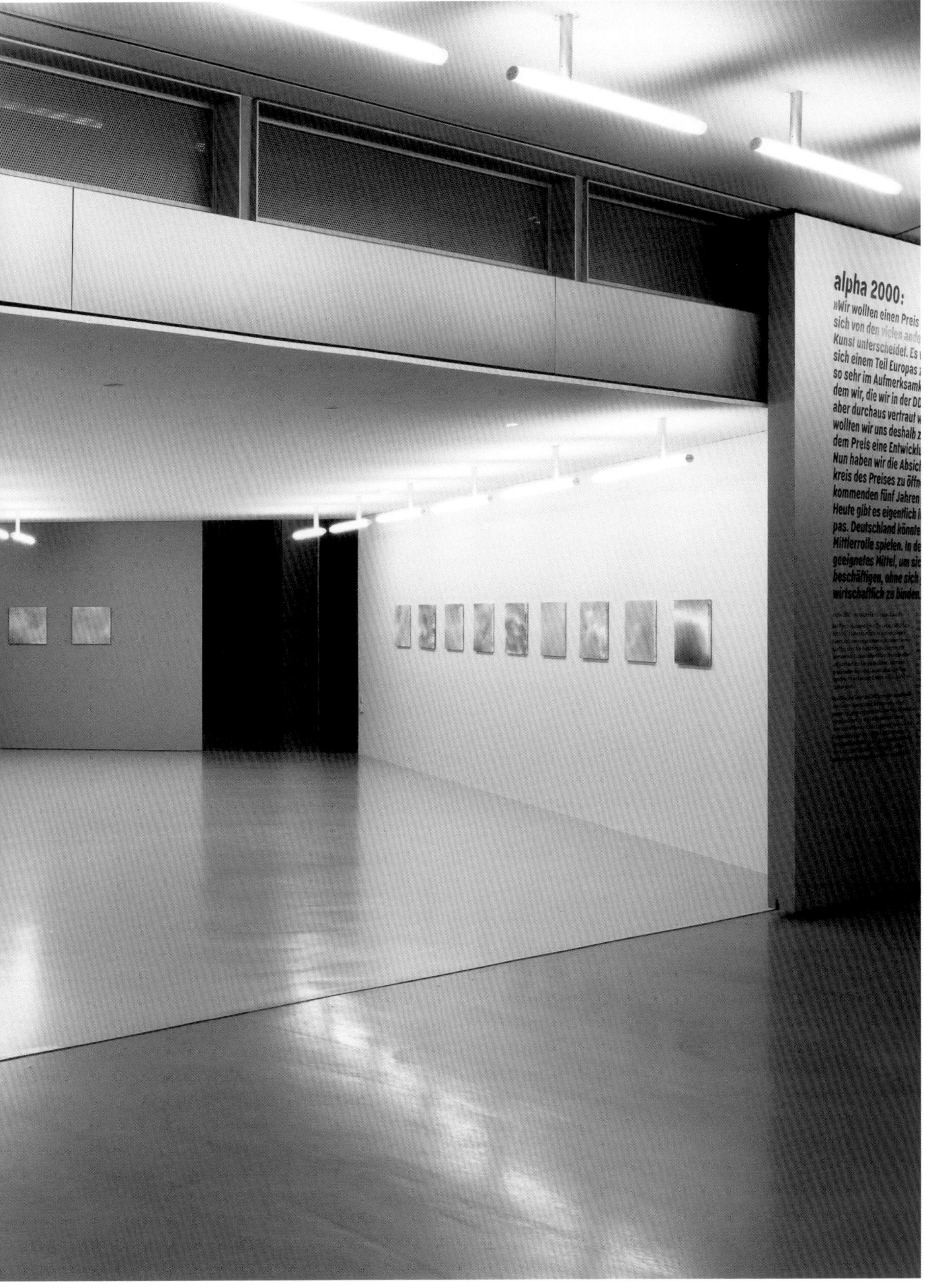

alpha 2000:
»Wir wollten einen Preis
sich von den vielen ande
Kunst unterscheidet. Es
sich einem Teil Europas z
so sehr im Aufmerksamk
dem wir, die wir in der DD
aber durchaus vertraut w
wollten wir uns deshalb z
dem Preis eine Entwicklu
Nun haben wir die Absich
kreis des Preises zu öffn
kommenden fünf Jahren
Heute gibt es eigentlich i
pas. Deutschland könnte
Mittlerrolle spielen. In de
geeignetes Mittel, um sic
beschäftigen, ohne sich
wirtschaftlich zu binden.

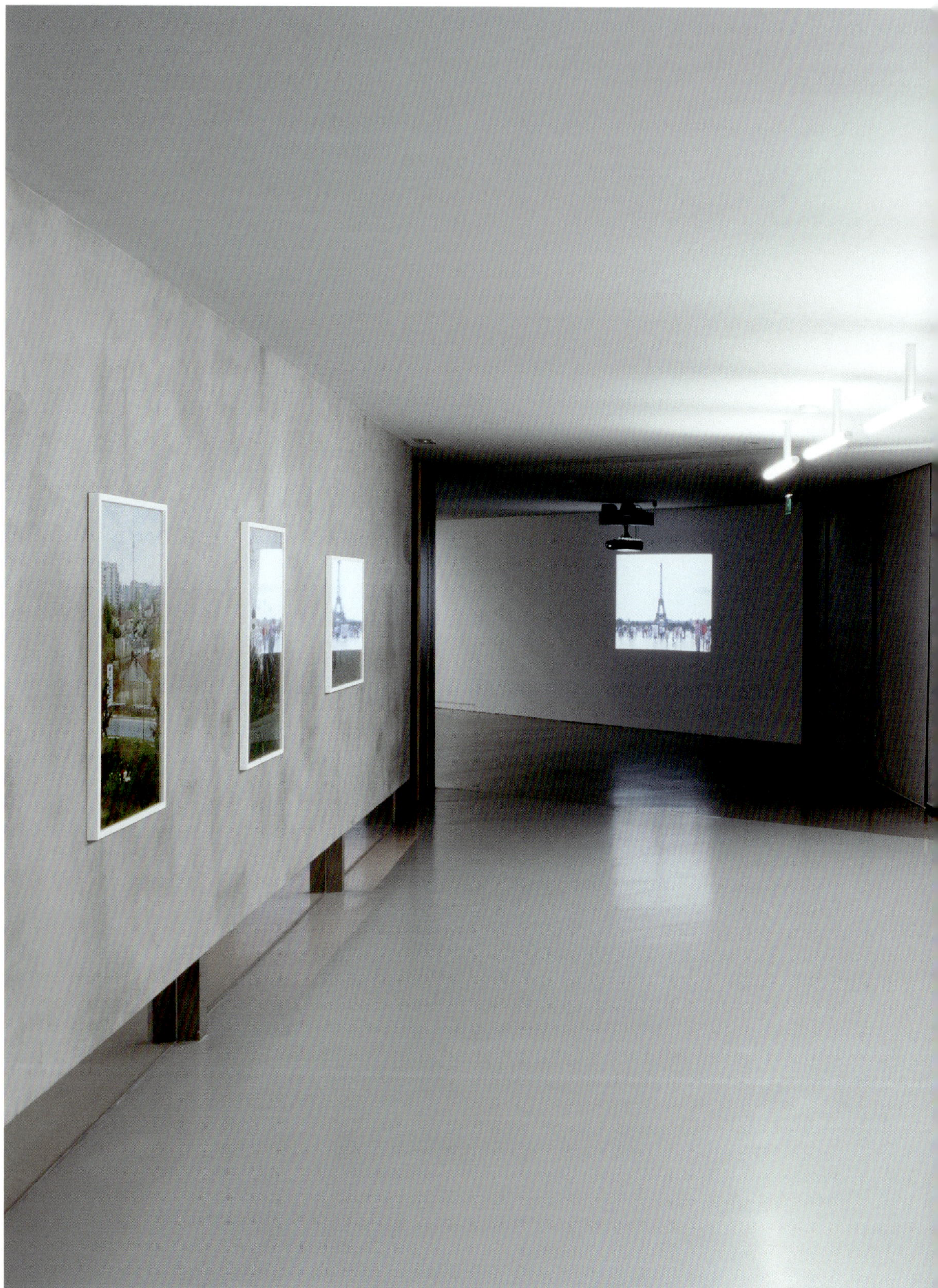

   The Captured Museum   Installation Views

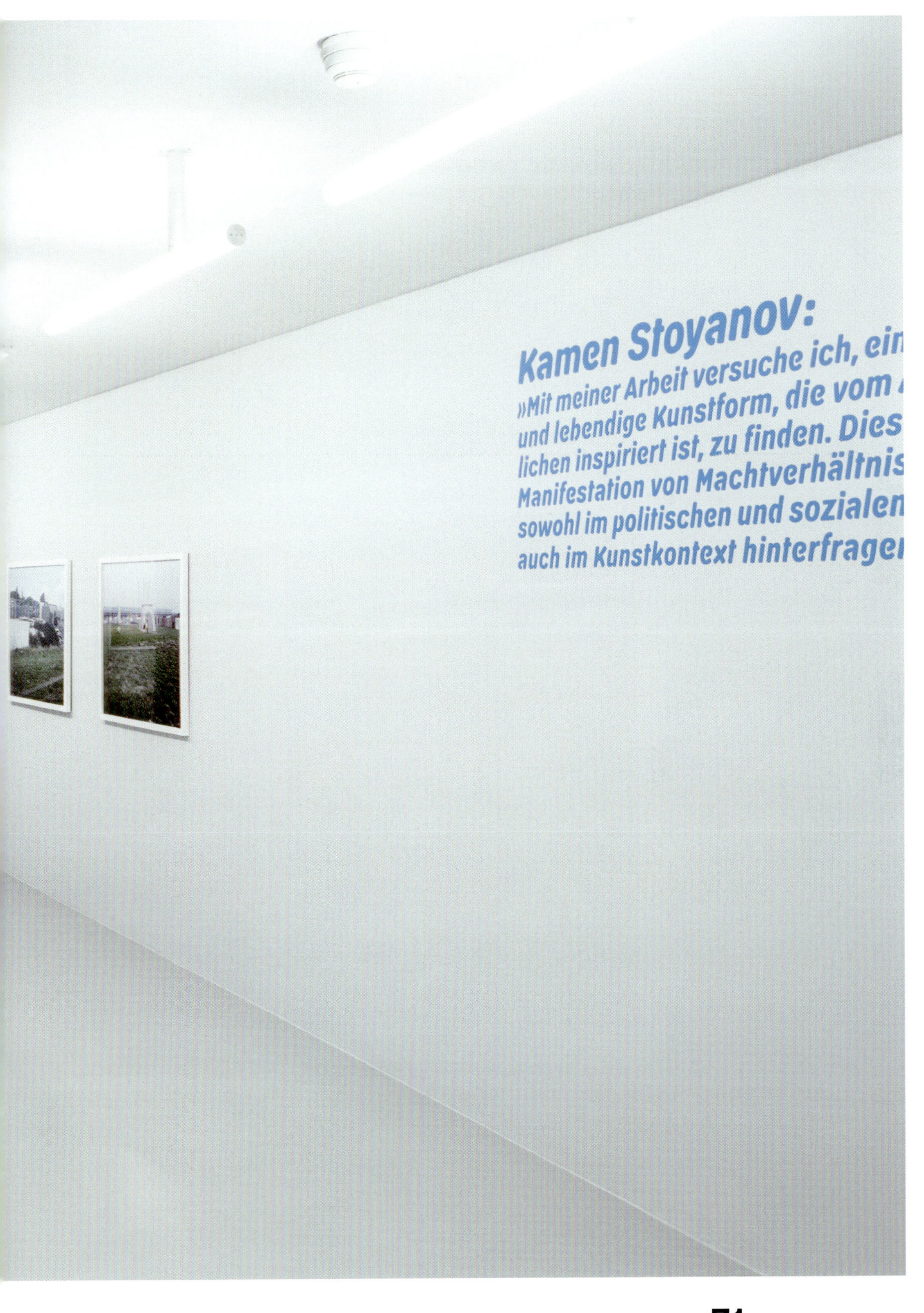
Kamen Stoyanov:
»Mit meiner Arbeit versuche ich, ein
und lebendige Kunstform, die vom
lichen inspiriert ist, zu finden. Dies
Manifestation von Machtverhältnis
sowohl im politischen und sozialen
auch im Kunstkontext hinterfrage

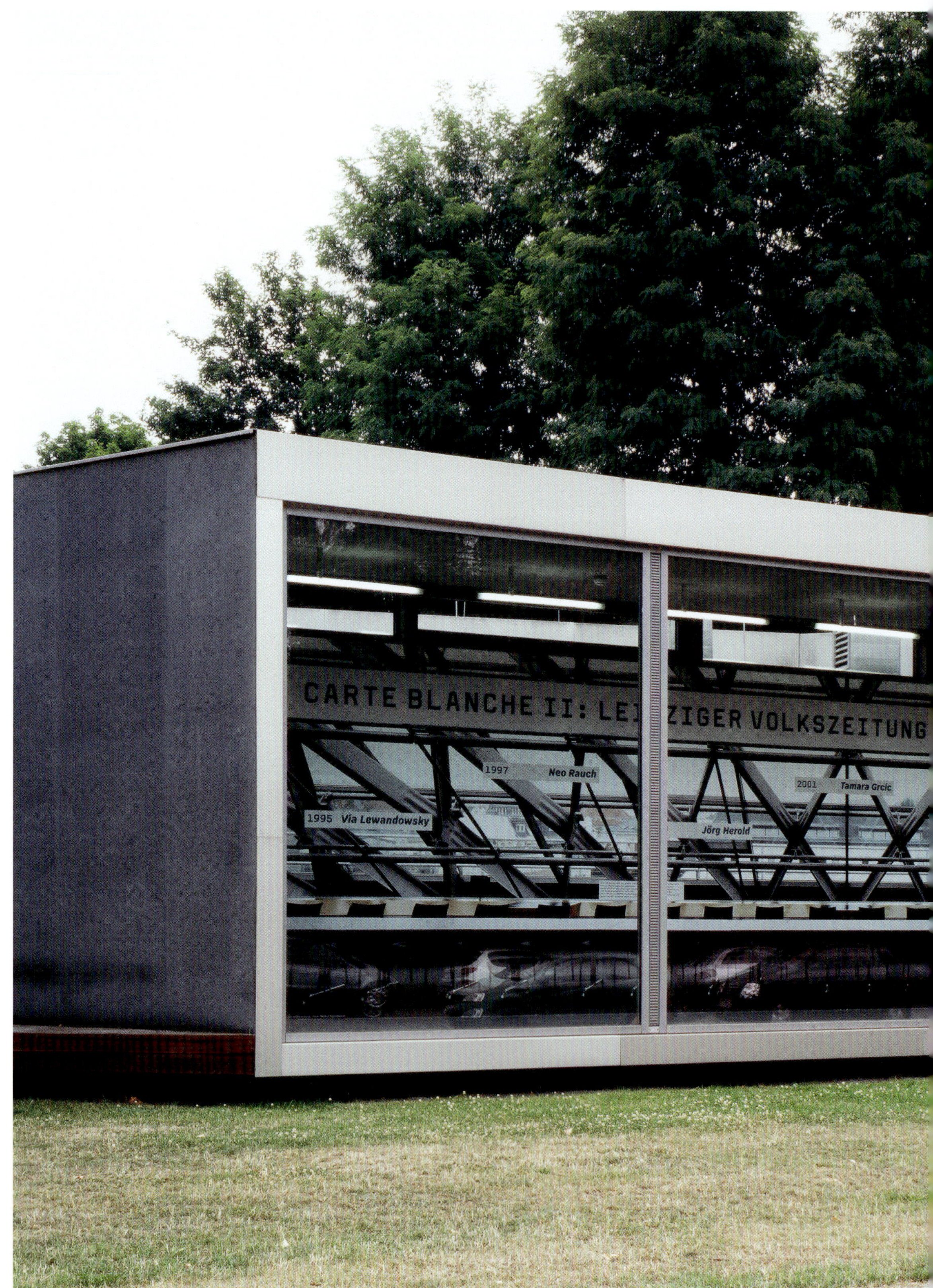

CARTE BLANCHE II: LEIPZIGER VOLKSZEITUNG
1997 Neo Rauch
1995 Via Lewandowsky
2001 Tamara Grcic
Jörg Herold

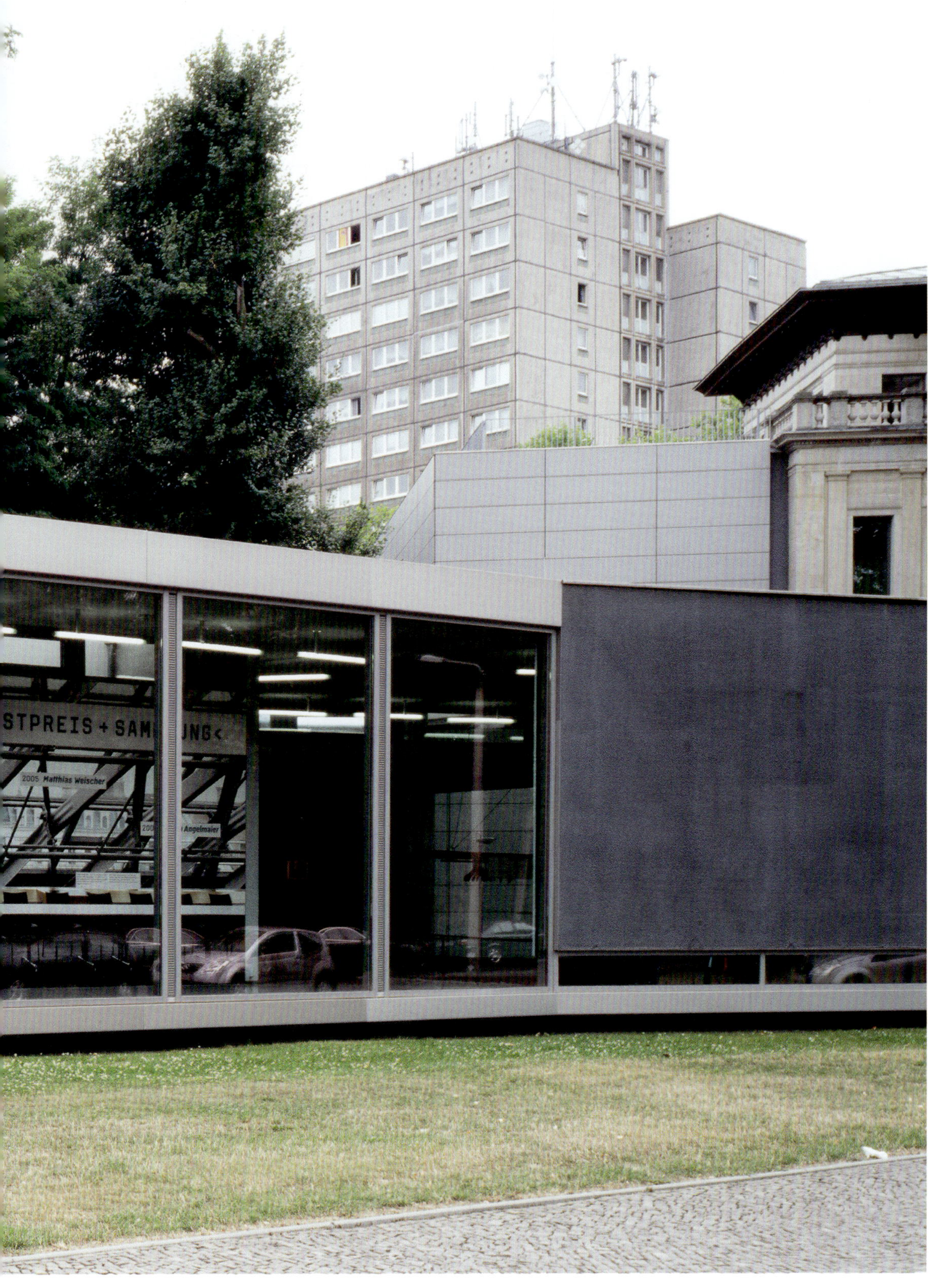
STPREIS + SAM   UNG<
2005 Matthias Weischer
200   Angelmaier

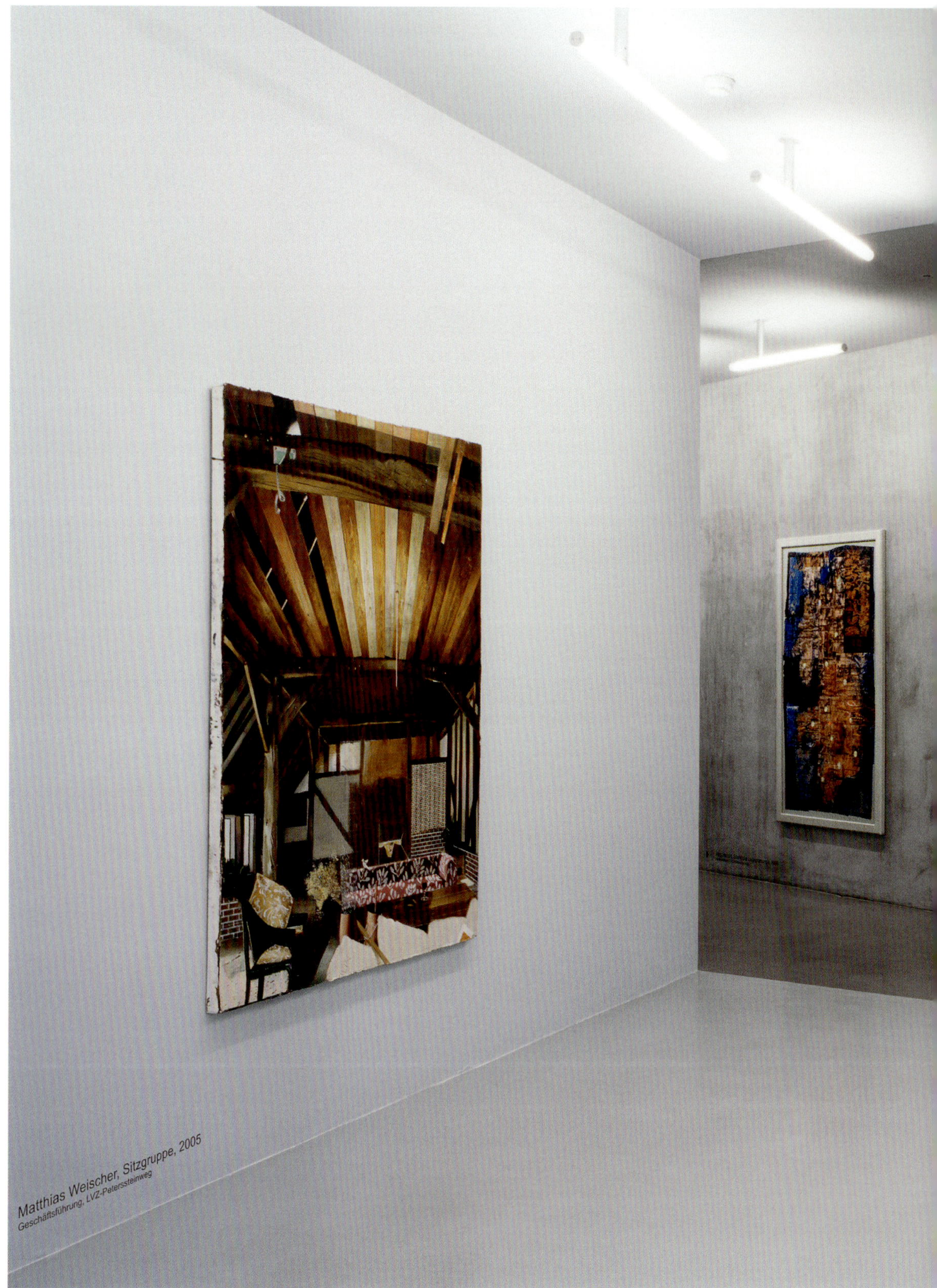

Matthias Weischer, Sitzgruppe, 2005
Geschäftsführung, LVZ-Peterssteinweg

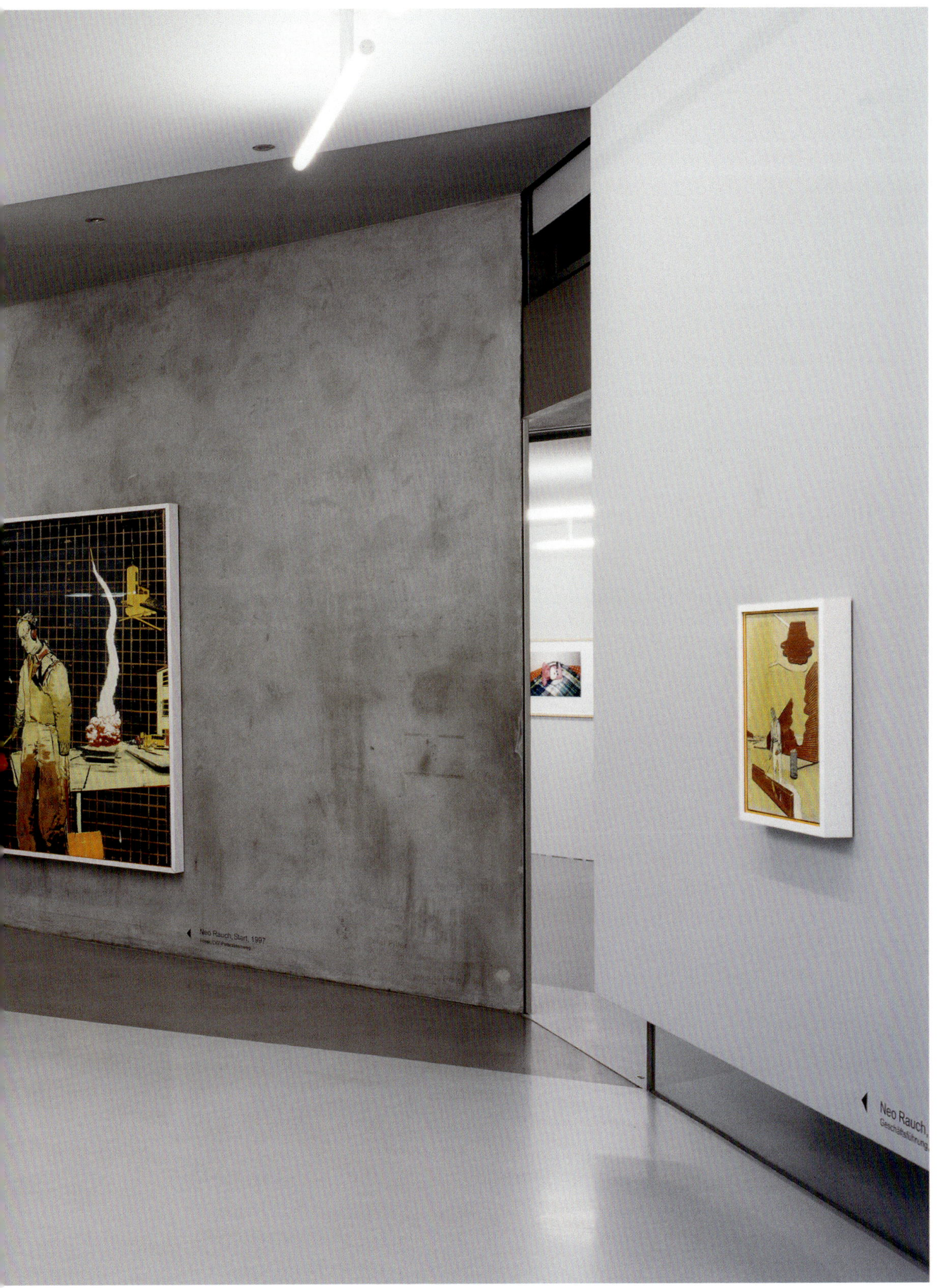

Neo Rauch, Start, 1997
Neo Rauch,

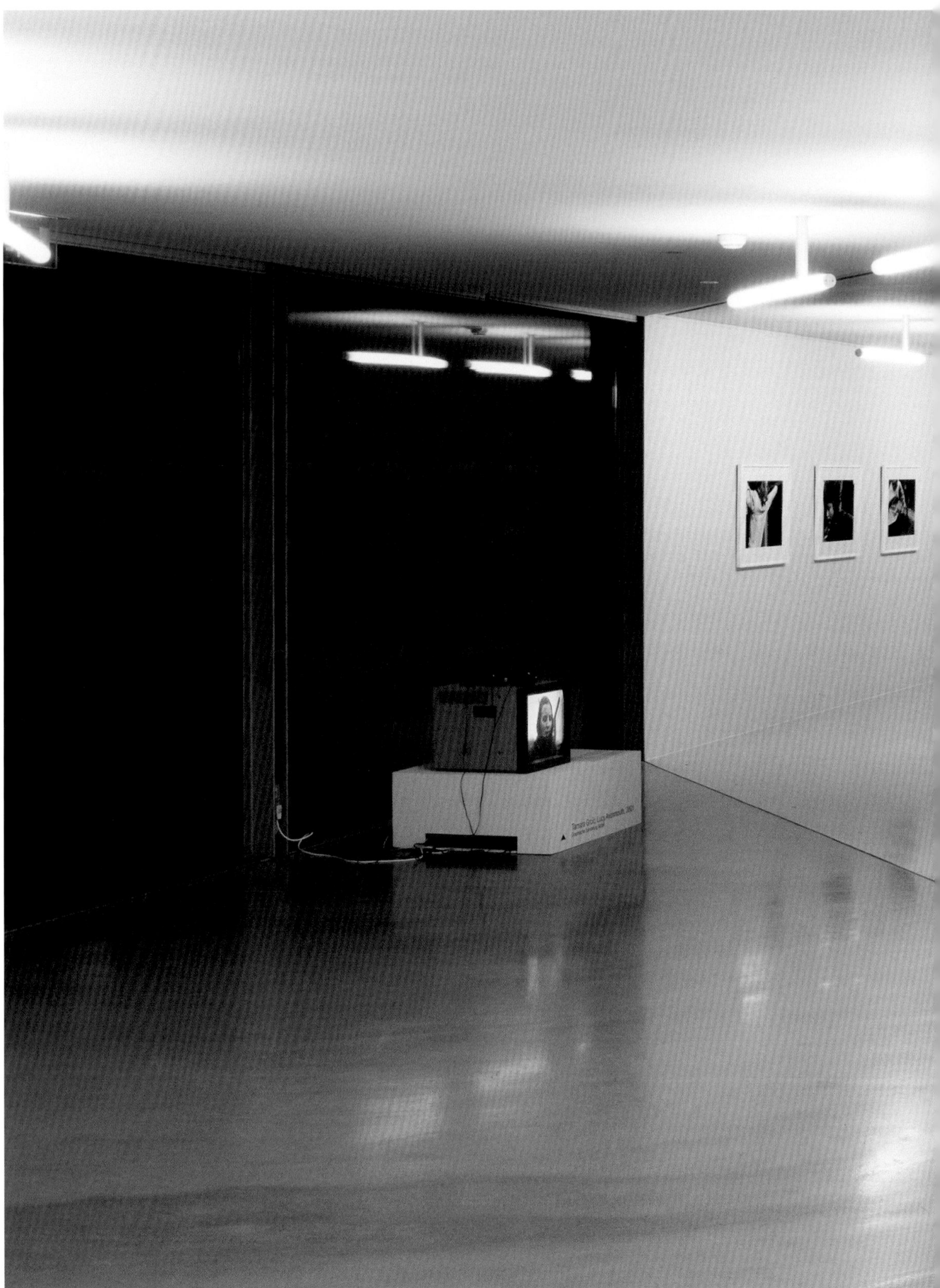

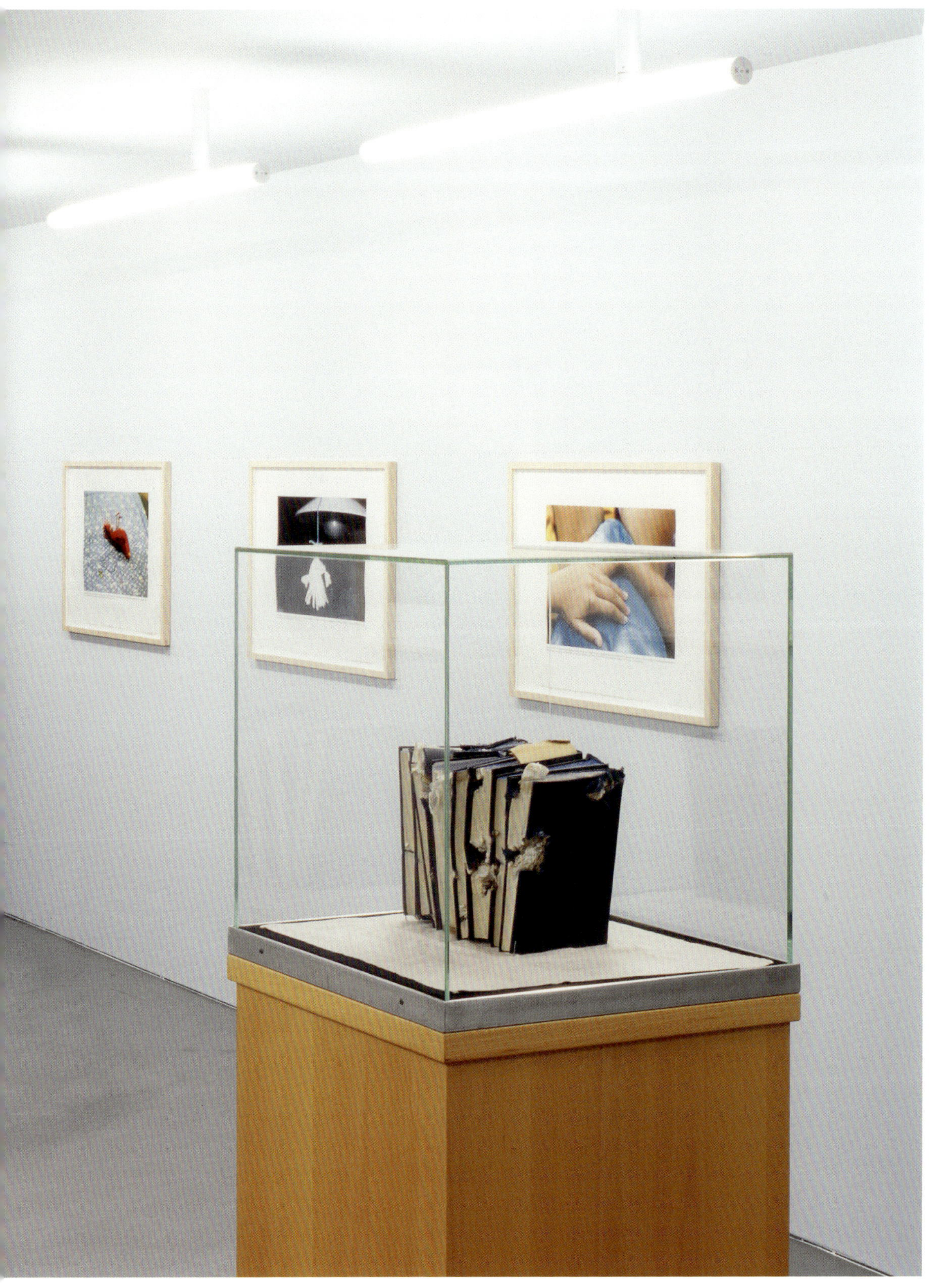

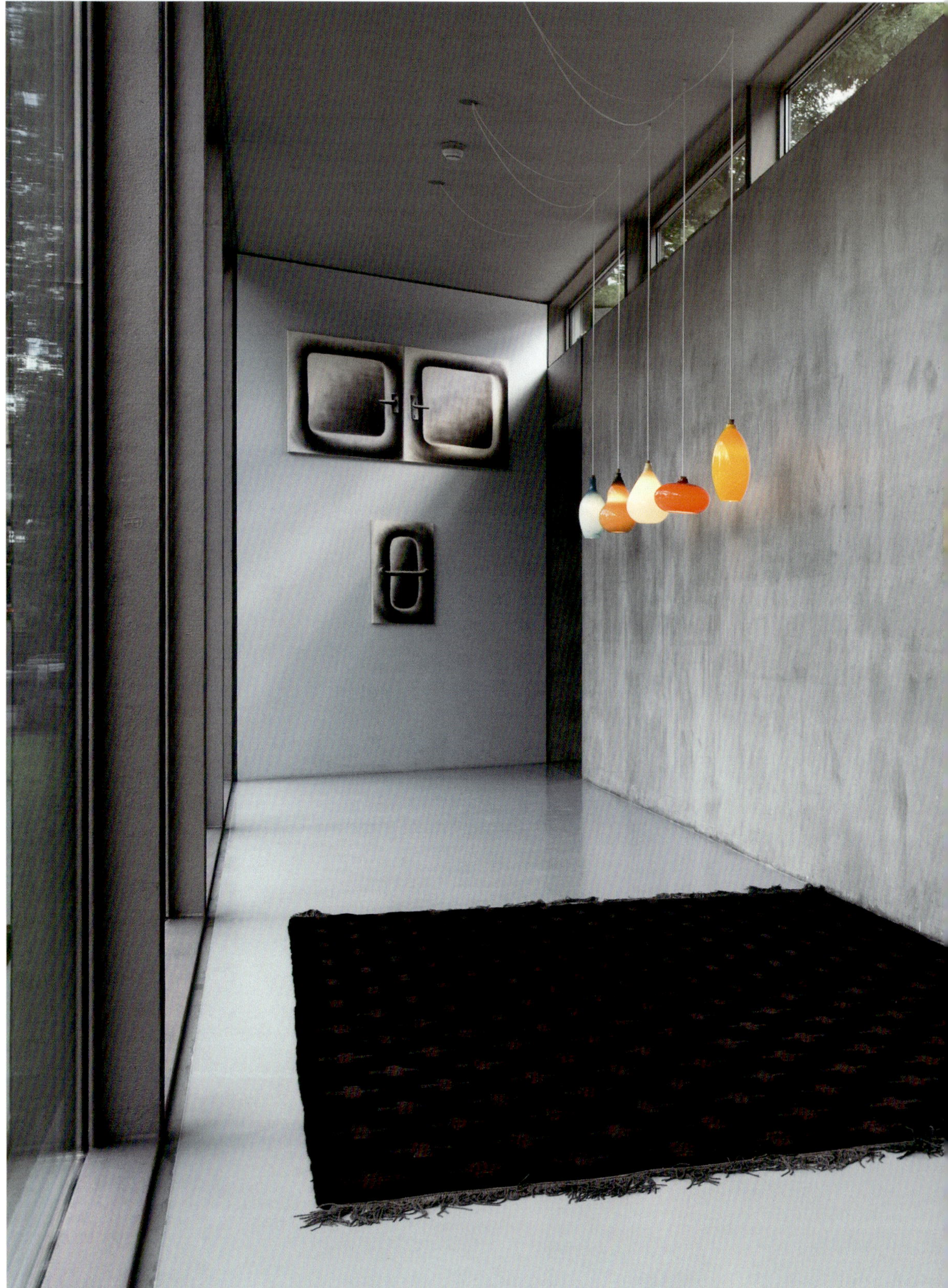

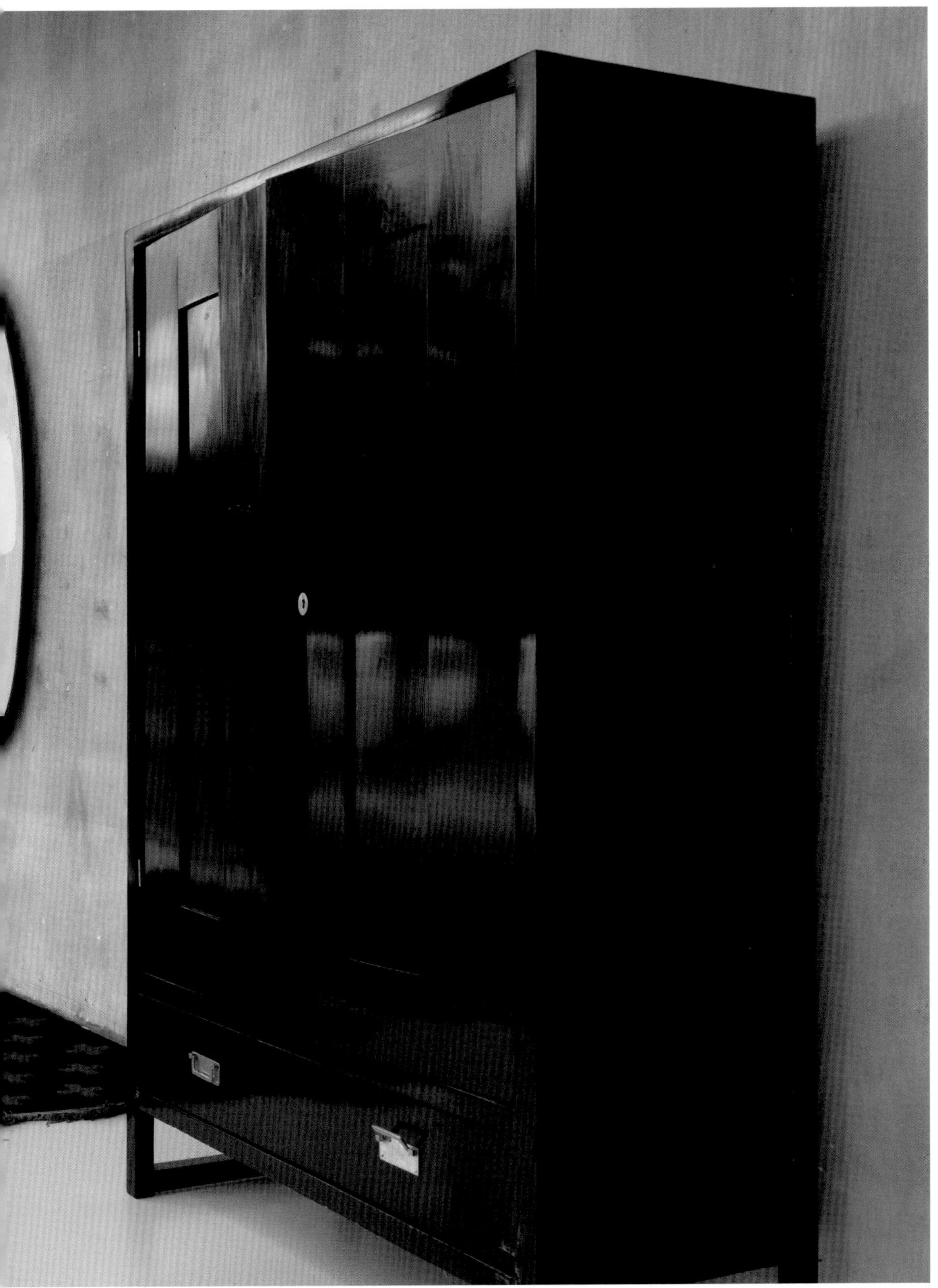

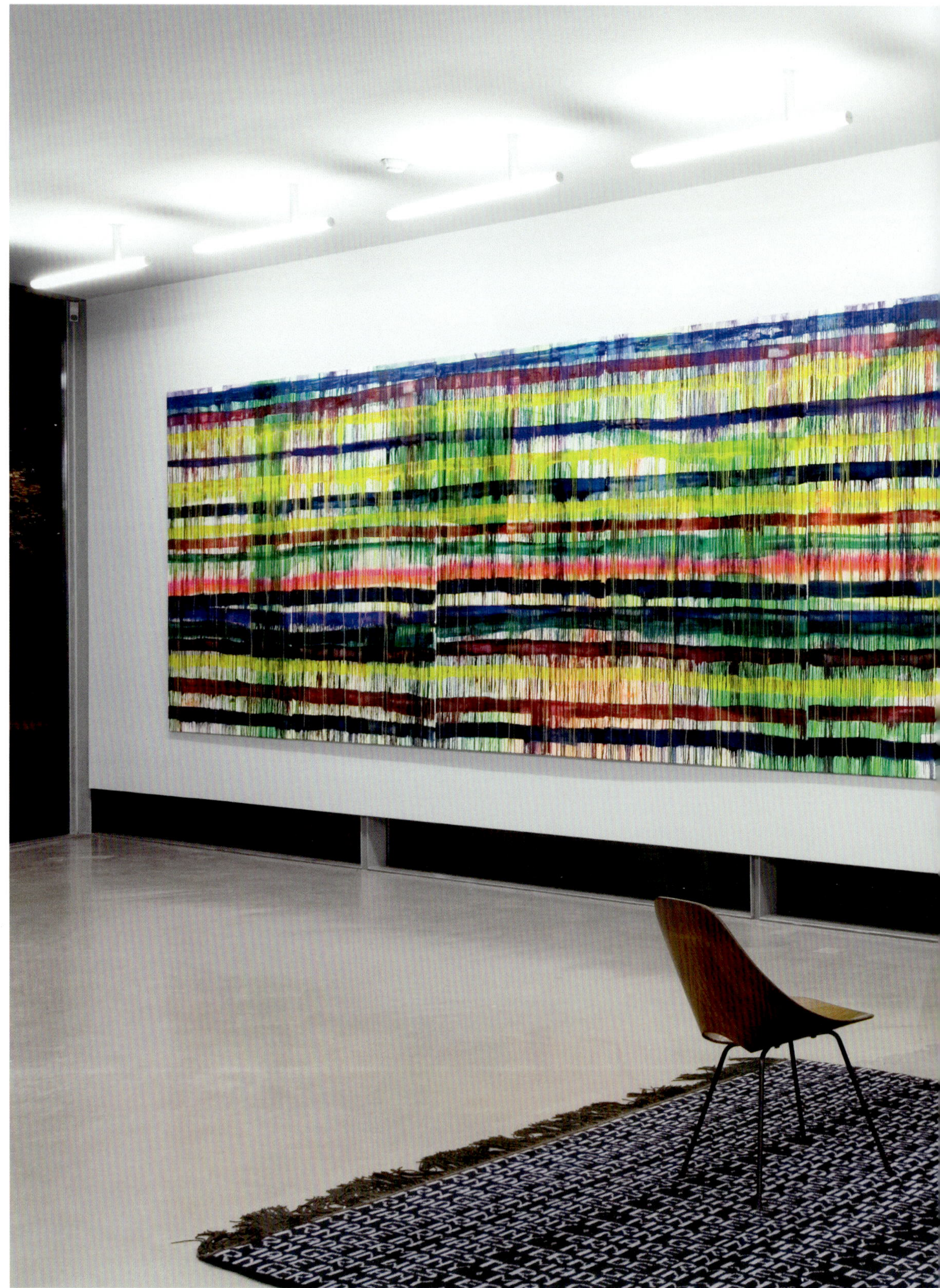

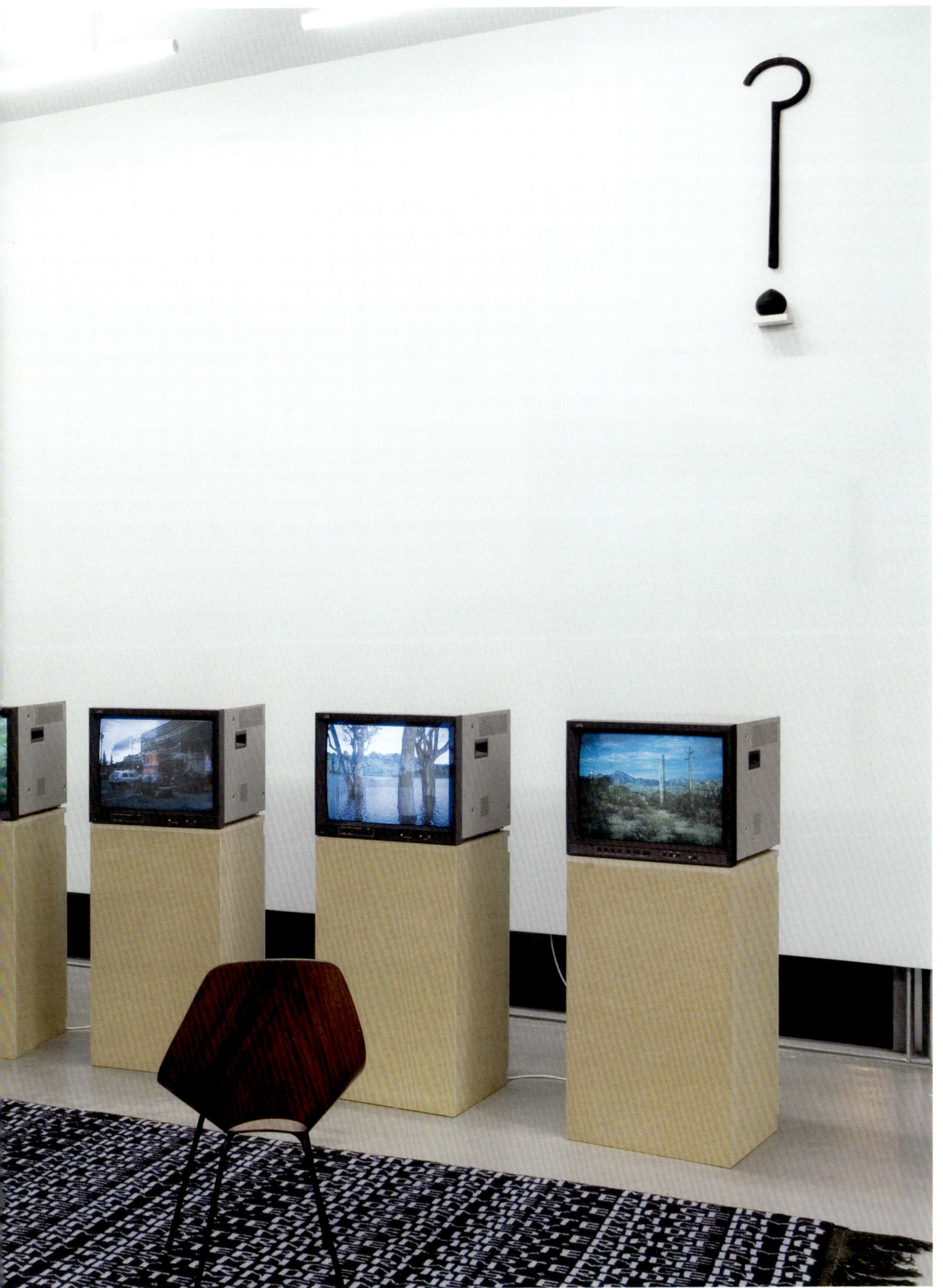

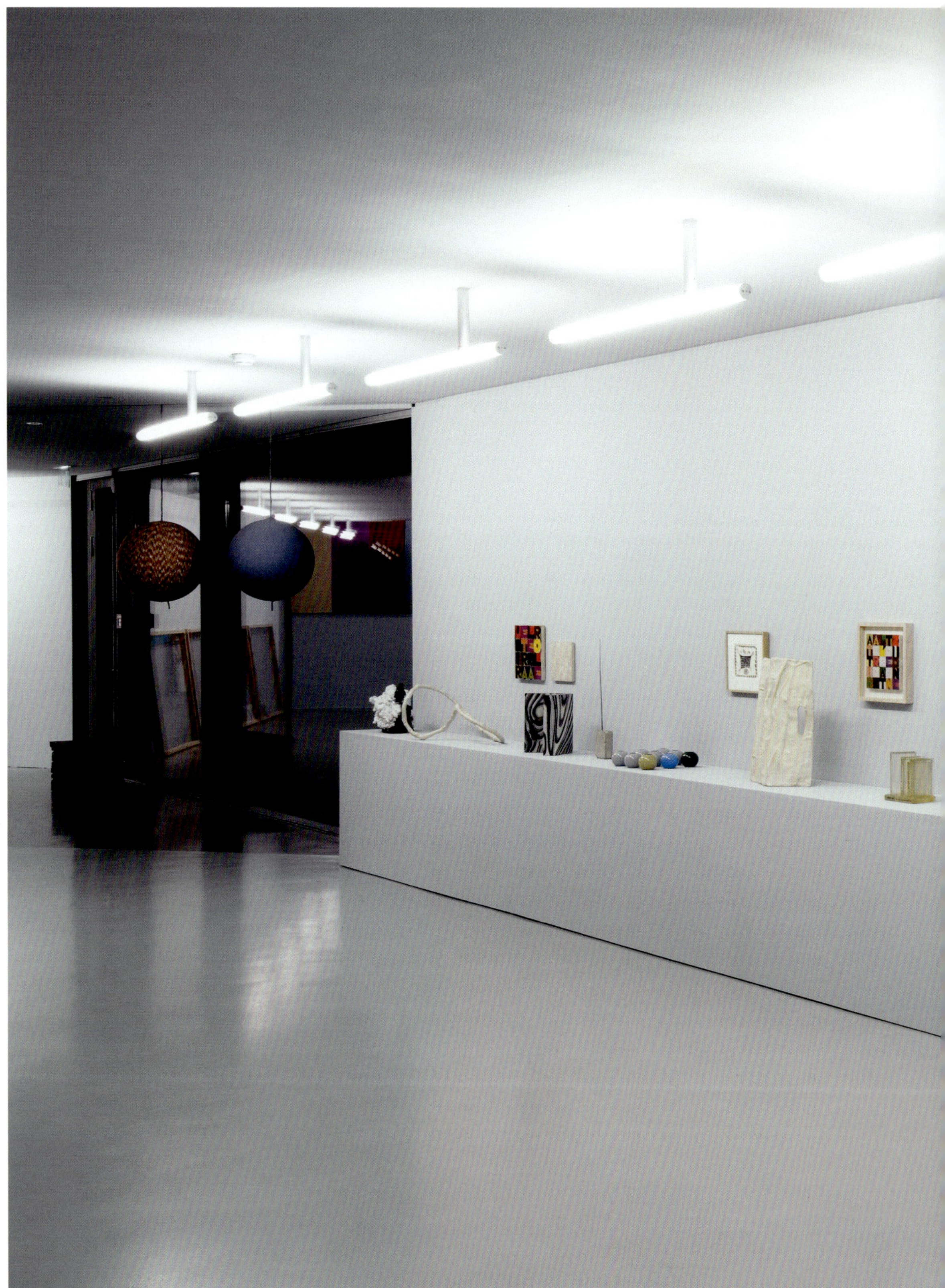

The Captured Museum   Installation Views

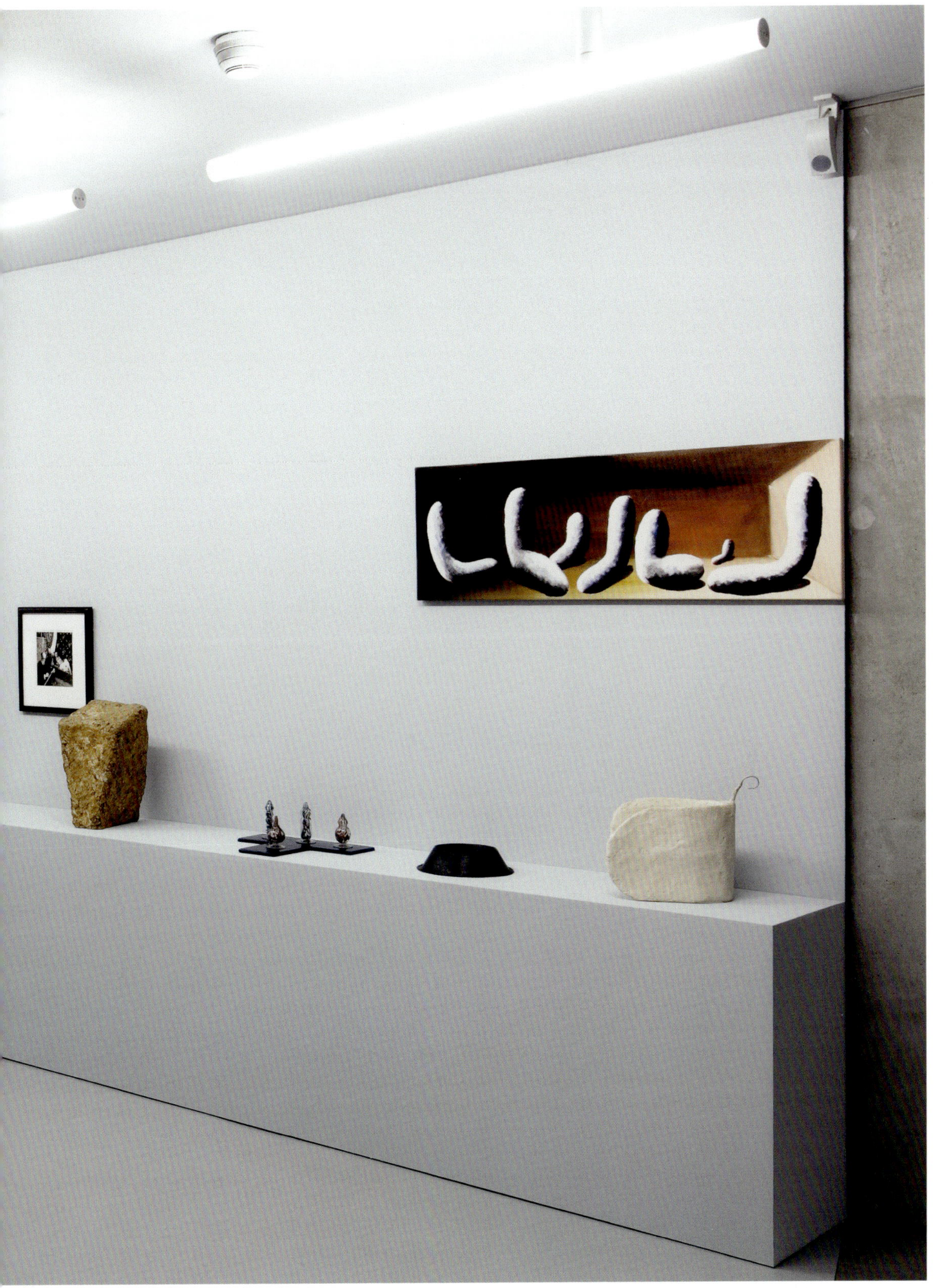

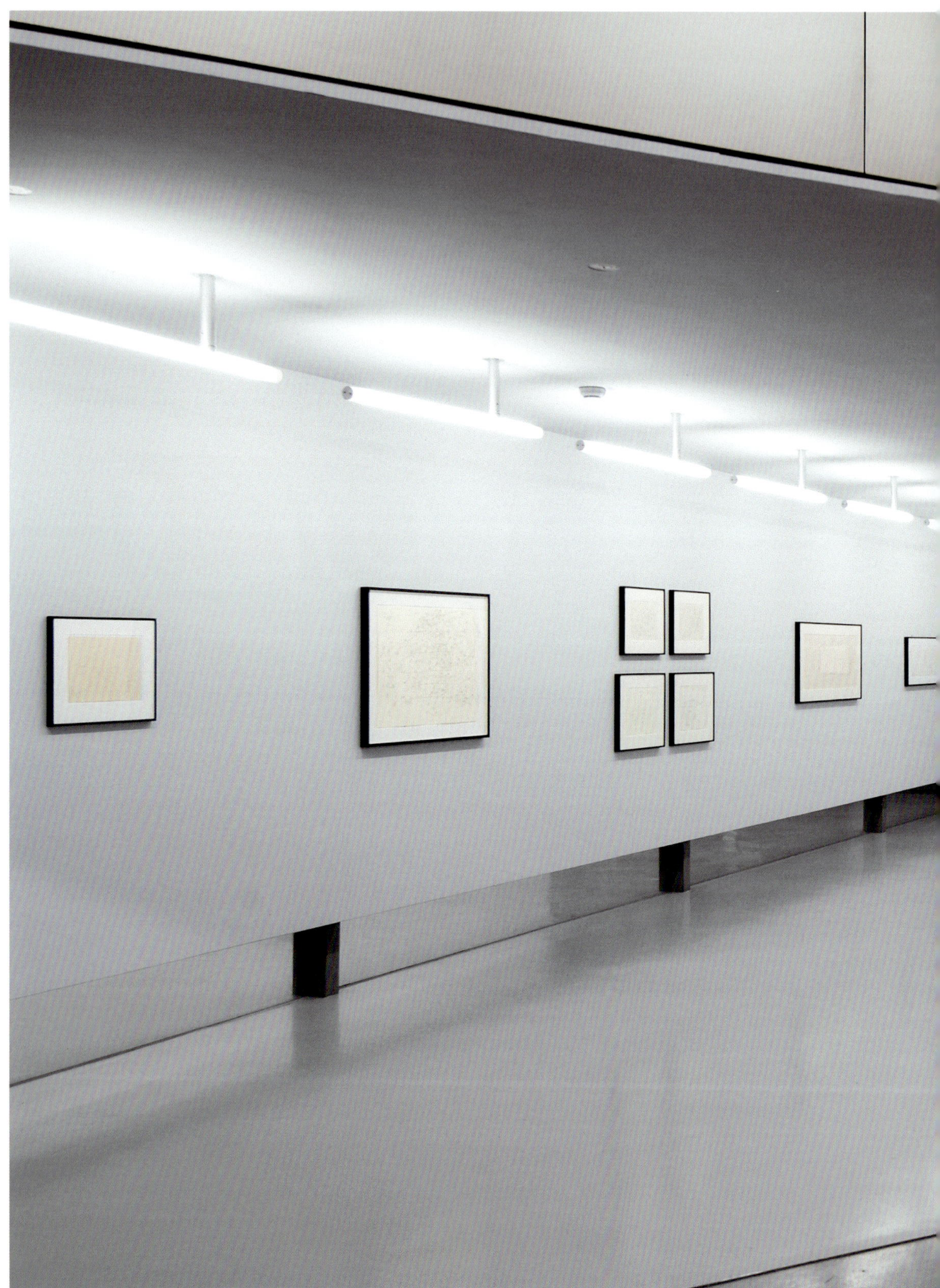

 The Captured Museum   Installation Views

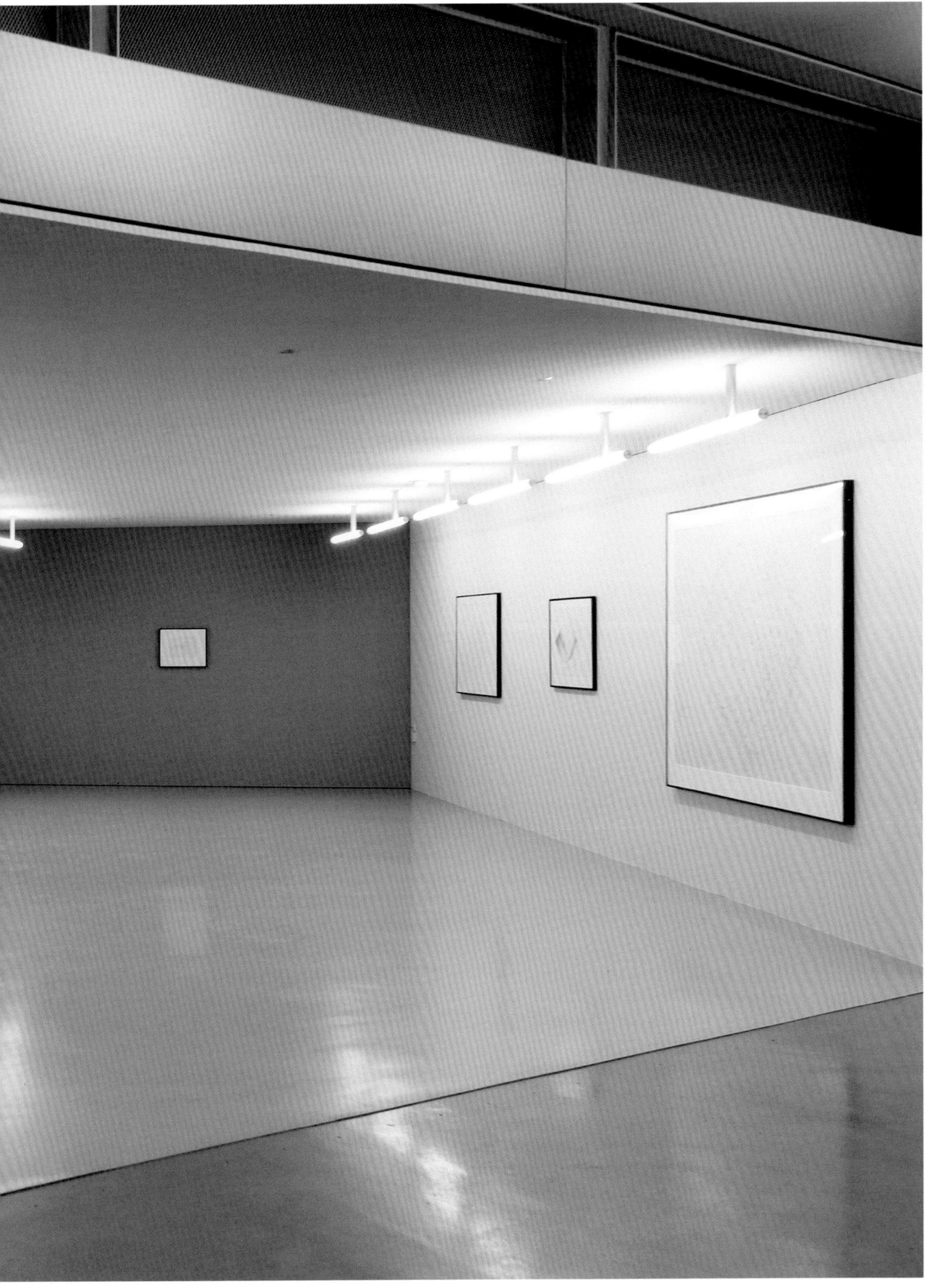

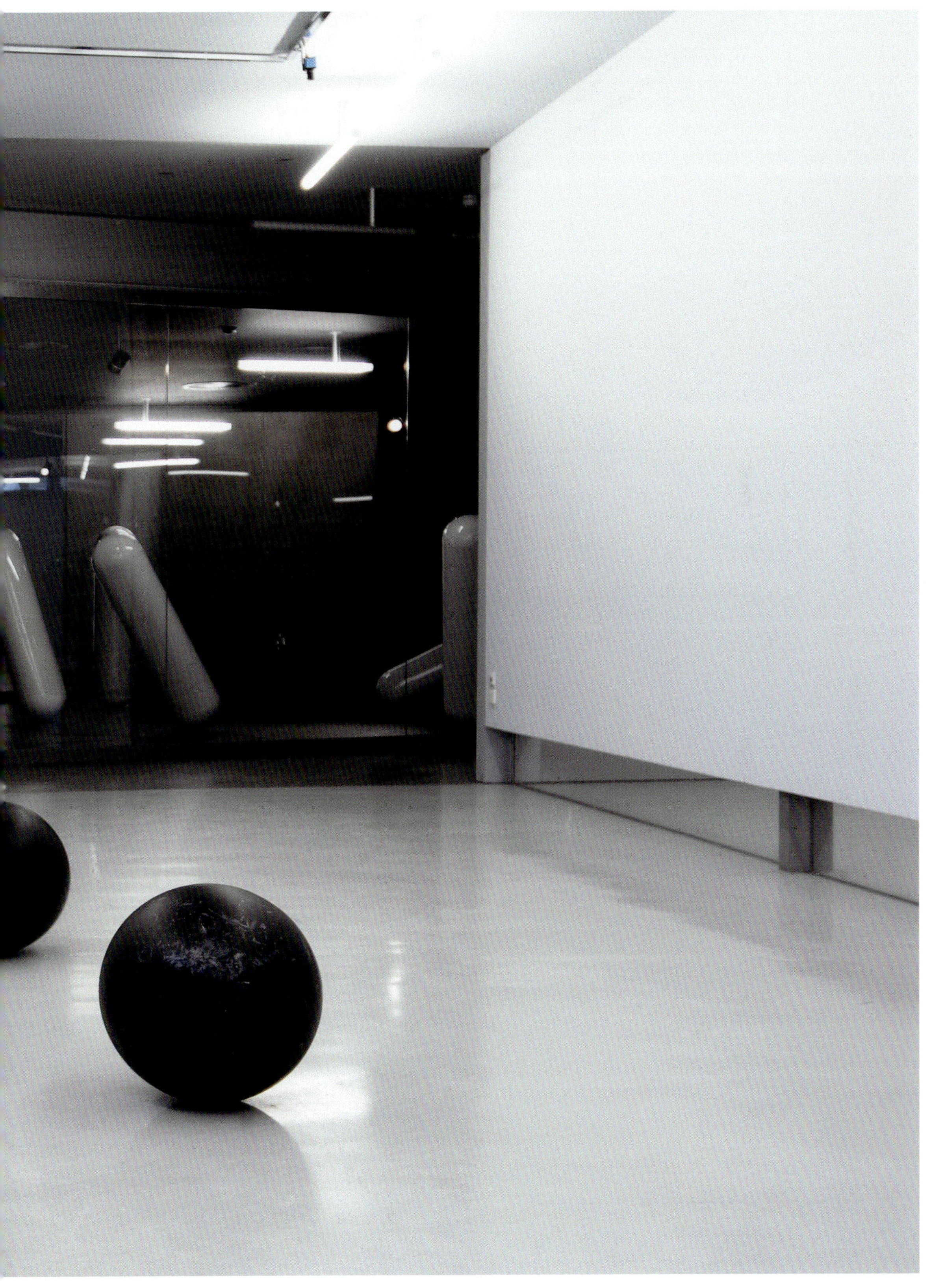

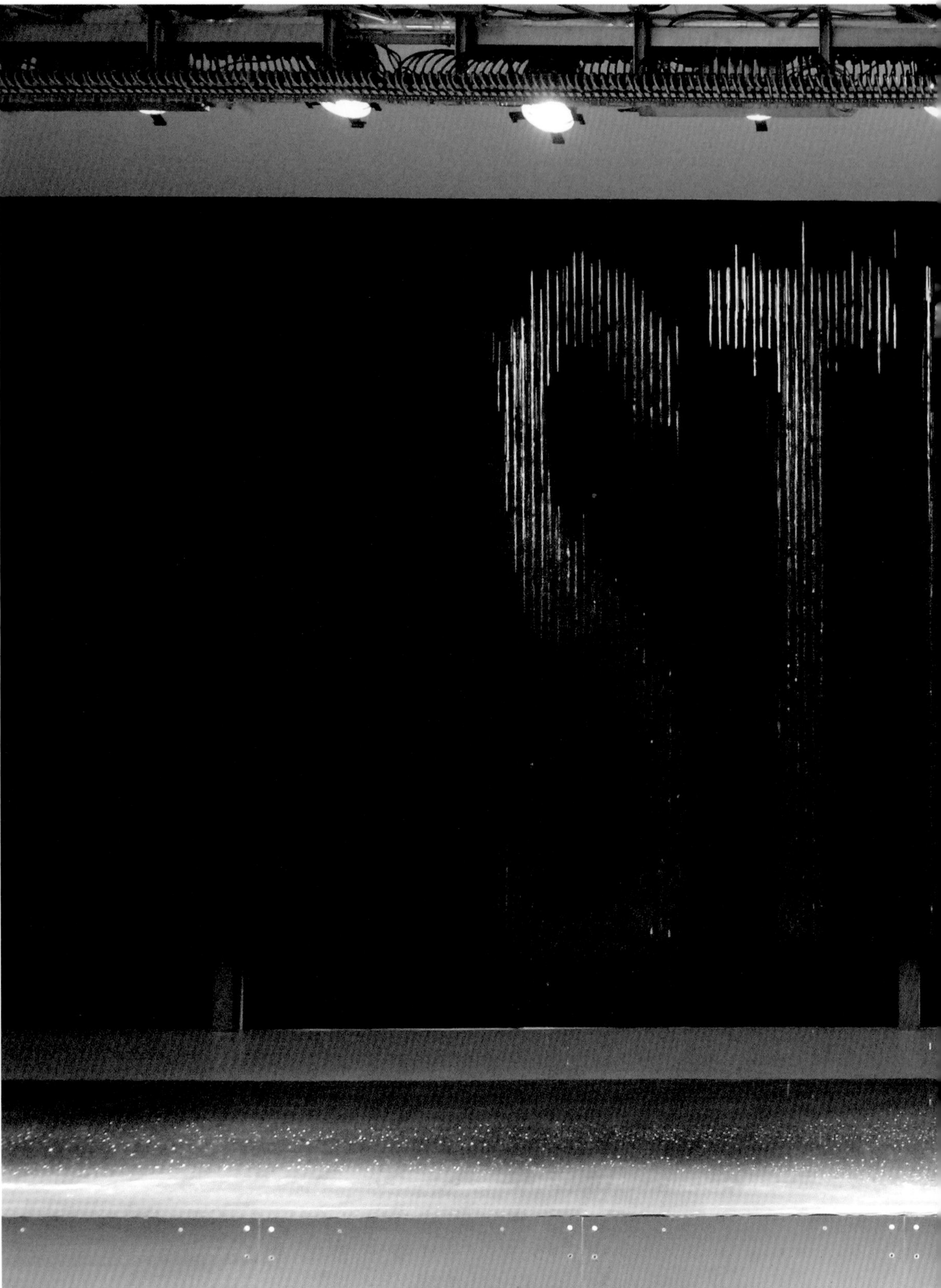

The Captured Museum   Installation Views

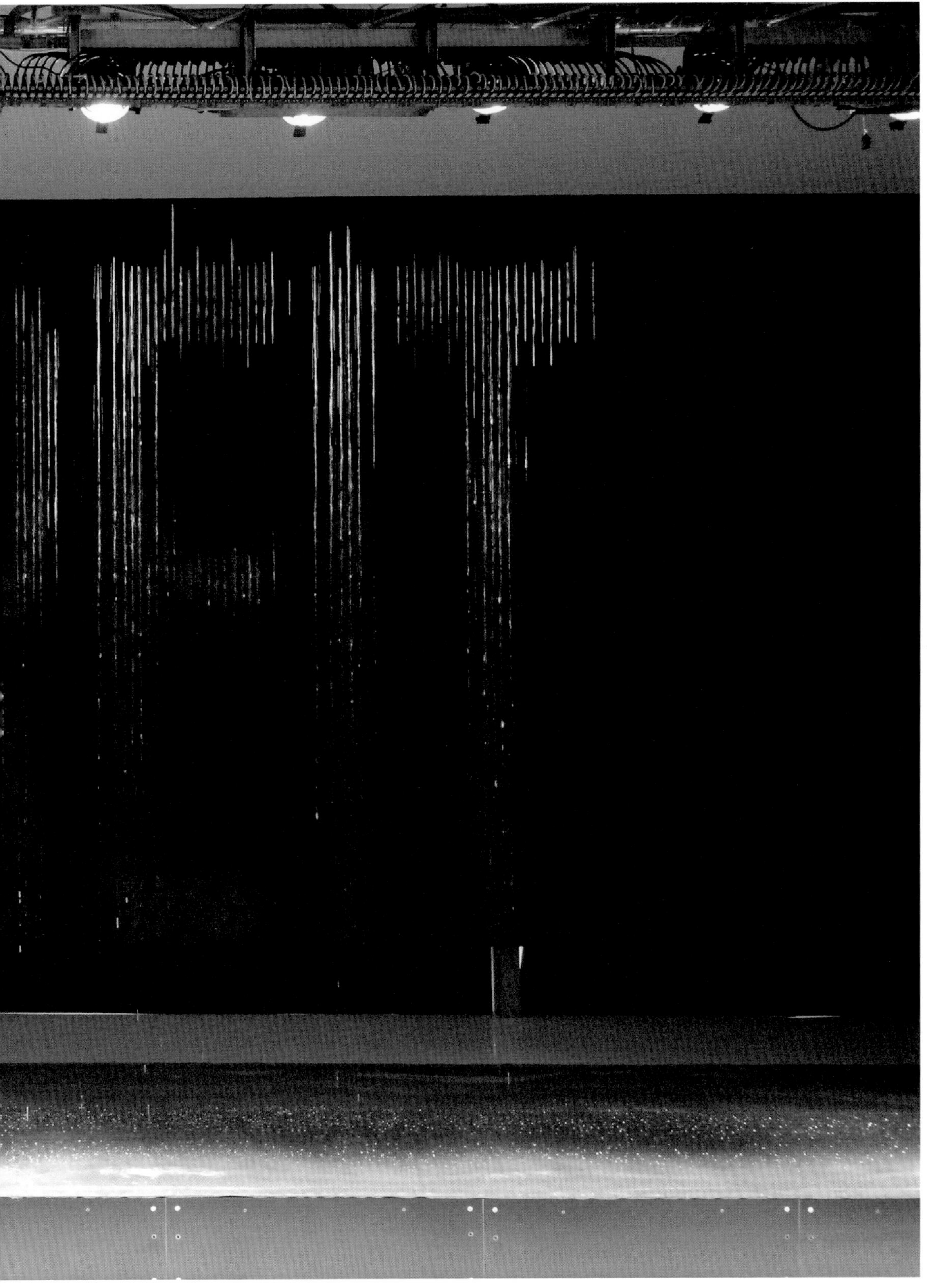

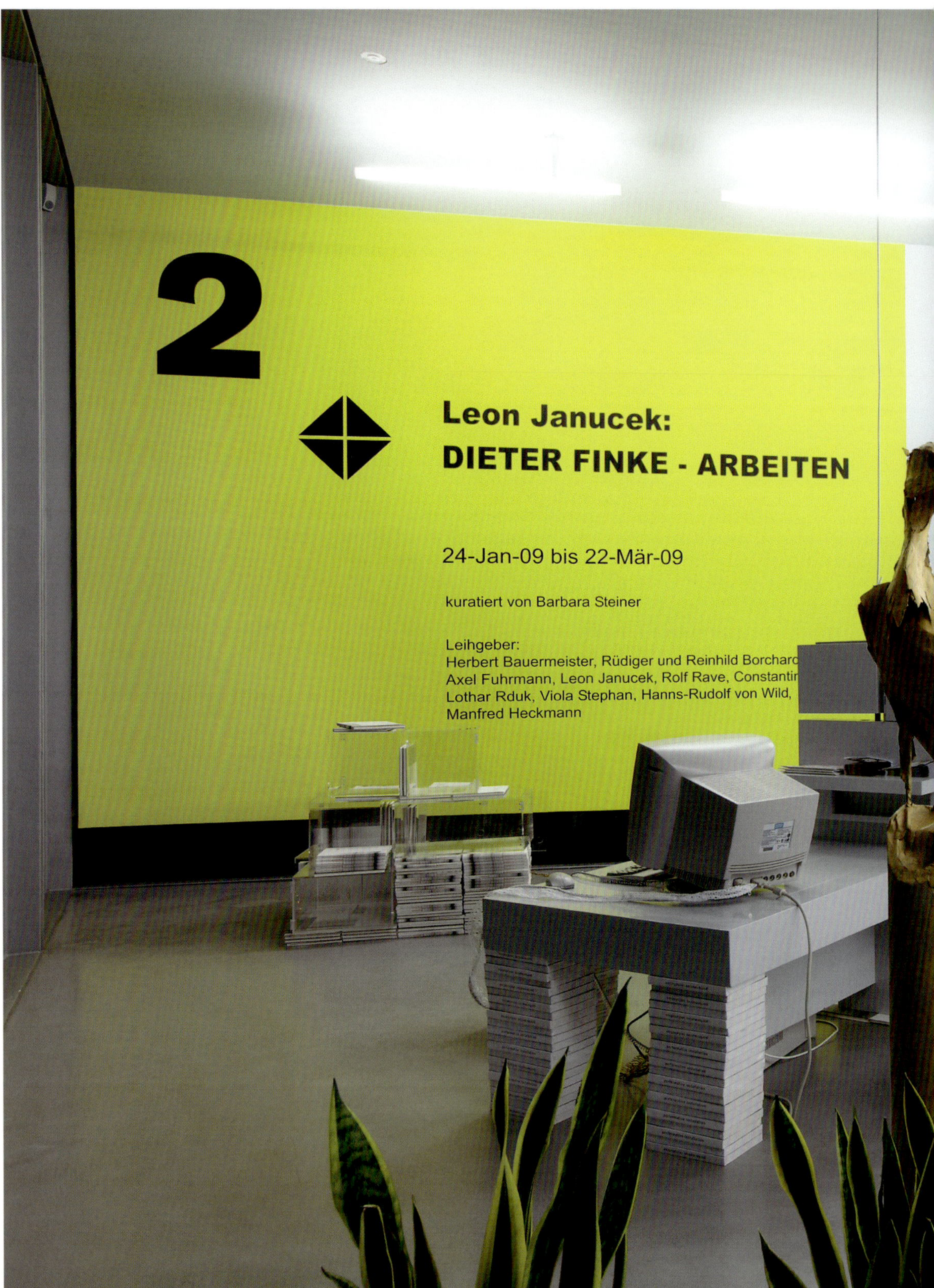
2
Leon Janucek:
DIETER FINKE - ARBEITEN

24-Jan-09 bis 22-Mär-09

kuratiert von Barbara Steiner

Leihgeber:
Herbert Bauermeister, Rüdiger und Reinhild Borchard
Axel Fuhrmann, Leon Janucek, Rolf Rave, Constantin
Lothar Rduk, Viola Stephan, Hanns-Rudolf von Wild,
Manfred Heckmann

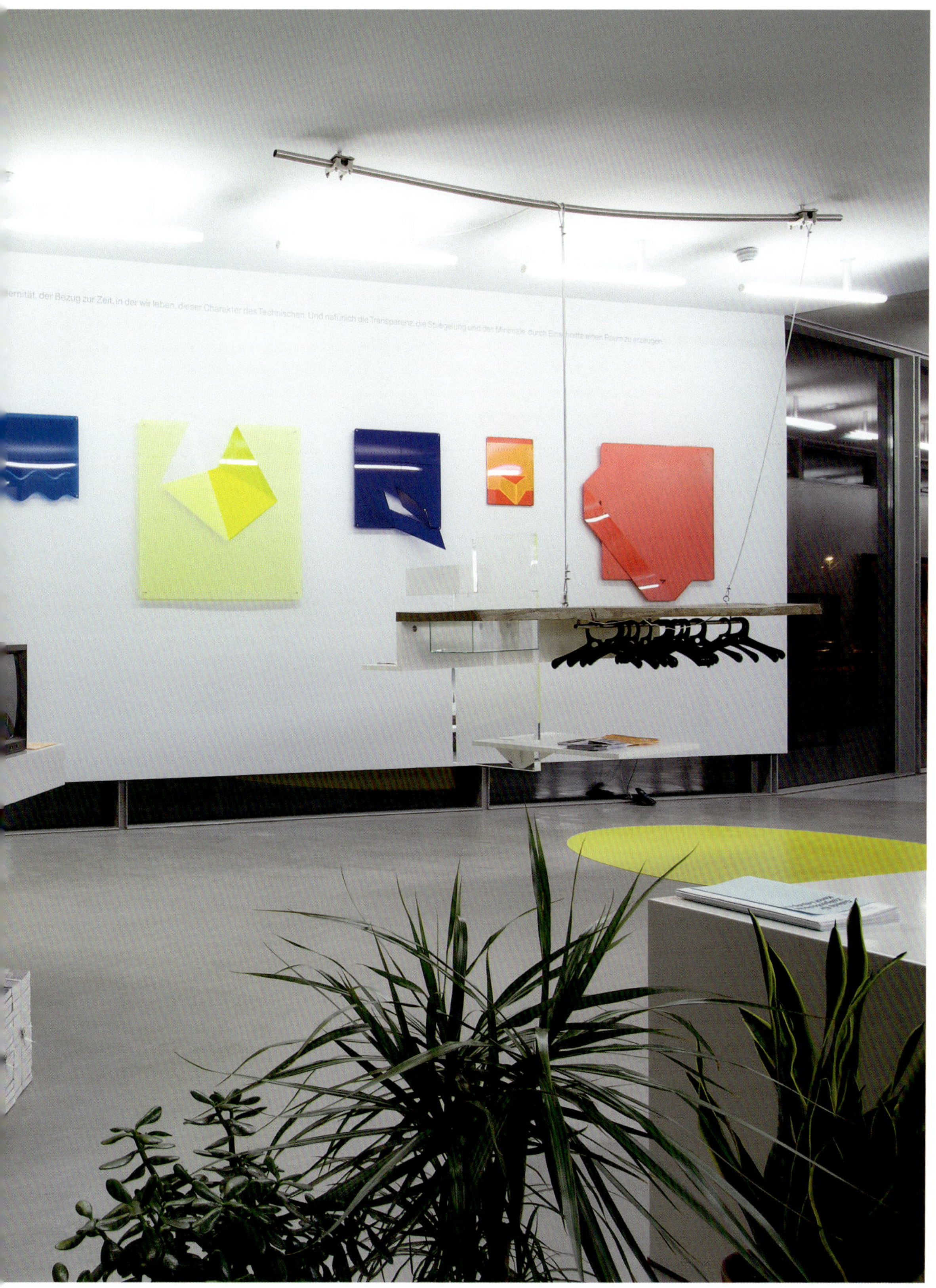
ernität, der Bezug zur Zeit, in der wir leben, dieser Charakter des Technischen. Und natürlich die Transparenz, die Spiegelung und das Minimale, durch Einschnitte einen Raum zu erzeugen.

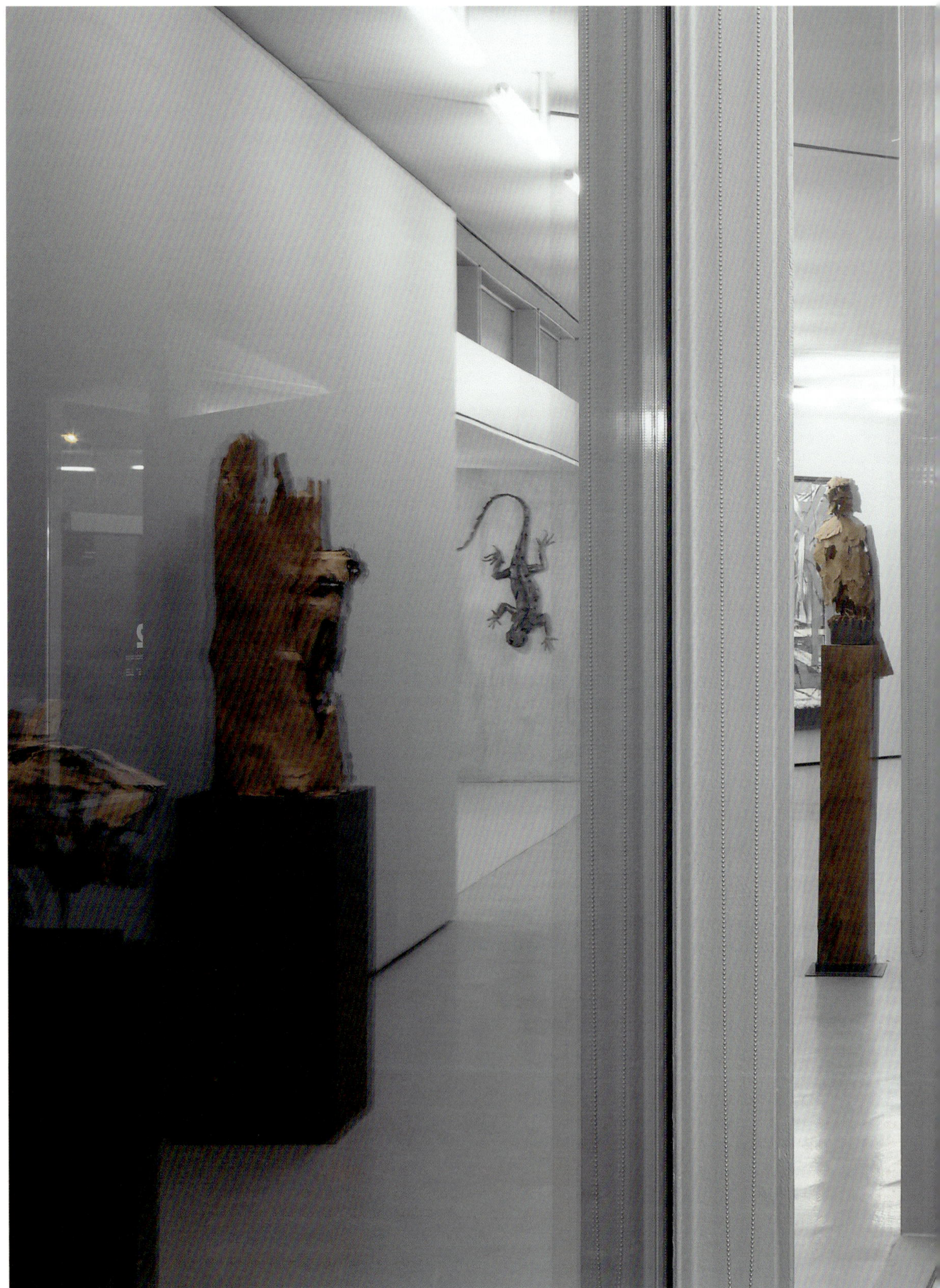

The Captured Museum   Installation Views

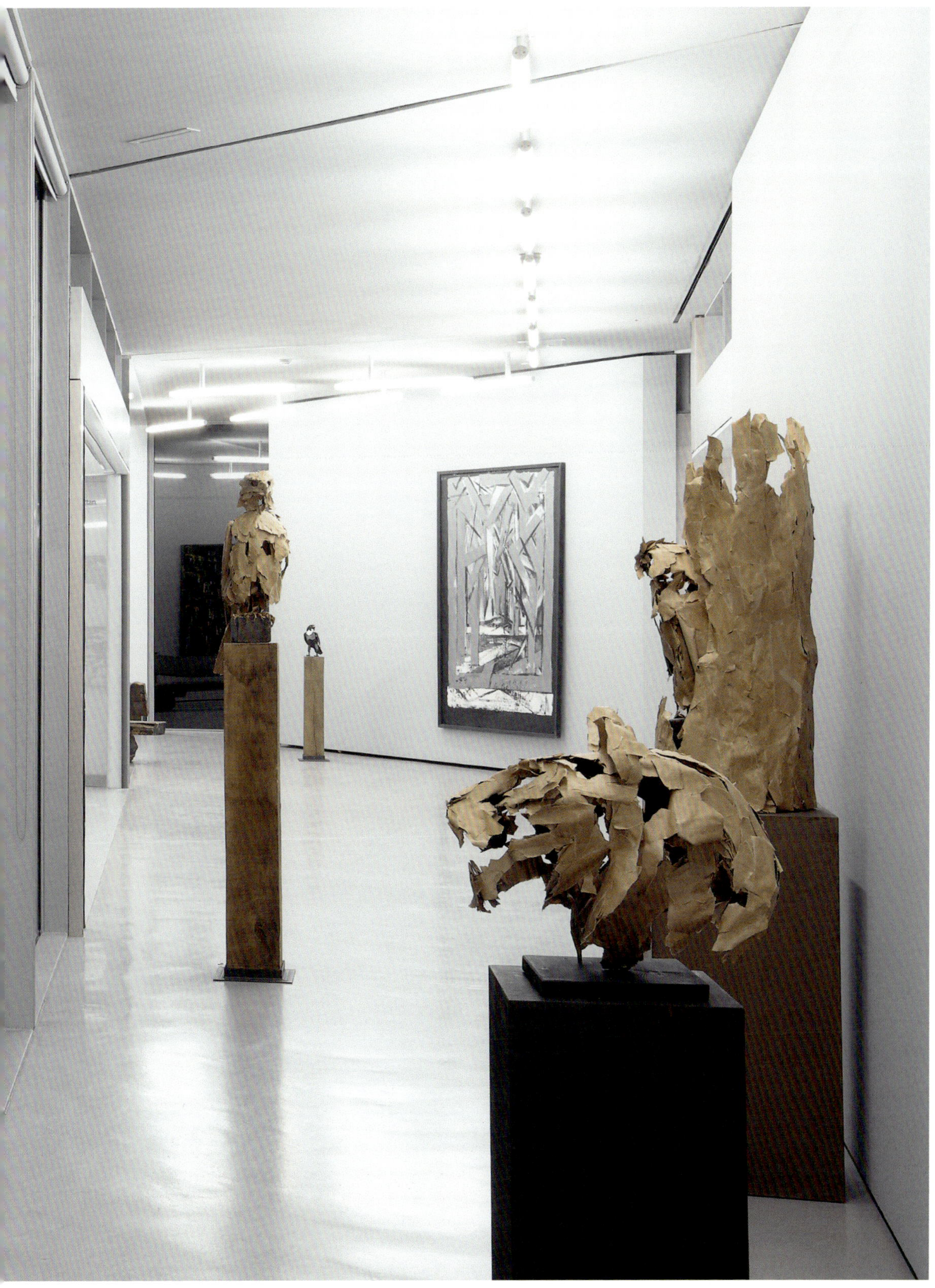

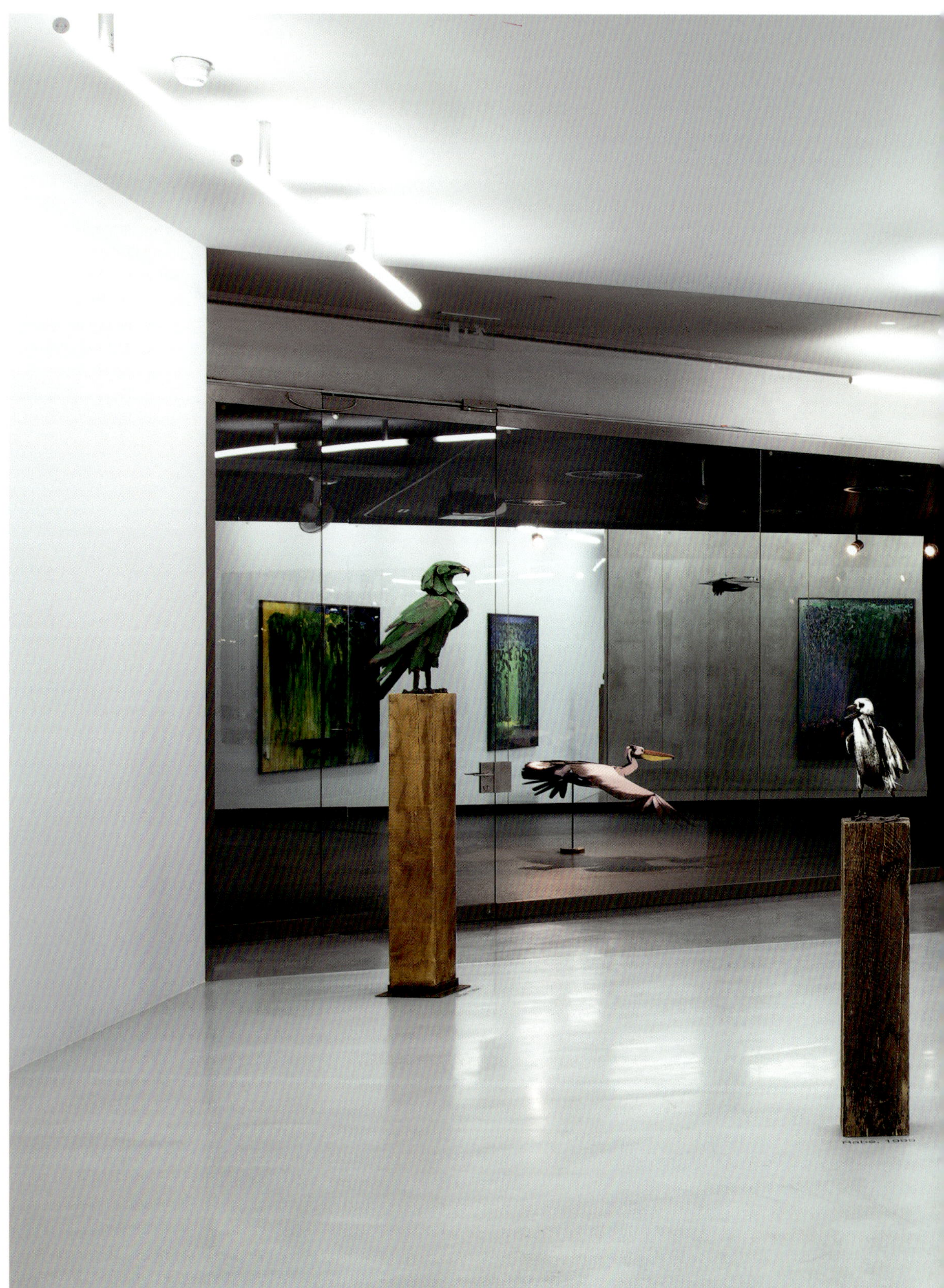

     The Captured Museum   Installation Views

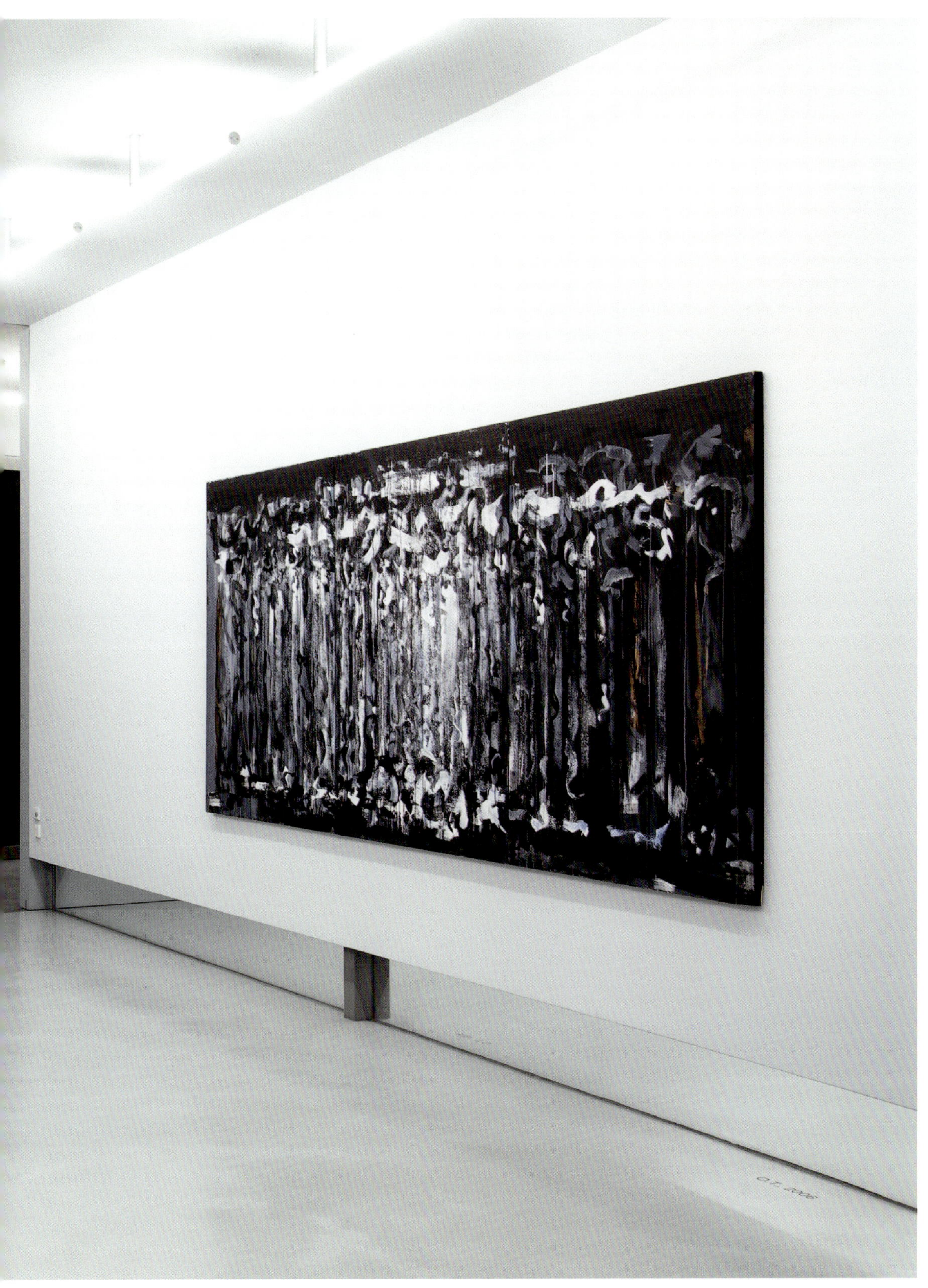

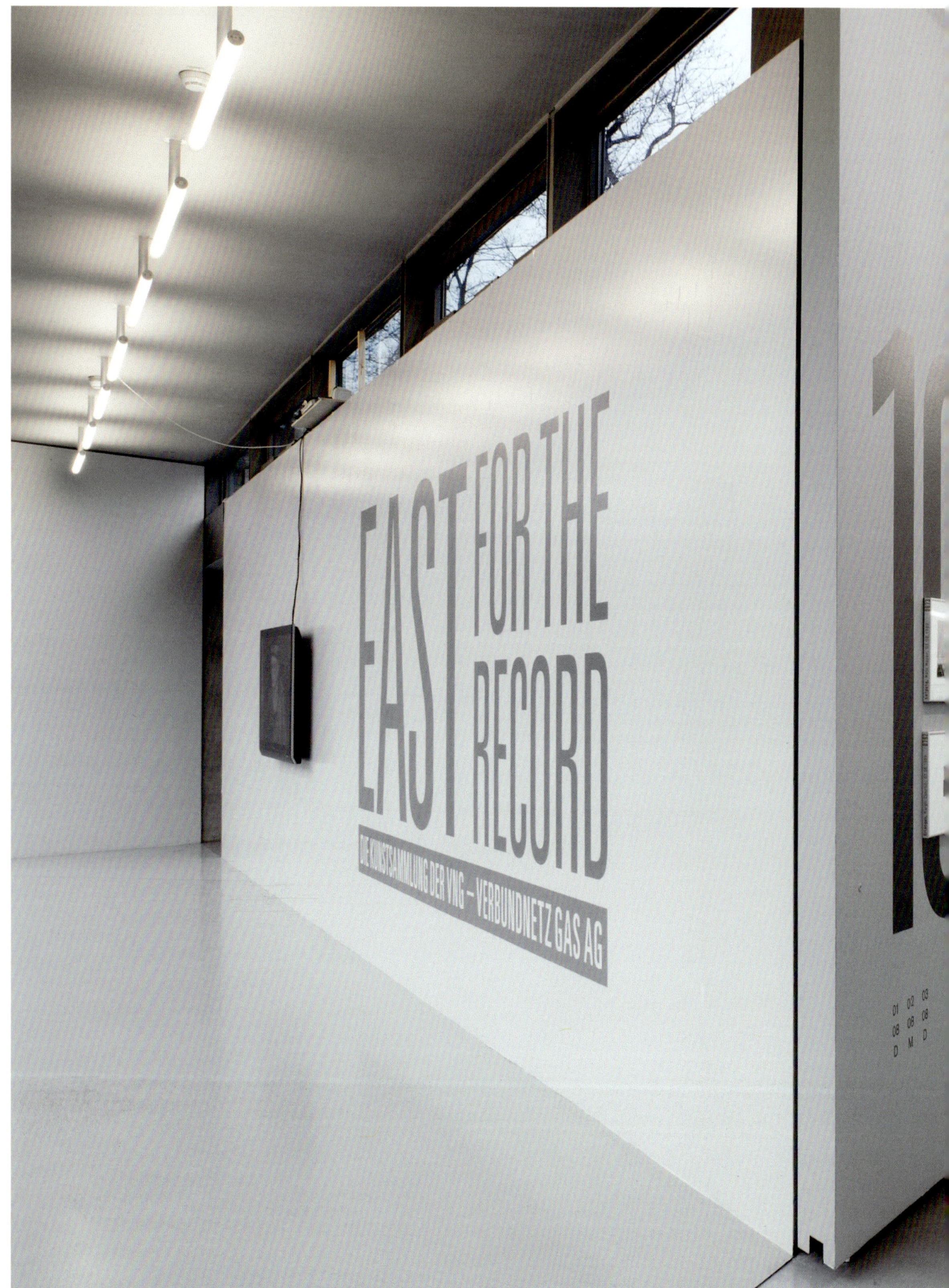

EAST FOR THE RECORD
DIE KUNSTSAMMLUNG DER VNG – VERBUNDNETZ GAS AG

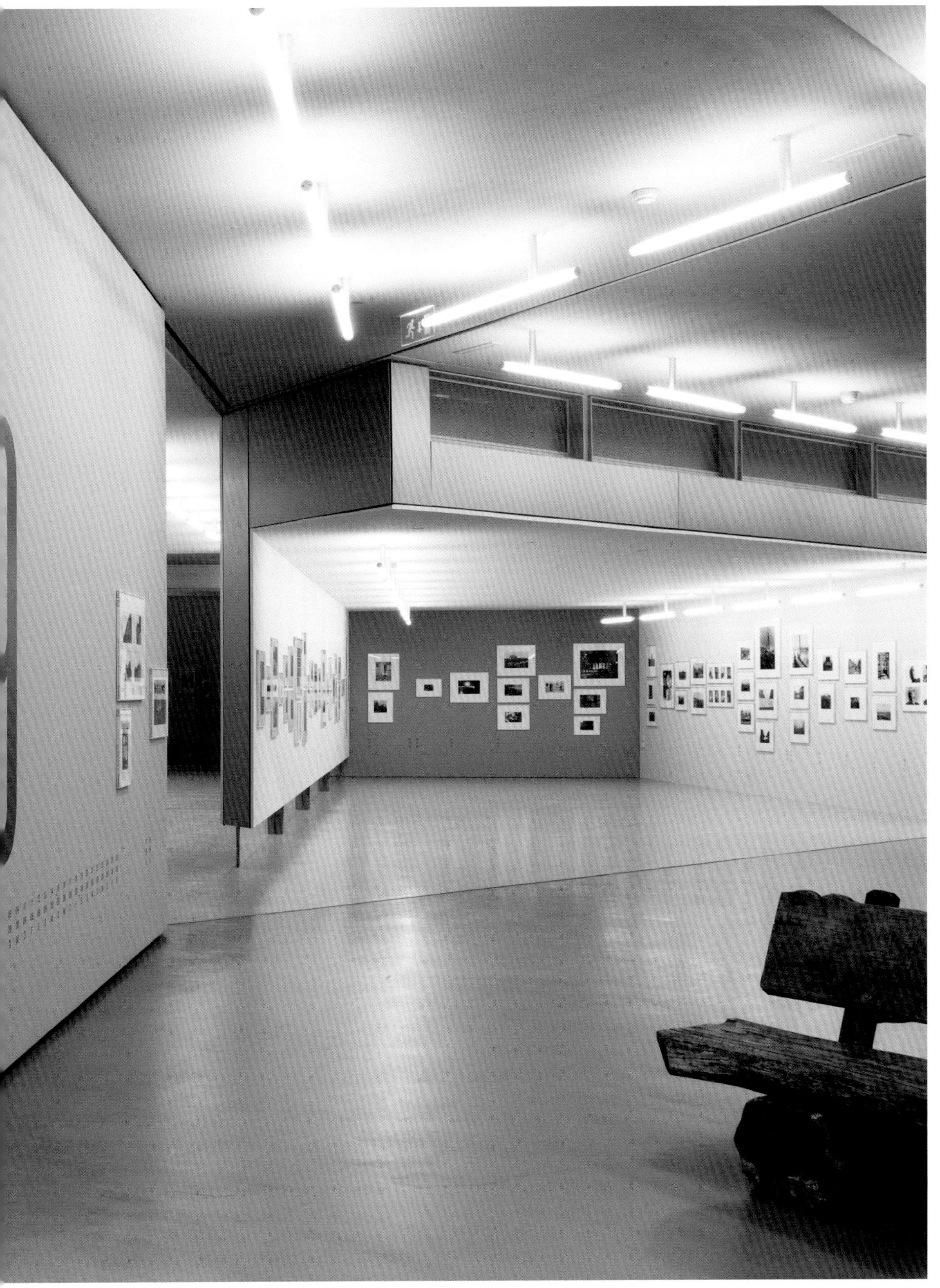

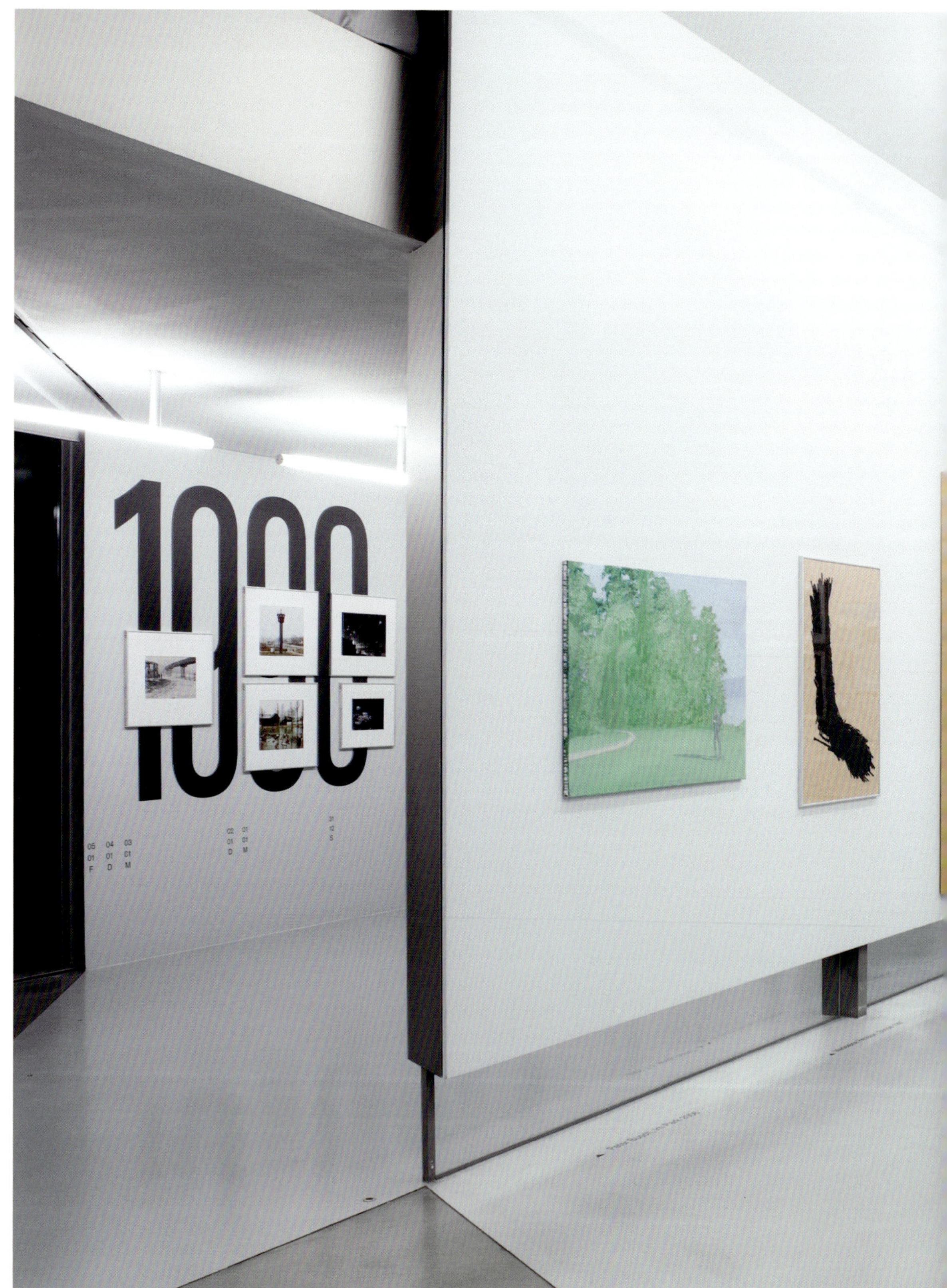

The Captured Museum   Installation Views

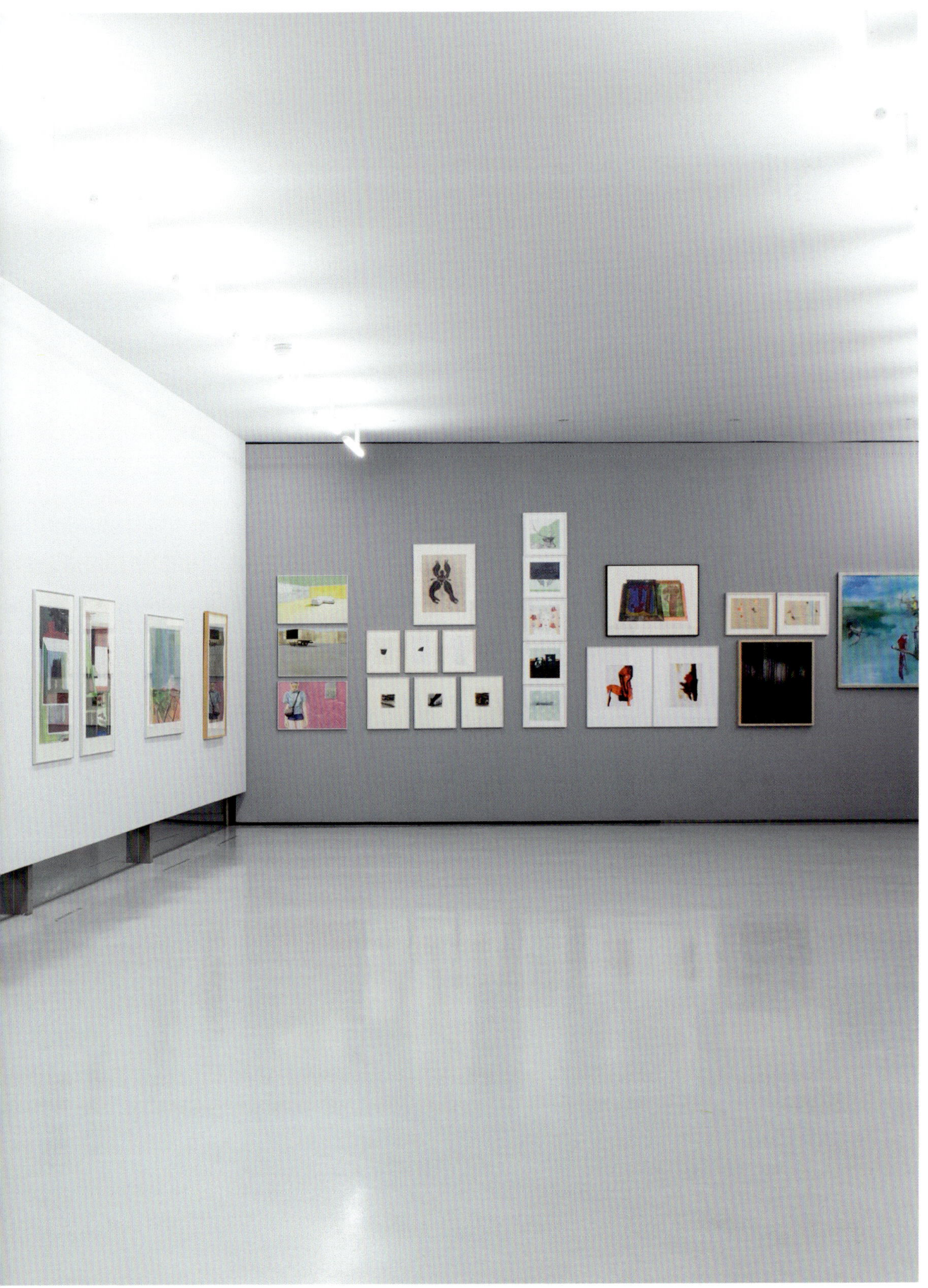

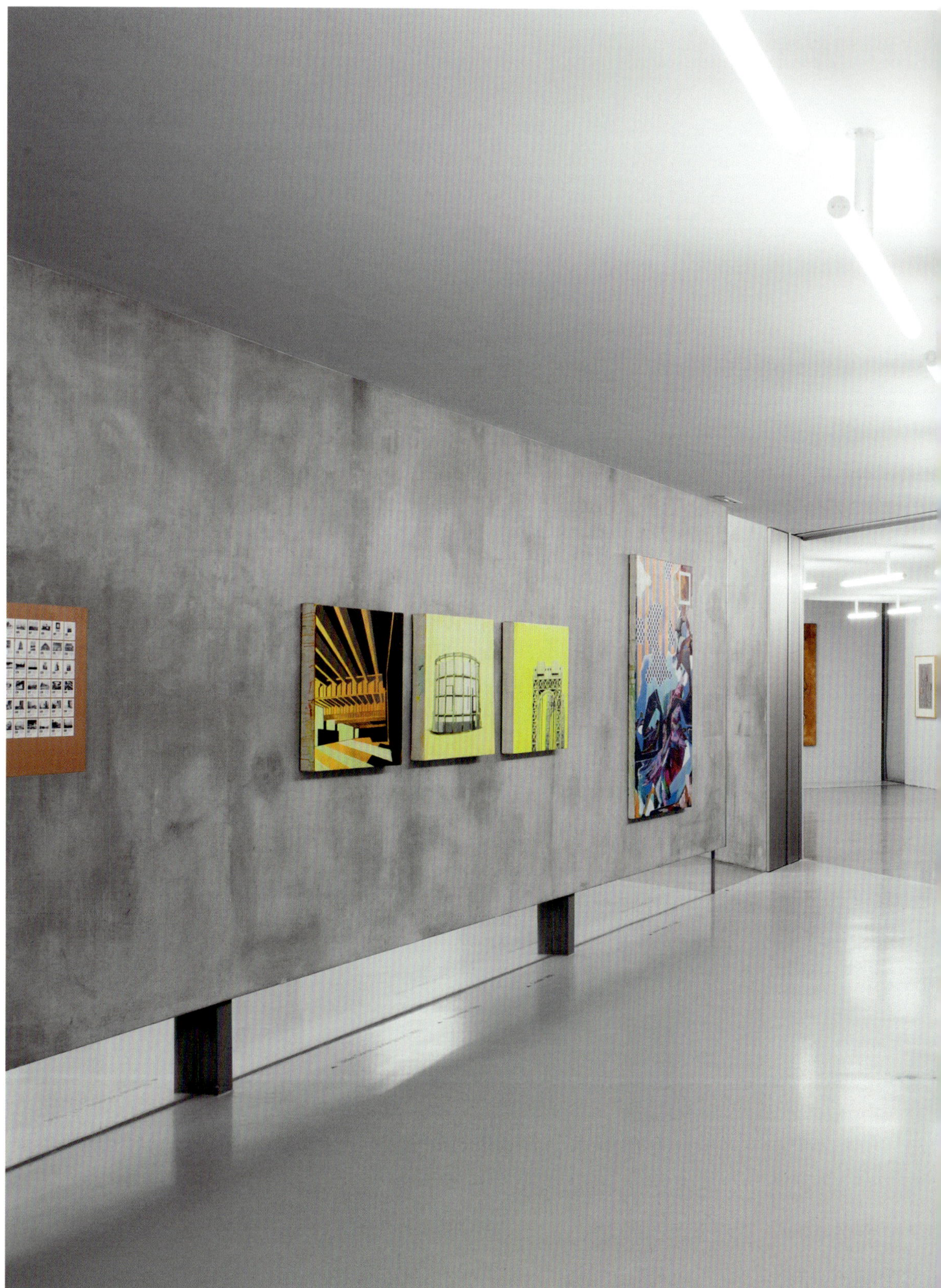

The Captured Museum   Installation Views

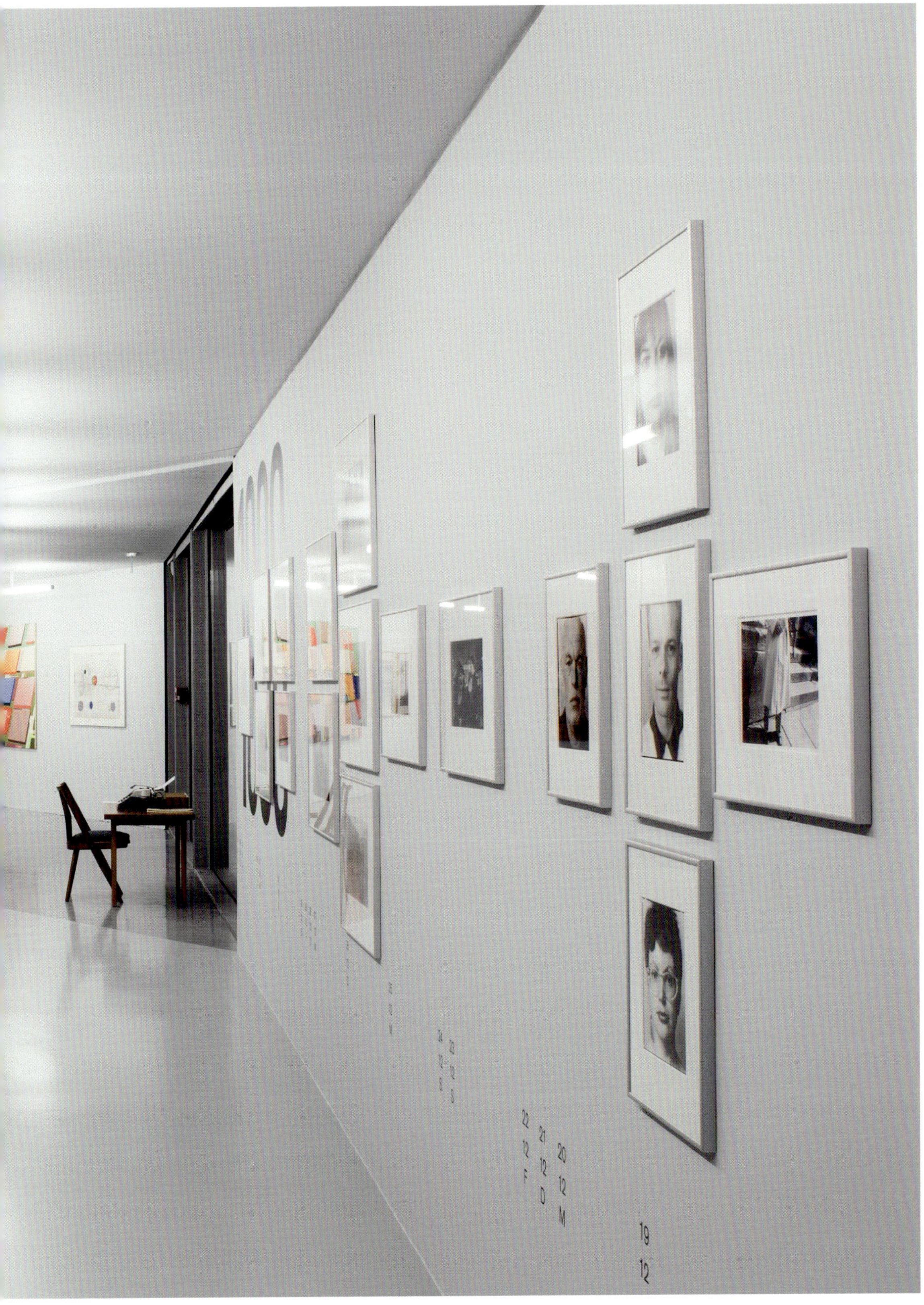

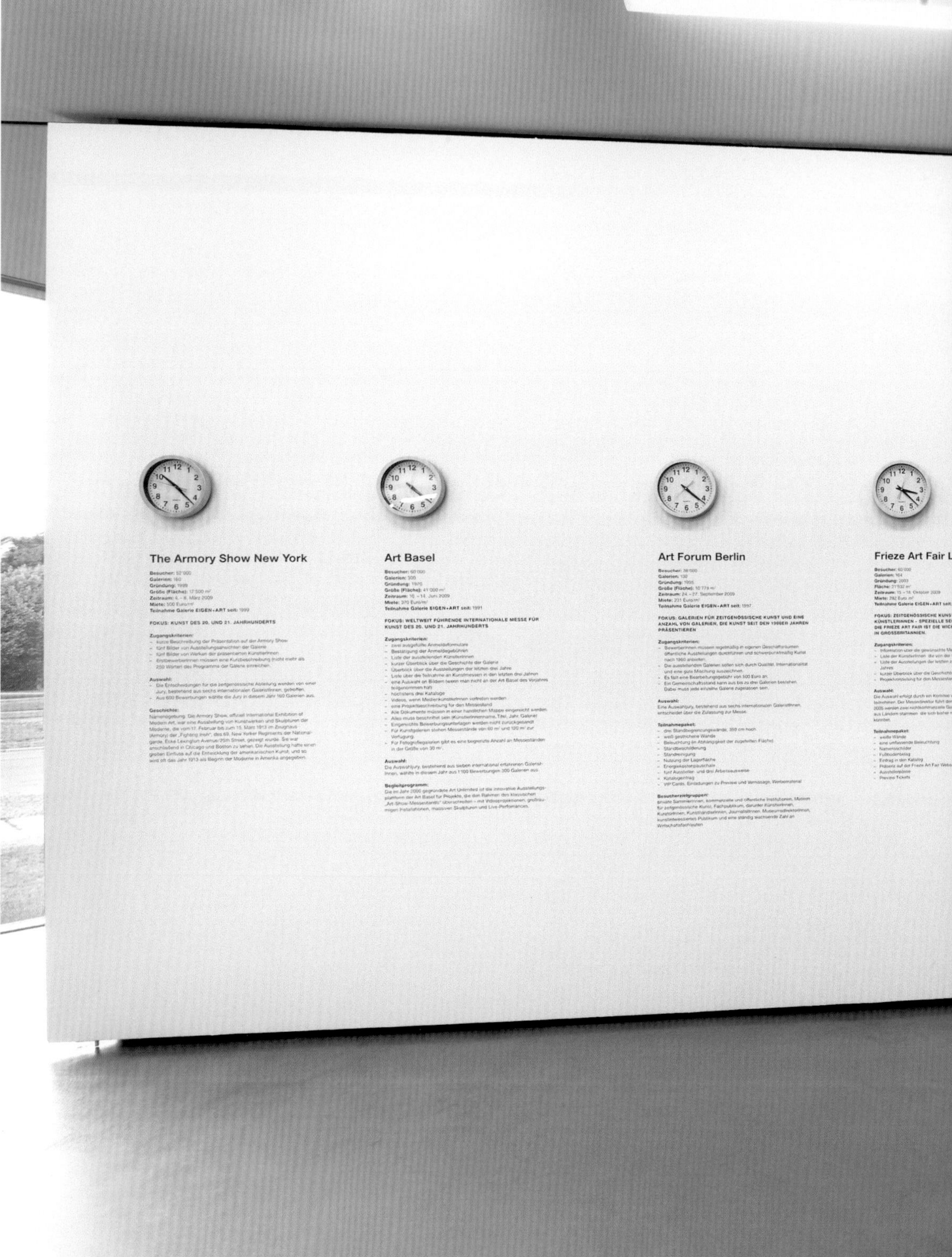

The Armory Show New York

Besucher: 52'000
Galerien: 160
Gründung: 1999
Größe (Fläche): 17'500 m²
Zeitraum: 4. – 8. März 2009
Miete: 500 Euro/m²
Teilnahme Galerie EIGEN + ART seit: 1999

FOKUS: KUNST DES 20. UND 21. JAHRHUNDERTS

Zugangskriterien:
– kurze Beschreibung der Präsentation auf der Armory Show
– fünf Bilder von Ausstellungsansichten der Galerie
– fünf Bilder von Werken der präsentierten KünstlerInnen
– ErstbewerberInnen müssen eine Kurzbeschreibung (nicht mehr als
  250 Wörter) des Programms der Galerie einreichen.

Auswahl:
– Die Entscheidungen für die zeitgenössische Abteilung werden von einer
  Jury, bestehend aus sechs internationalen GaleristInnen, getroffen.
– Aus 600 Bewerbungen wählte die Jury in diesem Jahr 160 Galerien aus.

Geschichte:
Namensgebung: Die Armory Show, offiziell International Exhibition of
Modern Art, war eine Ausstellung von Kunstwerken und Skulpturen der
Moderne, die vom 17. Februar bis zum 15. März 1913 im Zeughaus
(Armory) der „Fighting Irish", des 69. New Yorker Regiments der National-
garde, Ecke Lexington Avenue/25th Street, gezeigt wurde. Sie war
anschließend in Chicago und Boston zu sehen. Die Ausstellung hatte einen
großen Einfluss auf die Entwicklung der amerikanischen Kunst, und so
wird oft das Jahr 1913 als Beginn der Moderne in Amerika angegeben.

Art Basel

Besucher: 60 000
Galerien: 300
Gründung: 1970
Größe (Fläche): 41 000 m²
Zeitraum: 10. – 14. Juni 2009
Miete: 370 Euro/m²
Teilnahme Galerie EIGEN + ART seit: 1991

FOKUS: WELTWEIT FÜHRENDE INTERNATIONALE MESSE FÜR
KUNST DES 20. UND 21. JAHRHUNDERTS

Zugangskriterien:
– zwei ausgefüllte Anmeldeformulare
– Bestätigung der Anmeldegebühren
– Liste der ausstellenden KünstlerInnen
– kurzer Überblick über die Geschichte der Galerie
– Überblick über die Ausstellungen der letzten drei Jahre
– Liste über die Teilnahme an Kunstmessen in den letzten drei Jahren
– eine Auswahl an Bildern (wenn man nicht an der Art Basel des Vorjahres
  teilgenommen hat)
– höchstens drei Kataloge
– Videos, wenn MedienkünstlerInnen vertreten werden
– eine Projektbeschreibung für den Messestand
– Alle Dokumente müssen in einer handlichen Mappe eingereicht werden.
– Alles muss beschriftet sein (KünstlerInnenname, Titel, Jahr, Galerie)
– Eingereichte Bewerbungsunterlagen werden nicht zurückgesandt
– Für Kunstgalerien stehen Messestände von 60 m² und 120 m² zur
  Verfügung.
– Für Fotografiegalerien gibt es eine begrenzte Anzahl an Messeständen
  in der Größe von 30 m².

Auswahl:
Die Auswahljury, bestehend aus sieben international erfahrenen Galerist-
Innen, wählte in diesem Jahr aus 1'100 Bewerbungen 300 Galerien aus.

Begleitprogramm:
Die im Jahr 2000 gegründete Art Unlimited ist die innovative Ausstellungs-
plattform der Art Basel für Projekte, die den Rahmen des klassischen
„Art-Show-Messestands" überschreiten – mit Videoprojektionen, großräu-
migen Installationen, massiven Skulpturen und Live-Performances.

Art Forum Berlin

Besucher: 38'000
Galerien: 130
Gründung: 1995
Größe (Fläche): 10'779 m²
Zeitraum: 24. – 27. September 2009
Miete: 231 Euro/m²
Teilnahme Galerie EIGEN + ART seit: 1997

FOKUS: GALERIEN FÜR ZEITGENÖSSISCHE KUNST UND EINE
ANZAHL VON GALERIEN, DIE KUNST SEIT DEN 1960ER JAHREN
PRÄSENTIEREN

Zugangskriterien:
– BewerberInnen müssen regelmäßig in eigenen Geschäftsräumen
  öffentliche Ausstellungen durchführen und schwerpunktmäßig Kunst
  nach 1960 anbieten.
– Die ausstellenden Galerien sollen sich durch Qualität, Internationalität
  und eine gute Mischung auszeichnen.
– Es fällt eine Bearbeitungsgebühr von 500 Euro an.
– Ein Gemeinschaftsstand kann aus bis zu drei Galerien bestehen.
  Dabei muss jede einzelne Galerie zugelassen sein.

Auswahl:
Eine Auswahljury, bestehend aus sechs internationalen GaleristInnen,
entscheidet über die Zulassung zur Messe.

Teilnahmepaket:
– drei Standbegrenzungswände, 350 cm hoch
– weiß gestrichene Wände
– Beleuchtung in Abhängigkeit der zugeteilten Fläche
– Standbeschilderung
– Standreinigung
– Nutzung der Lagerfläche
– Energiekostenpauschale
– fünf Aussteller- und drei Arbeitsausweise
– Katalogeintrag
– VIP Cards, Einladungen zu Preview und Vernissage, Werbematerial

Besucherzielgruppen:
private SammlerInnen, kommerzielle und öffentliche Institutionen, Museen
für zeitgenössische Kunst, Fachpublikum, darunter KünstlerInnen,
KuratorInnen, KunsthändlerInnen, JournalistInnen, MuseumsdirektorInnen,
kunstinteressiertes Publikum und eine ständig wachsende Zahl an
Wirtschaftsfachleuten

Frieze Art Fair Lo

Besucher: 60 000
Galerien: 164
Gründung: 2003
Fläche: 21'932 m²
Zeitraum: 15. – 18. Oktober 2009
Miete: 282 Euro/m²
Teilnahme Galerie EIGEN + ART seit: 200

FOKUS: ZEITGENÖSSISCHE KUNST U
KÜNSTLERINNEN - SPEZIELLE SEKTIC
DIE FRIEZE ART FAIR IST DIE WICHTIC
IN GROSSBRITANNIEN.

Zugangskriterien:
– Information über die gewünschte Messe
– Liste der KünstlerInnen, die von der Gale
– Liste der Ausstellungen der letzten zwei
  Jahres
– kurzer Überblick über die Geschichte der
– Projektvorstellung für den Messestand

Auswahl:
Die Auswahl erfolgt durch ein Komitee von
teilnehmen. Der Messedirektor führt den Vor
2005 werden zwei nichtkommerzielle Galerien
aus Ländern stammen, die sich bisher nicht
kannten.

Teilnahmepaket:
– weiße Wände
– eine umfassende Beleuchtung
– Namensschilder
– Fußbodenbelag
– Eintrag in den Katalog
– Präsenz auf der Frieze Art Fair Website
– Ausstellerpässe
– Preview Tickets

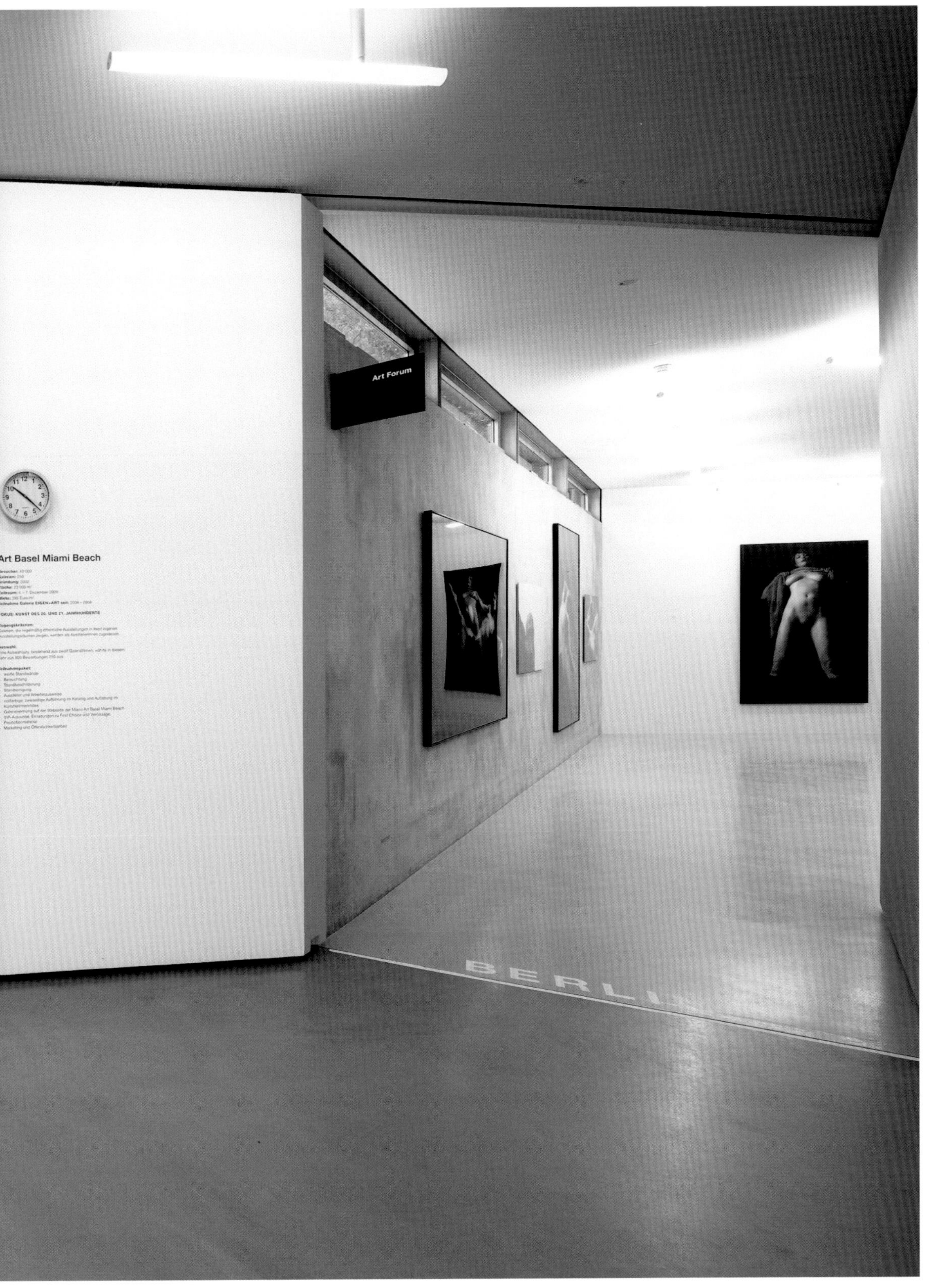
Art Forum
Art Basel Miami Beach
FOKUS: KUNST DES 20. UND 21. JAHRHUNDERTS
BERLIN

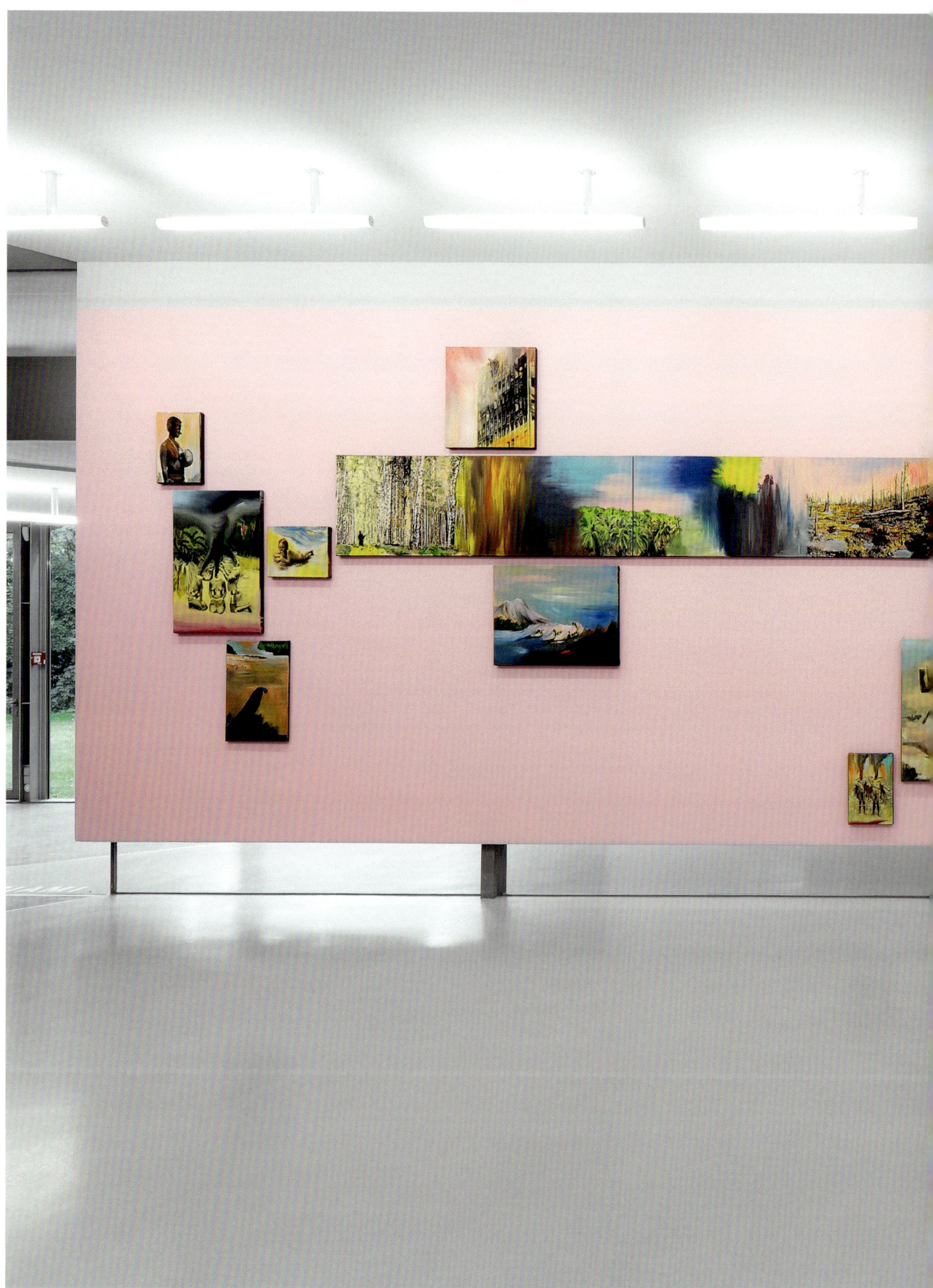

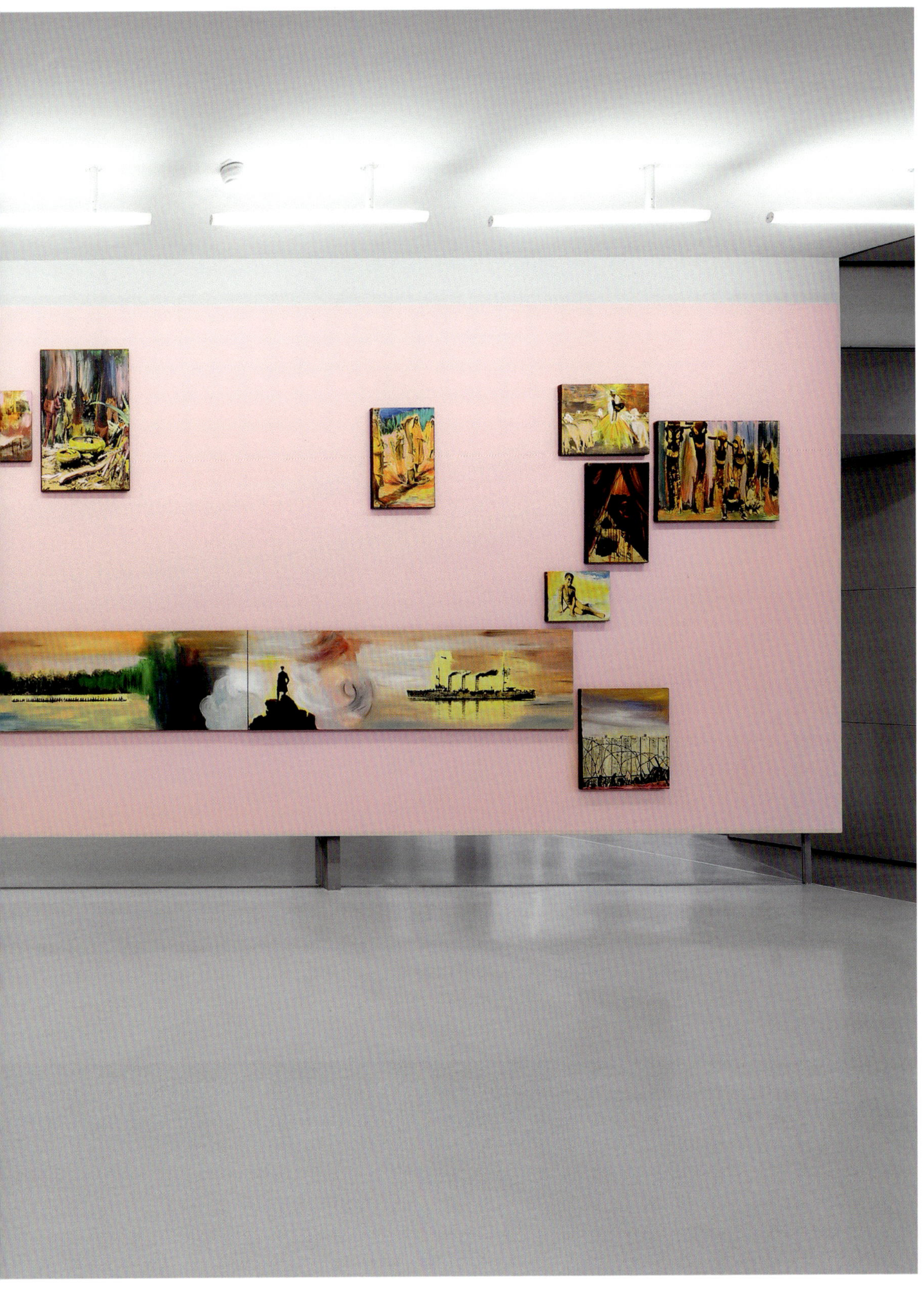

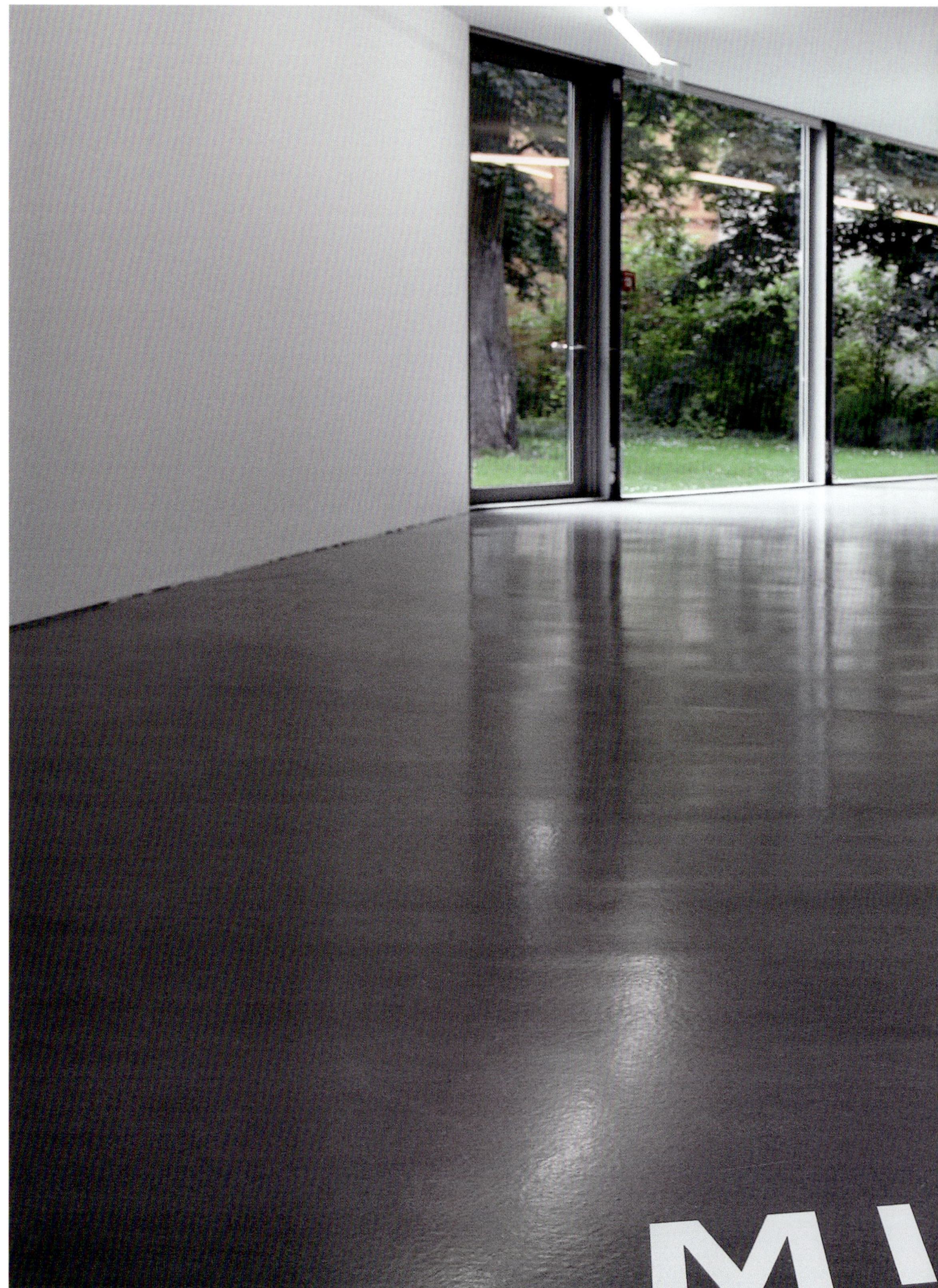

MU

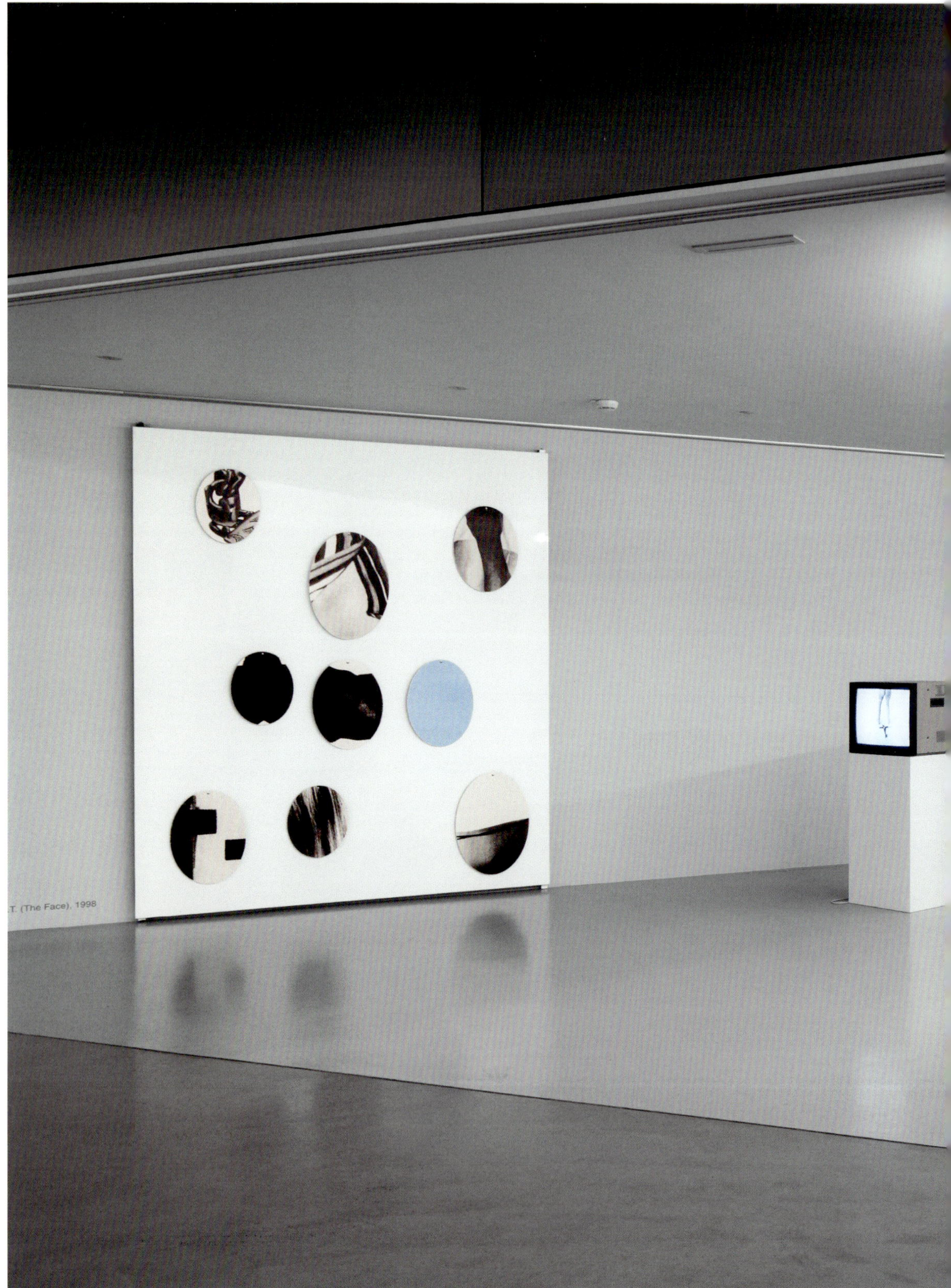

.T. (The Face), 1998

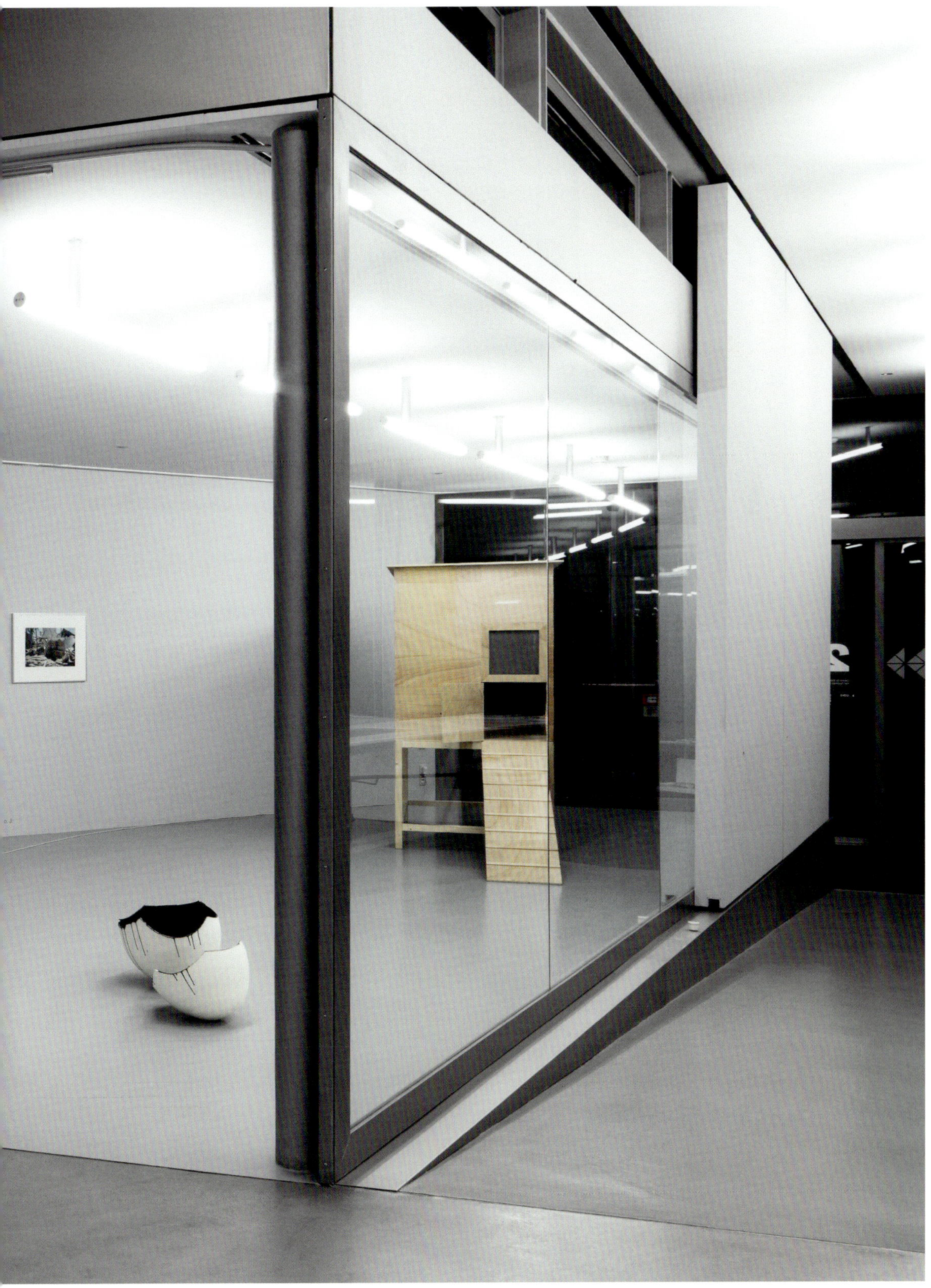

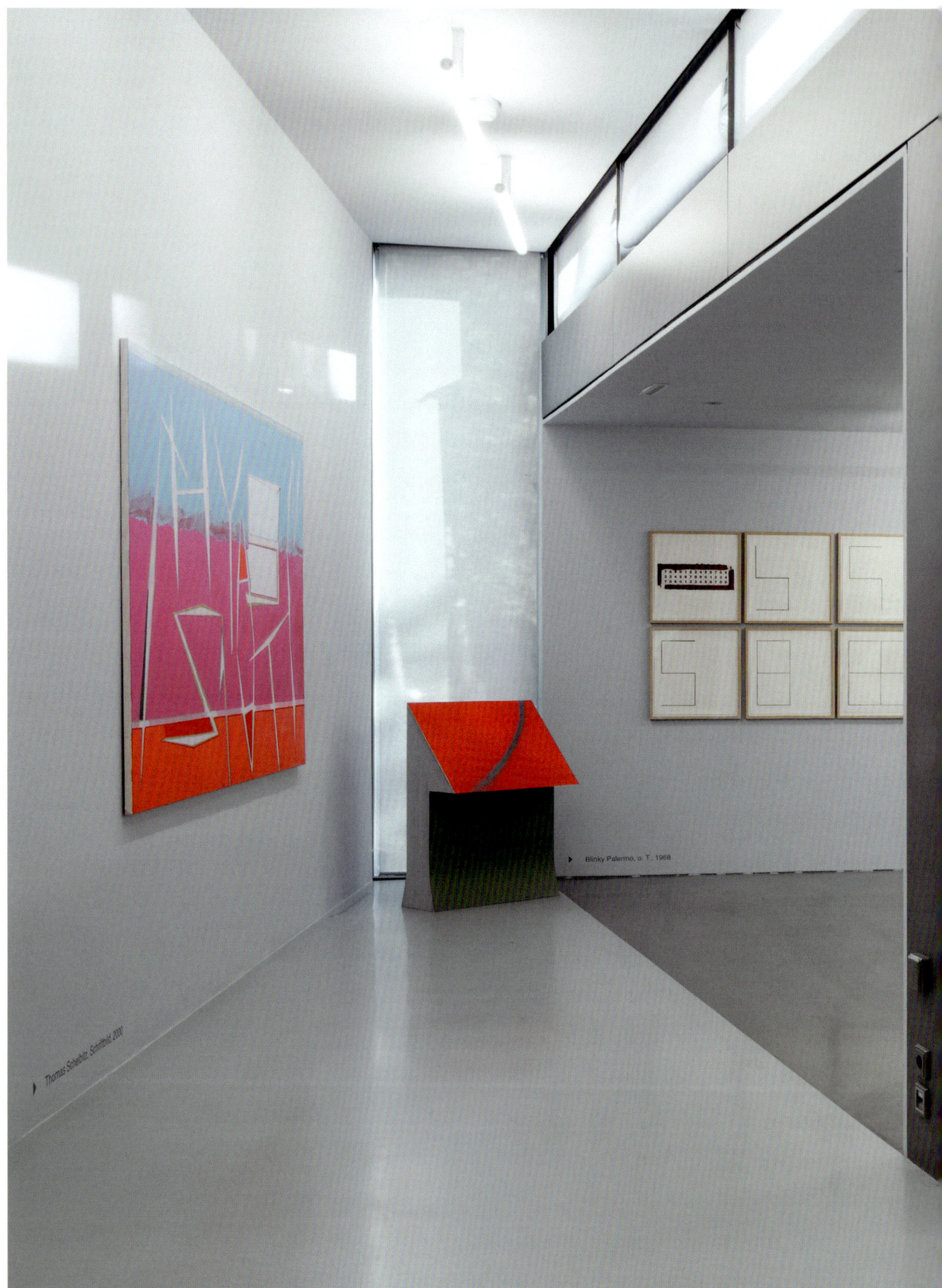

Thomas Scheibitz, Schlittsd, 2000
Blinky Palermo, o. T., 1968

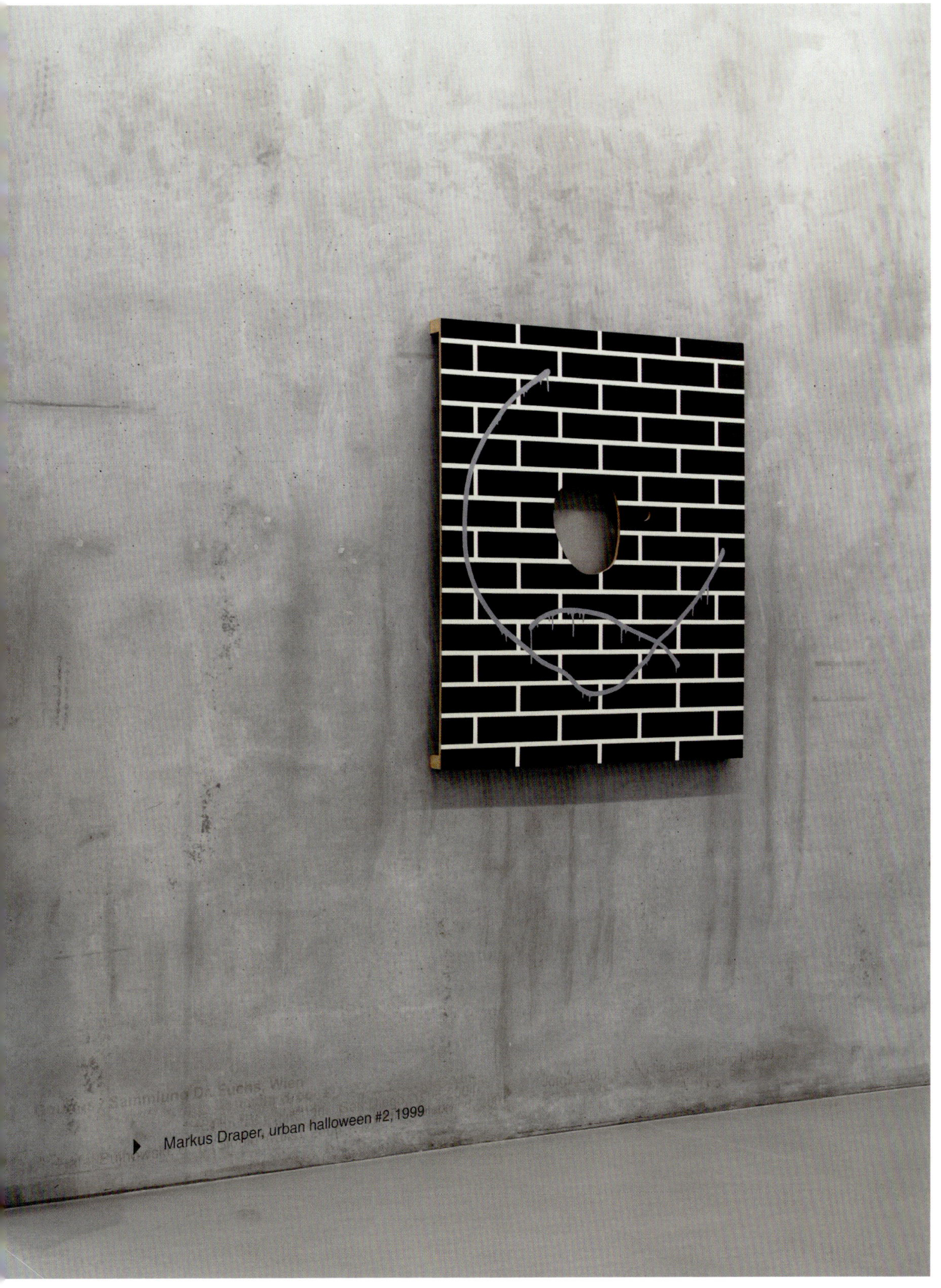

Markus Draper, urban halloween #2, 1999

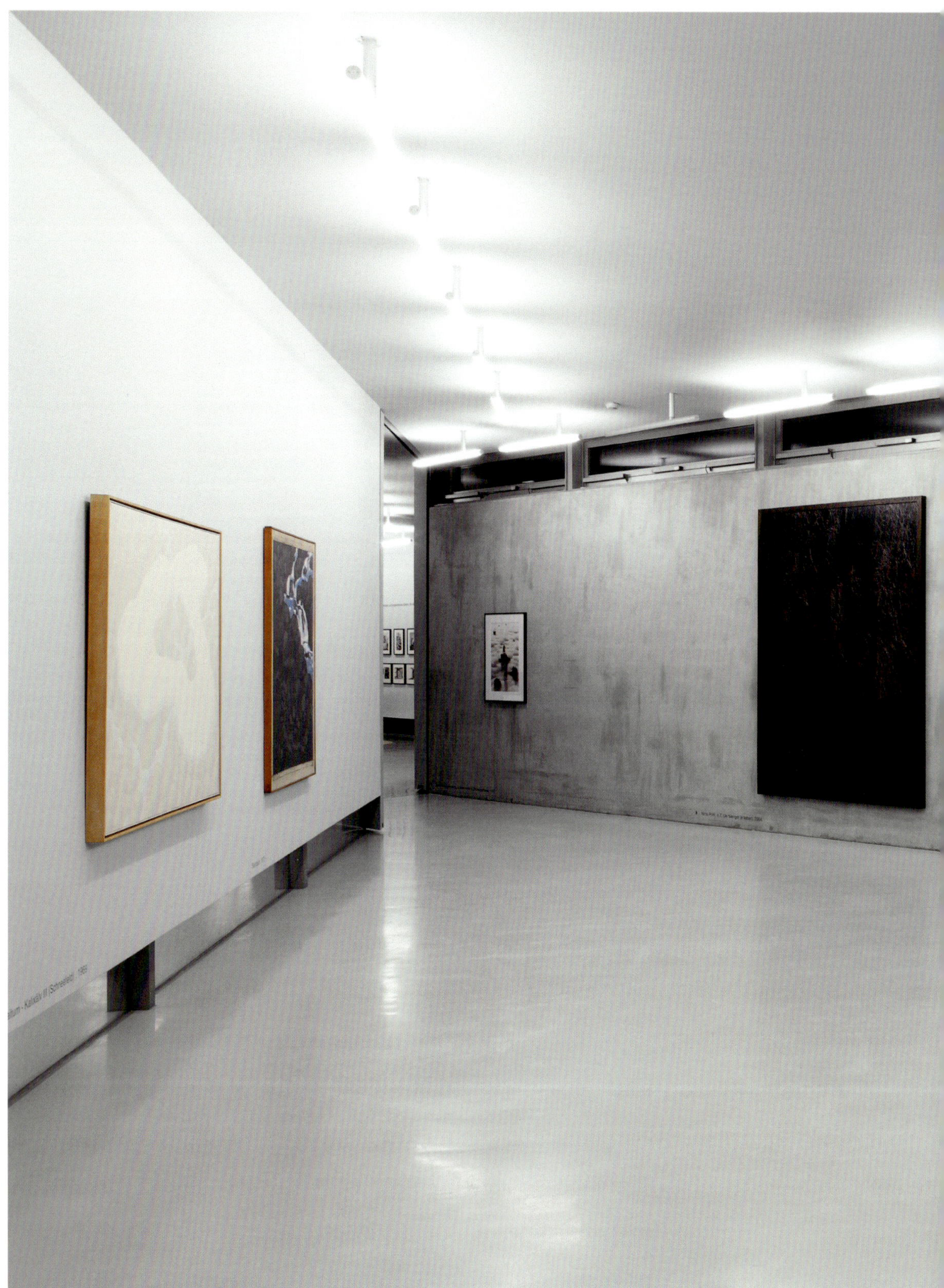

The Captured Museum   Installation Views

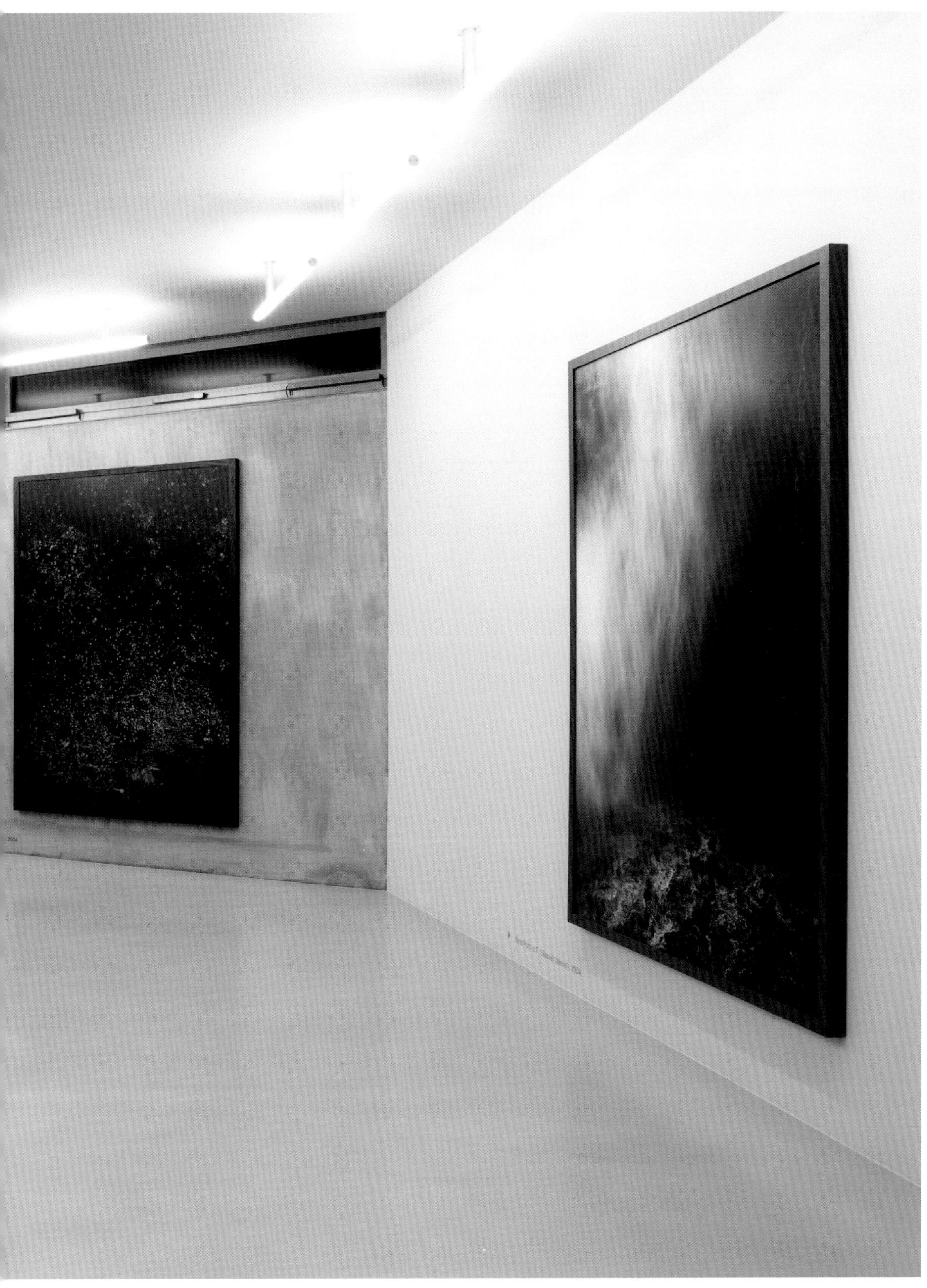

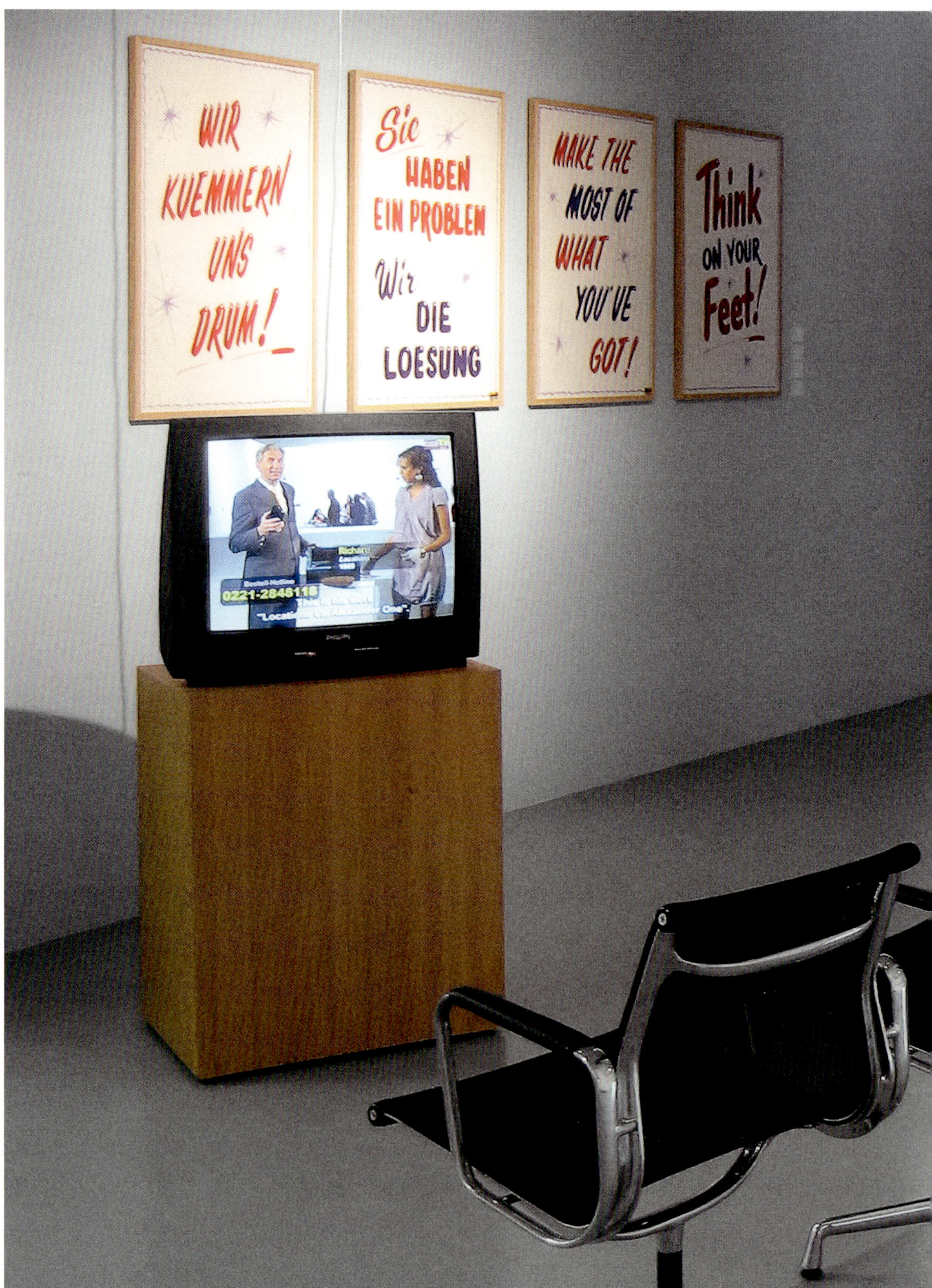

WIR
KUEMMERN
UNS
DRUM!

Sie
HABEN
EIN PROBLEM
Wir
DIE
LOESUNG

MAKE THE
MOST OF
WHAT
YOU'VE
GOT!

Think
ON YOUR
Feet!

0221-2848118

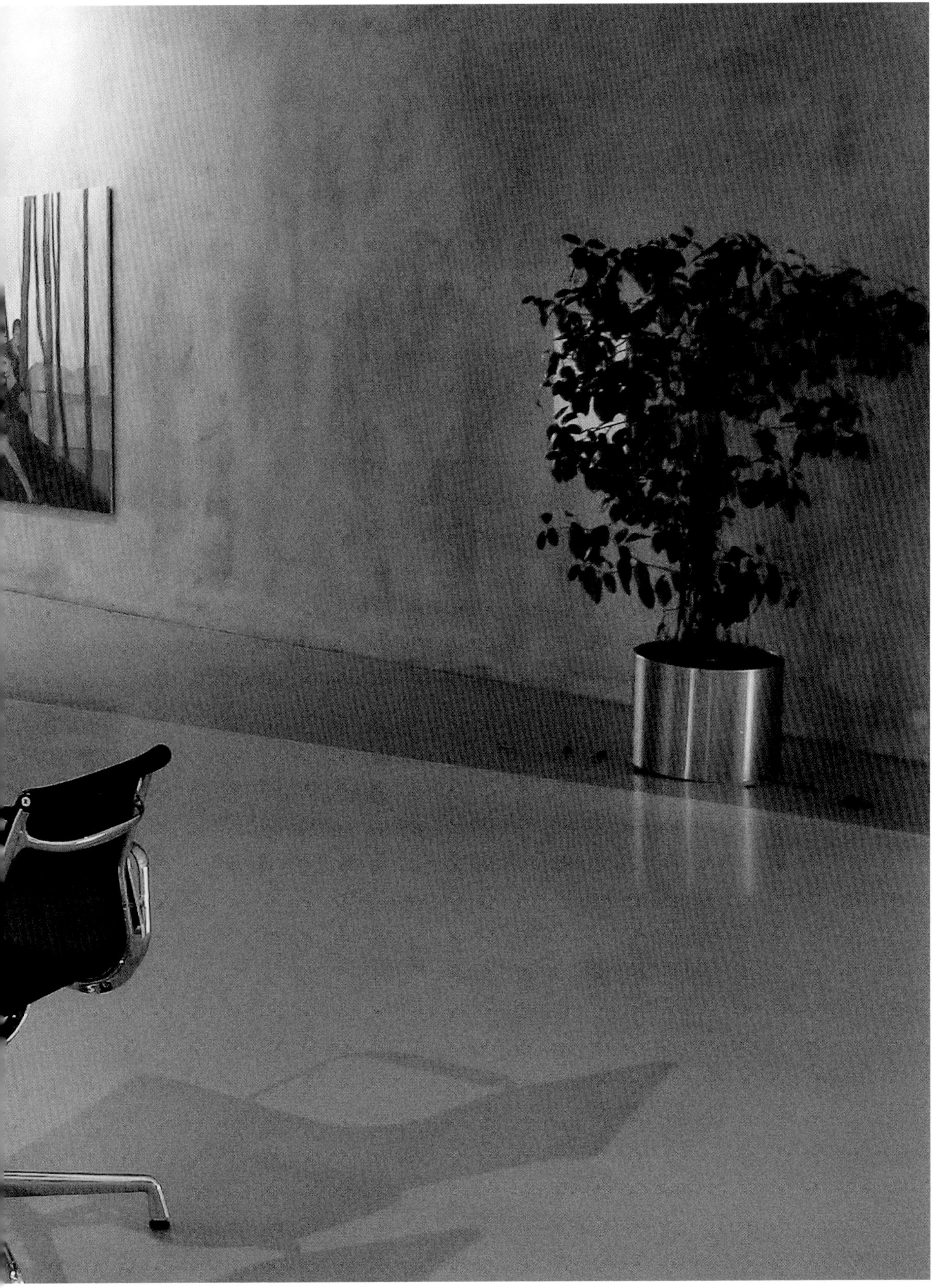

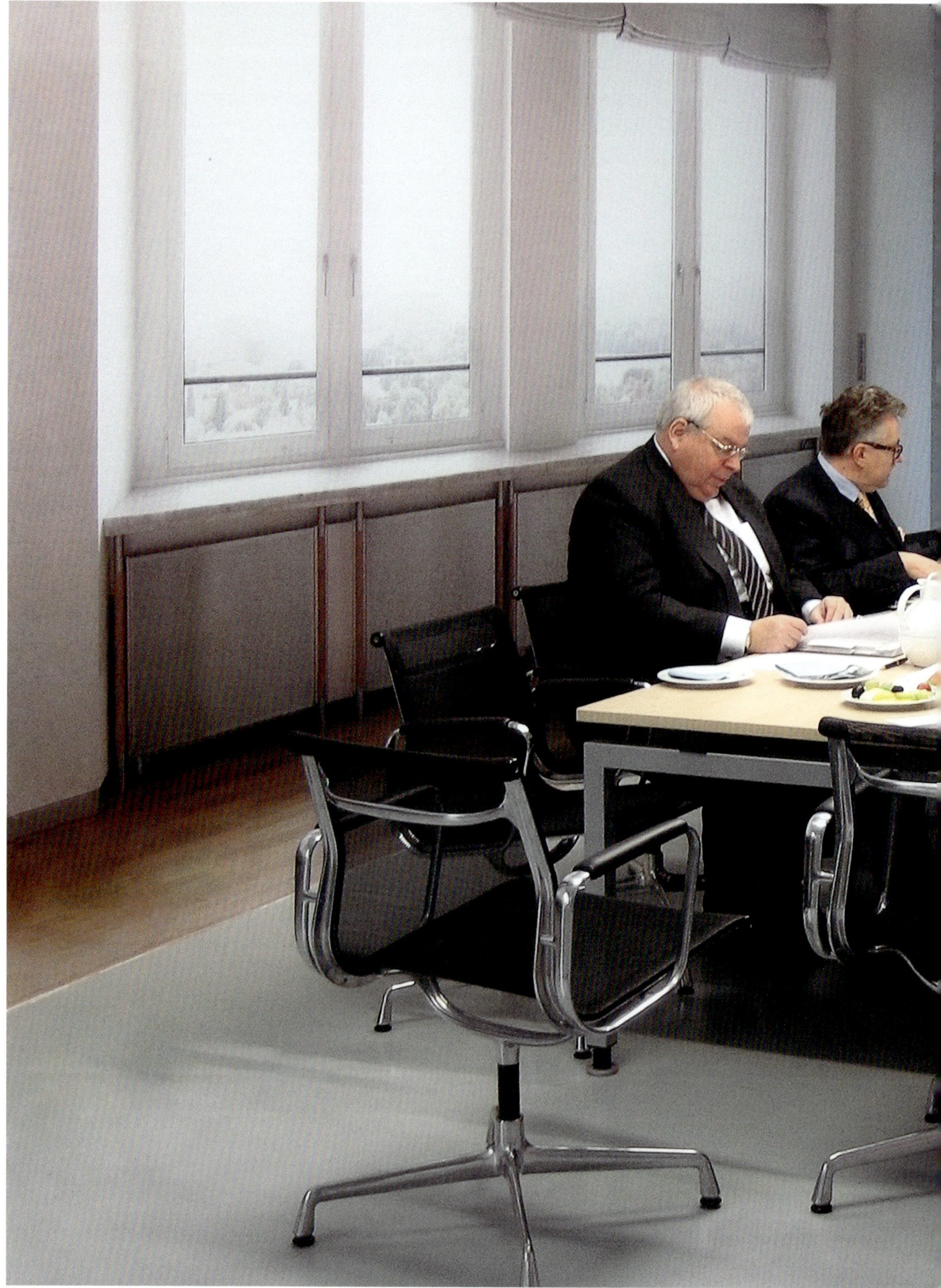

     The Captured Museum   Installation Views

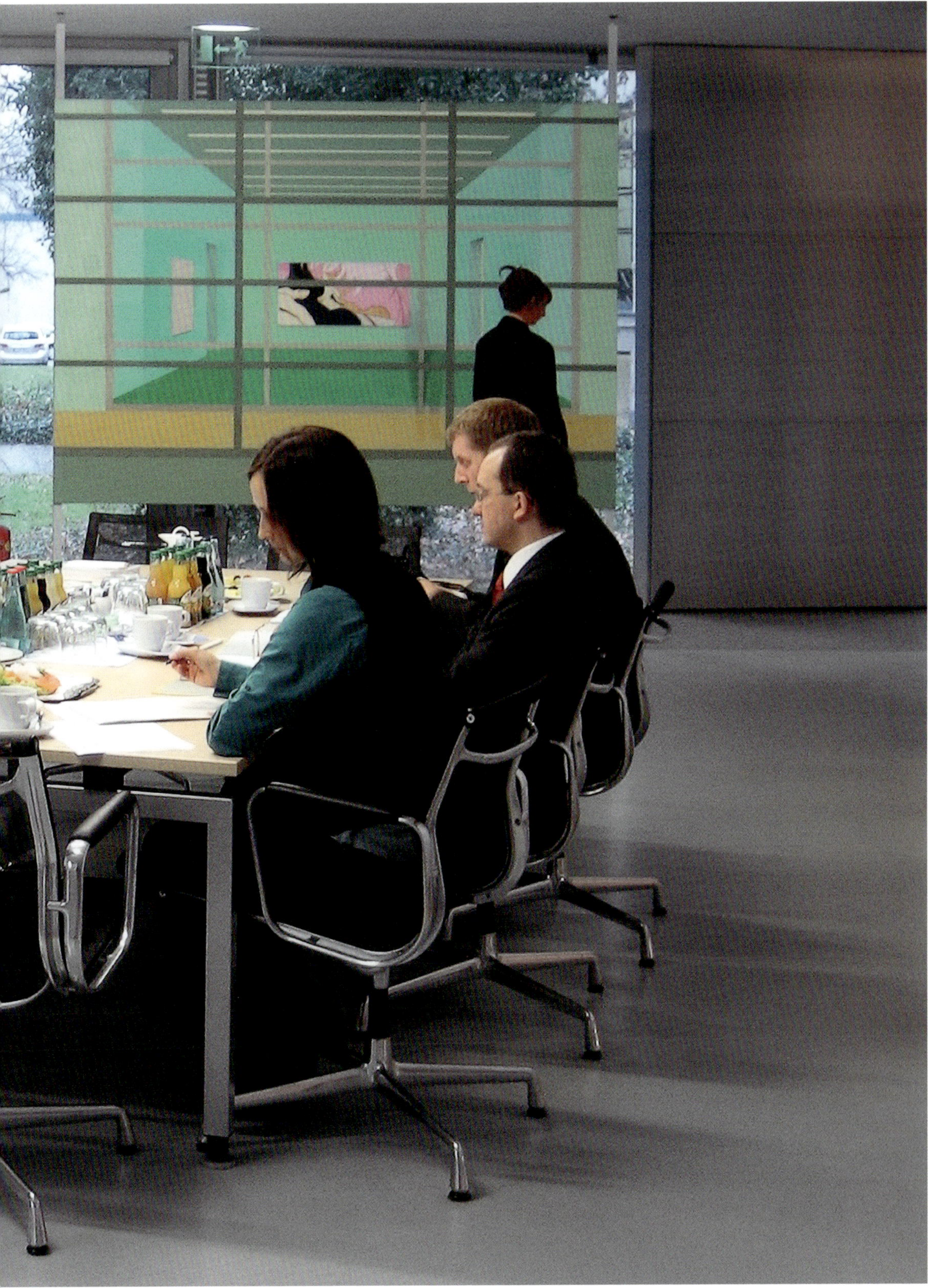

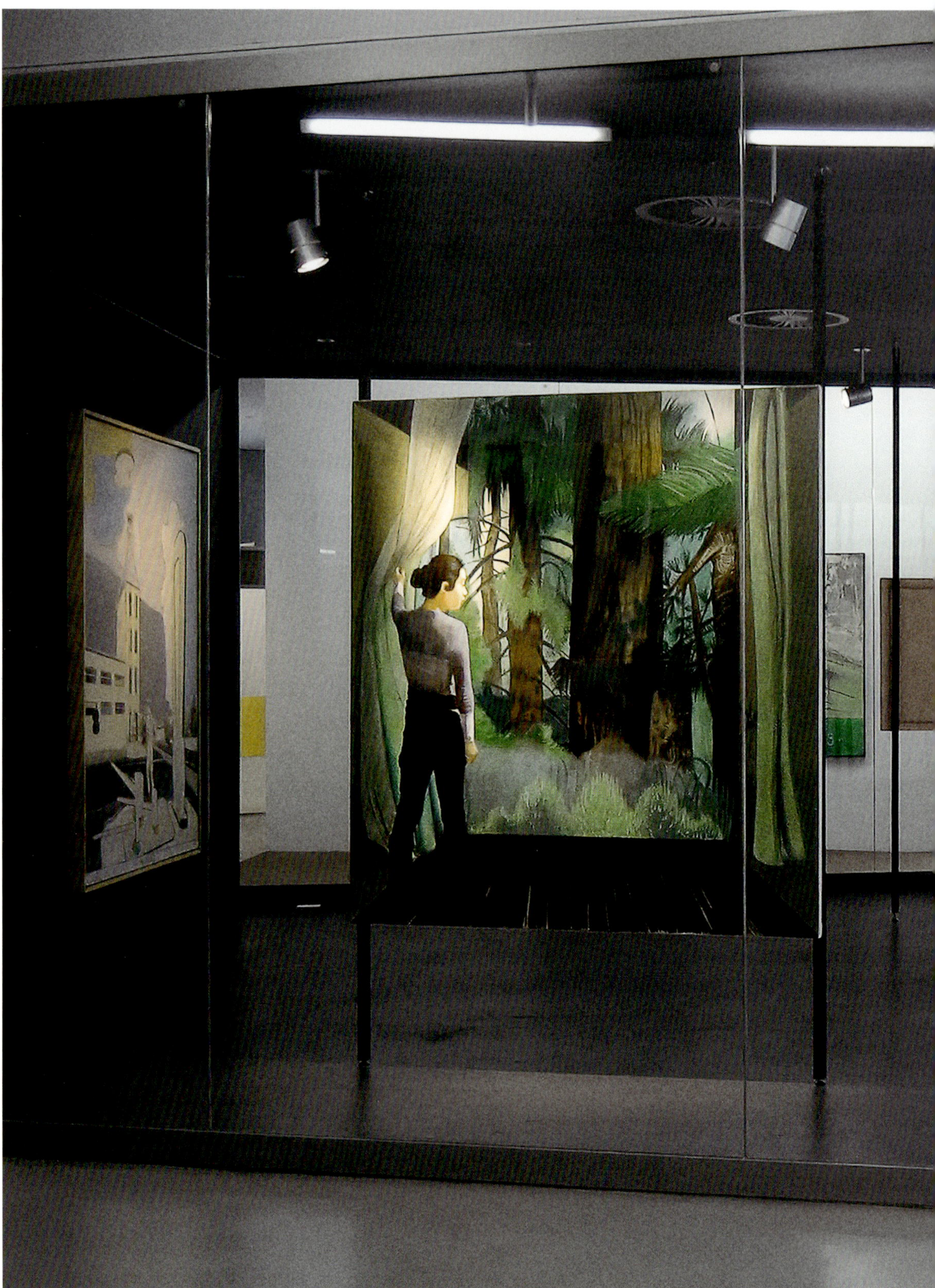

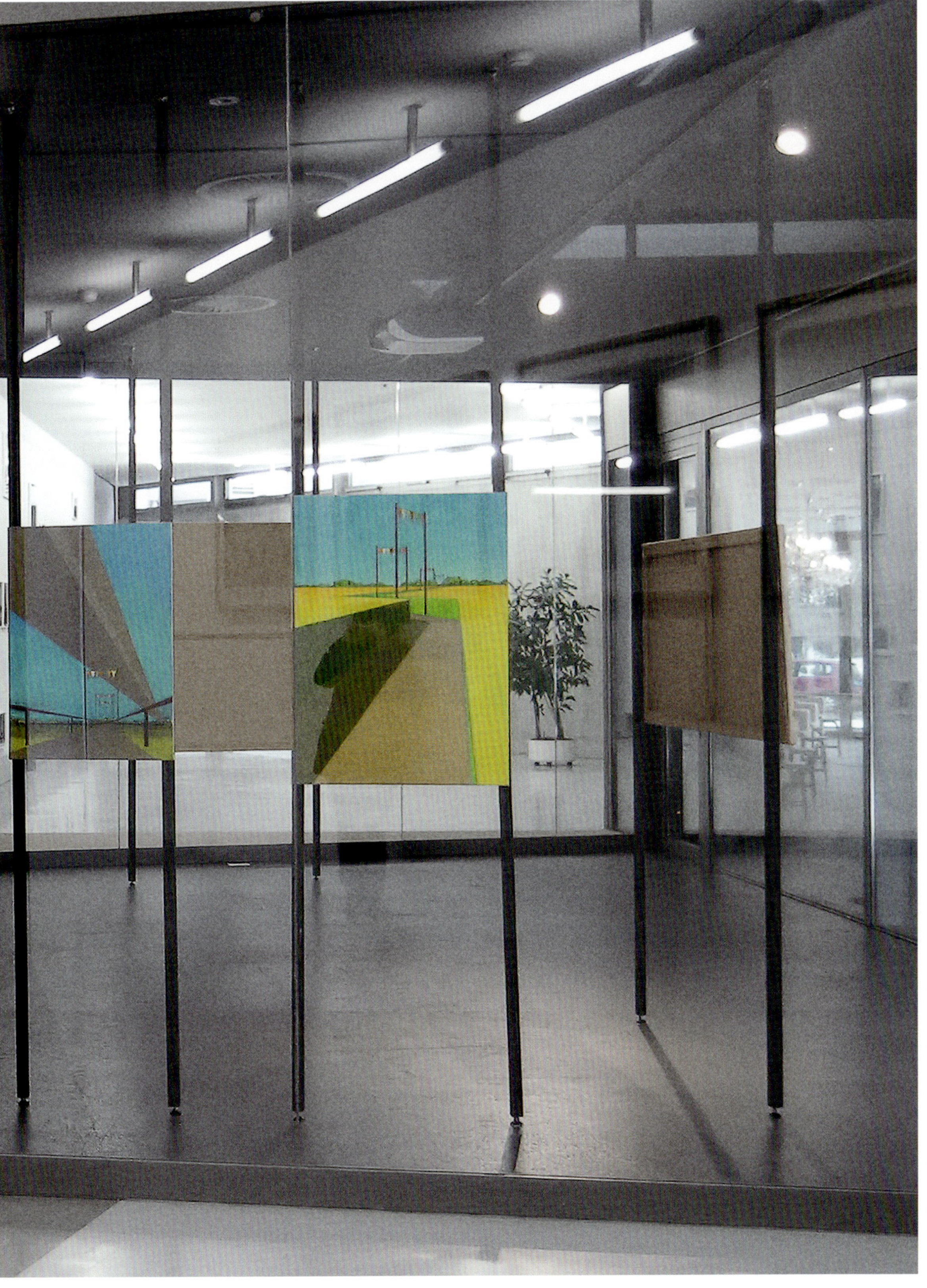

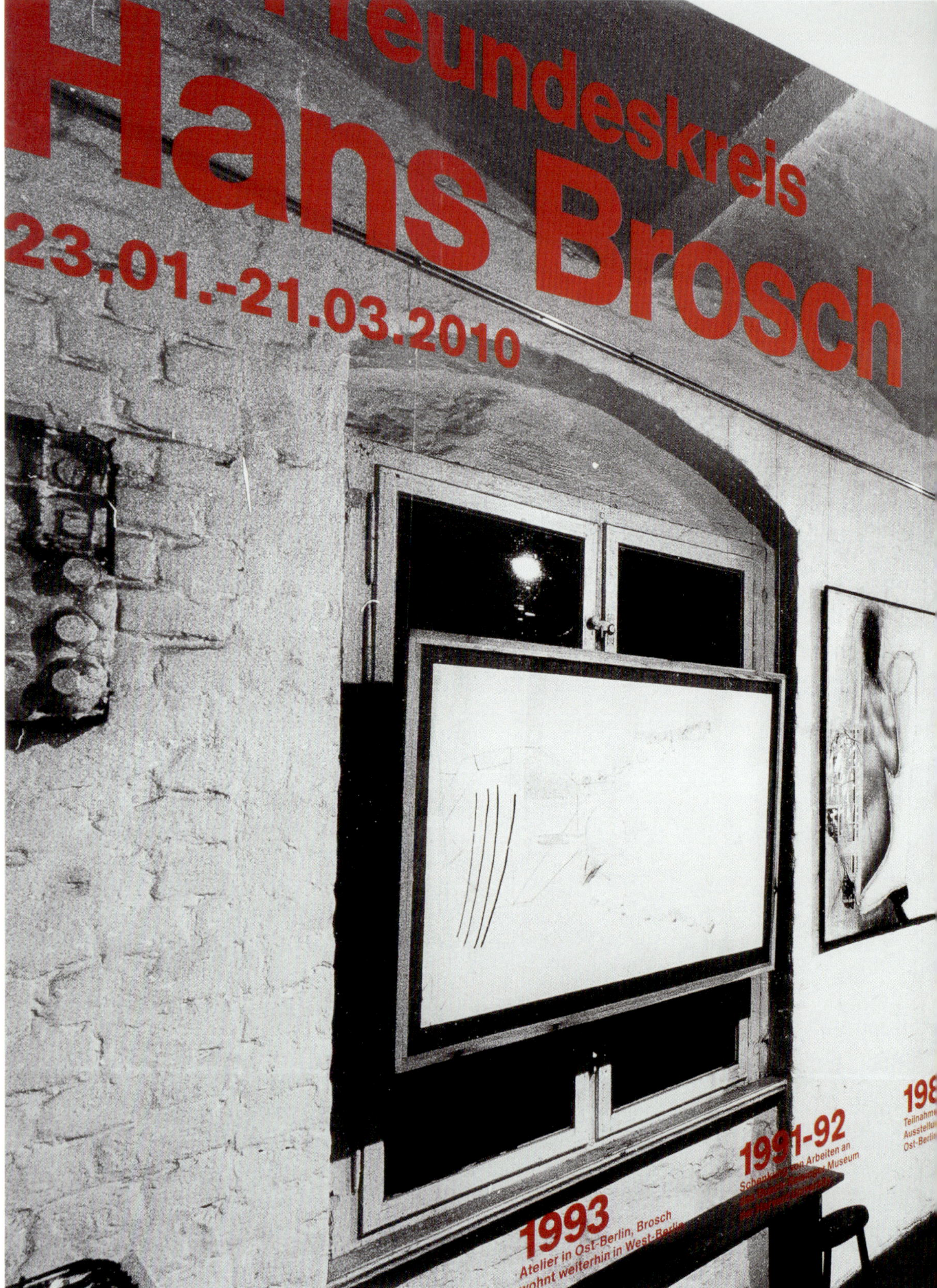
Freundeskreis
Hans Brosch
23.01.–21.03.2010
1993
Atelier in Ost-Berlin, Brosch
wohnt weiterhin in West-Berlin
1991-92
1988

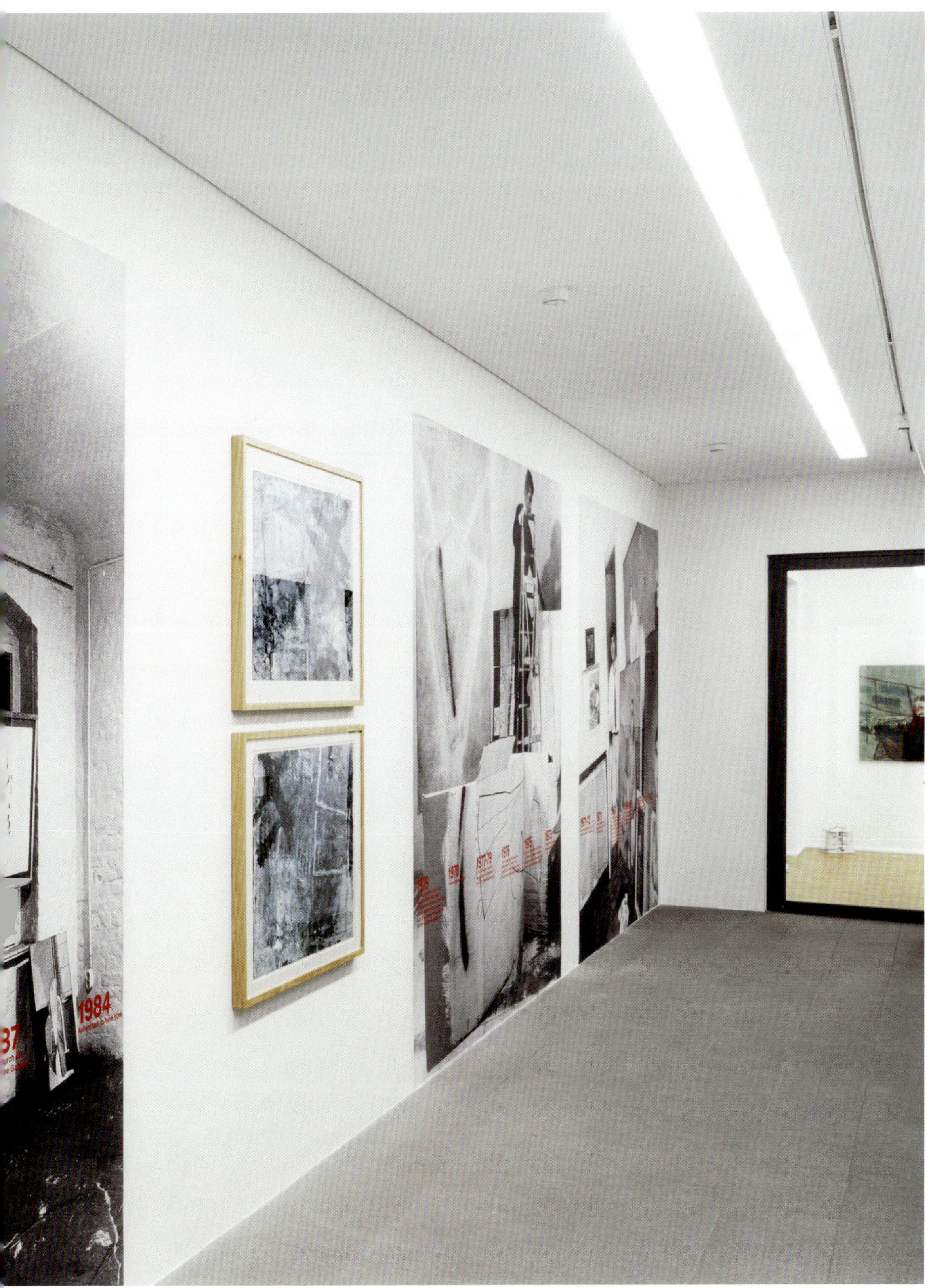

1984
1987

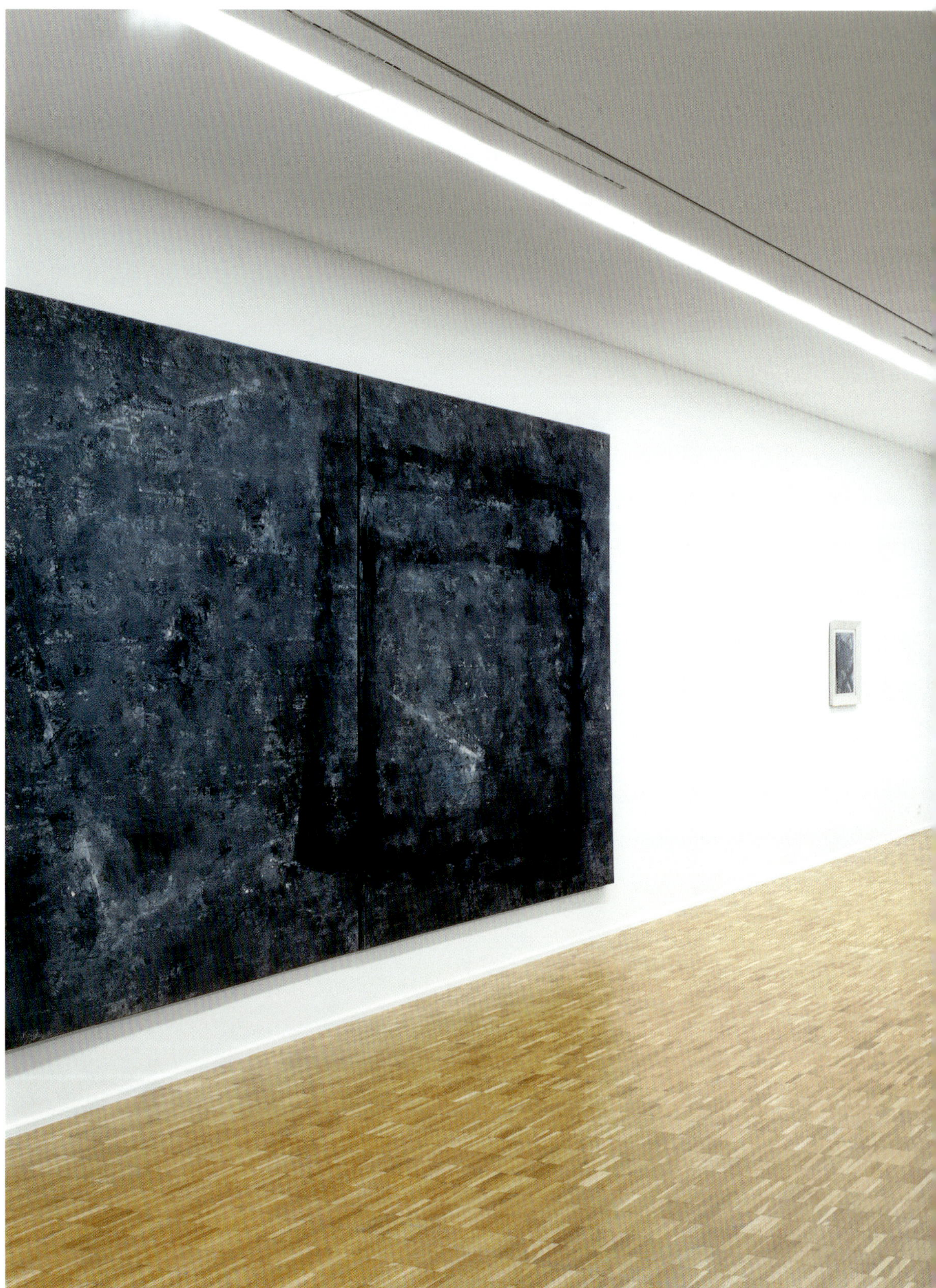

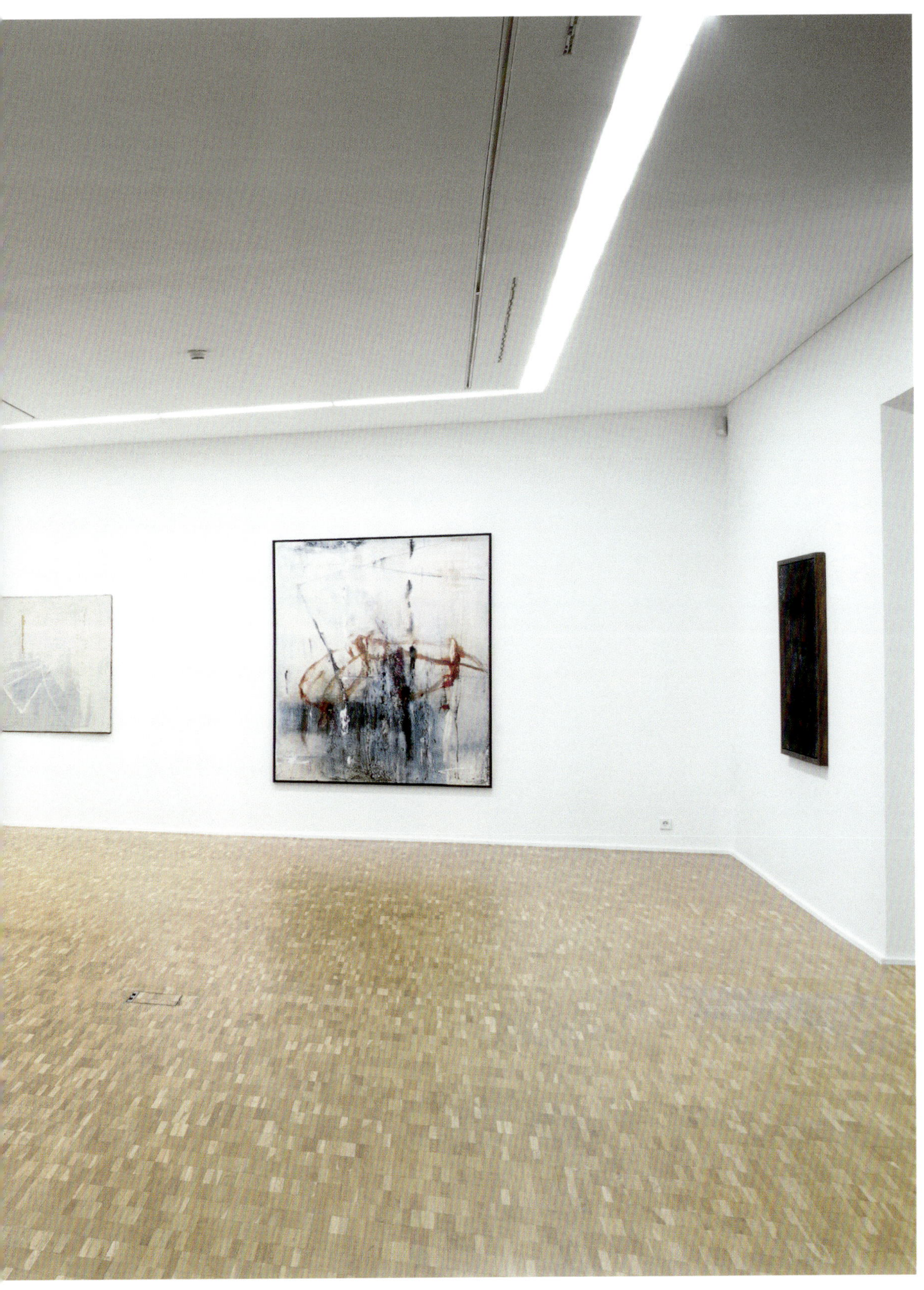

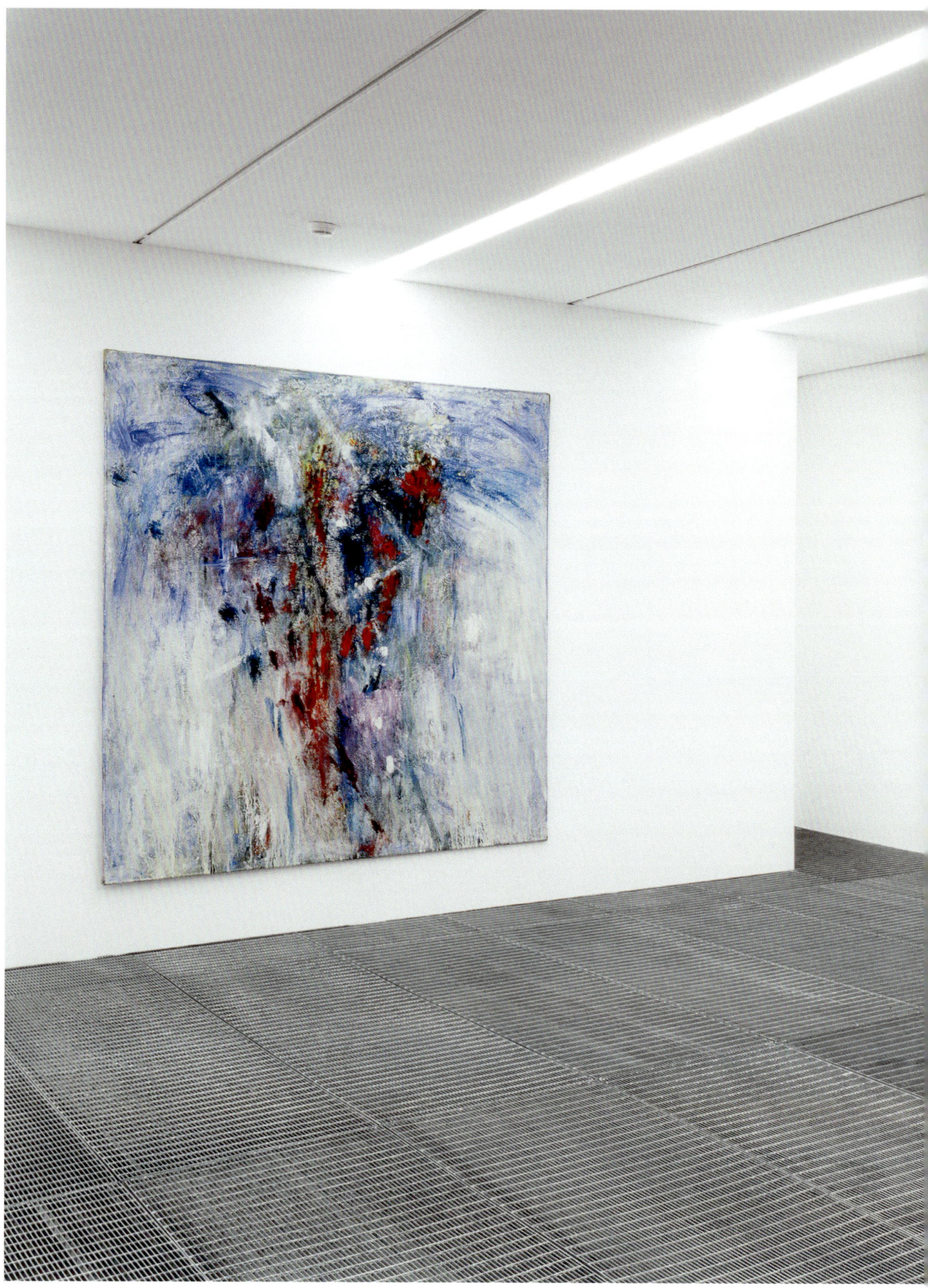

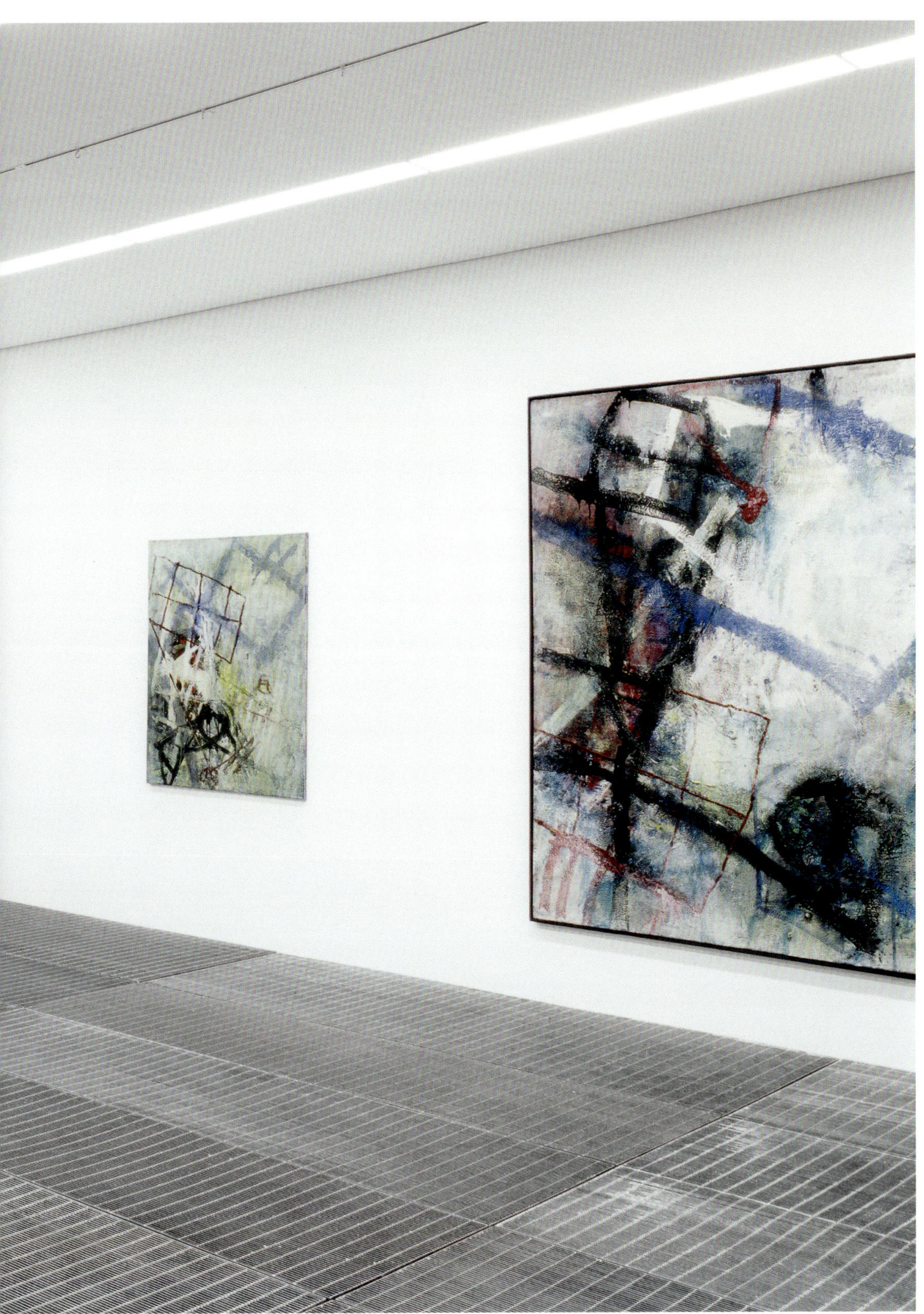

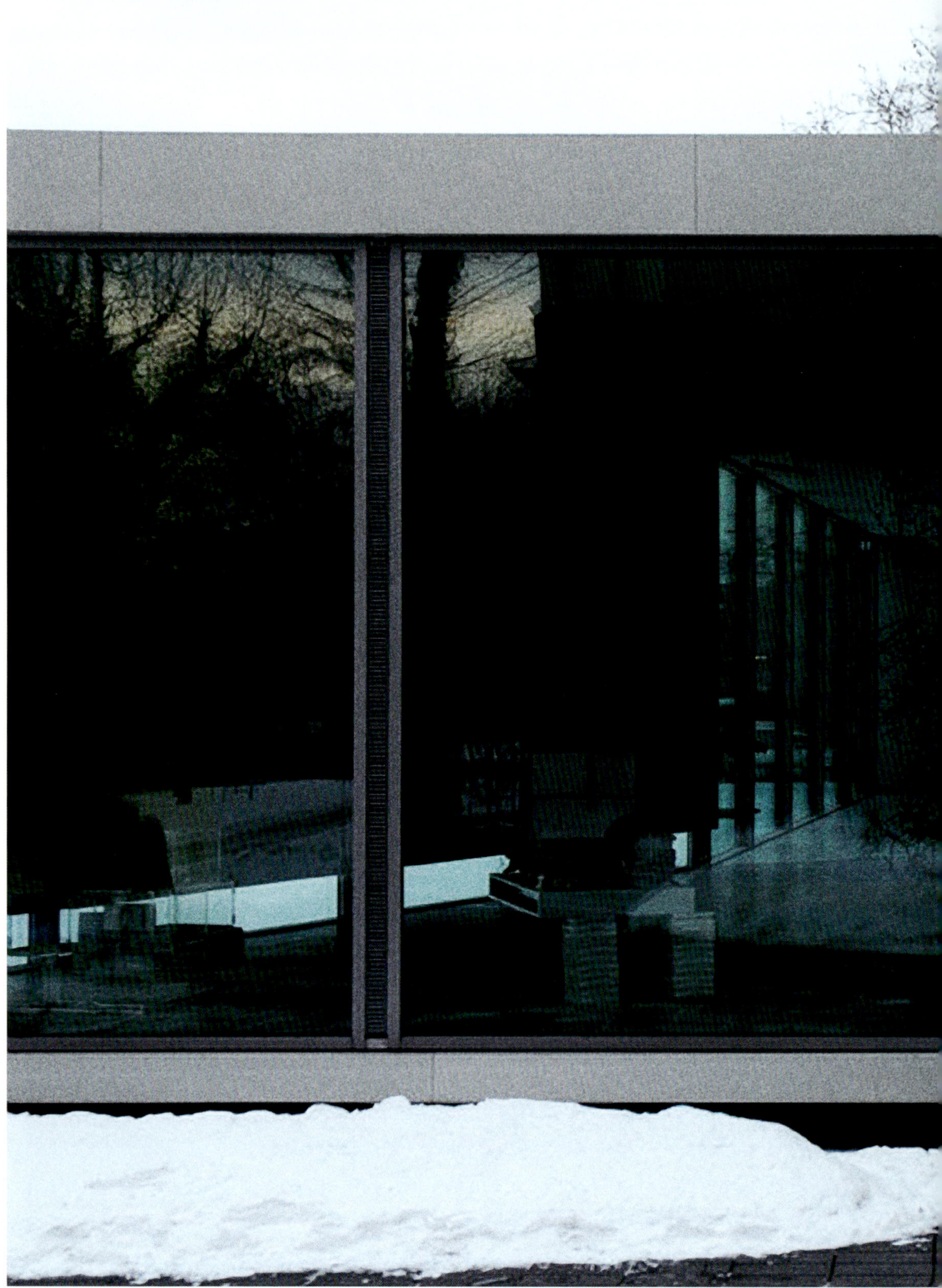

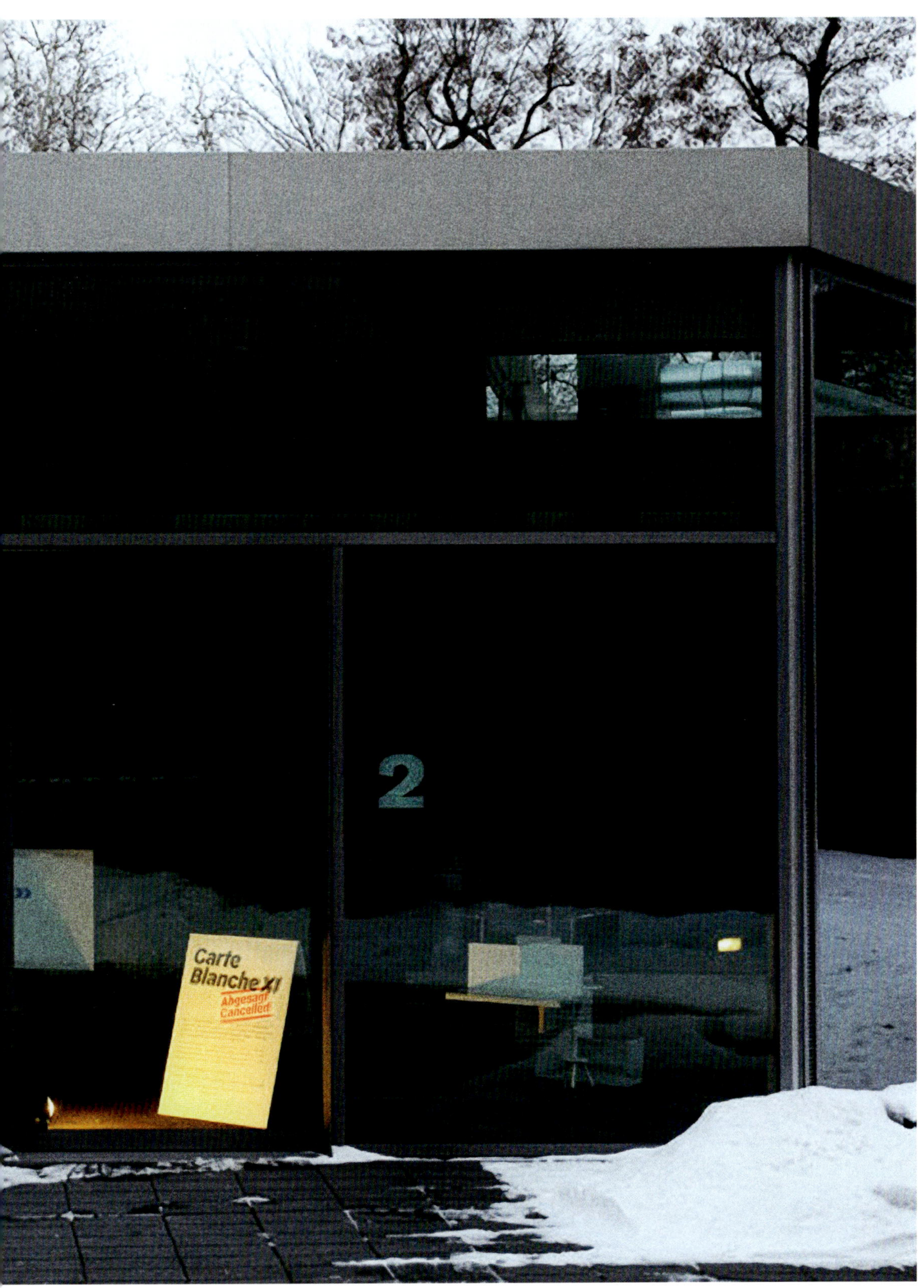

2
Carte
Blanche XI
Abgesagt
Cancelled

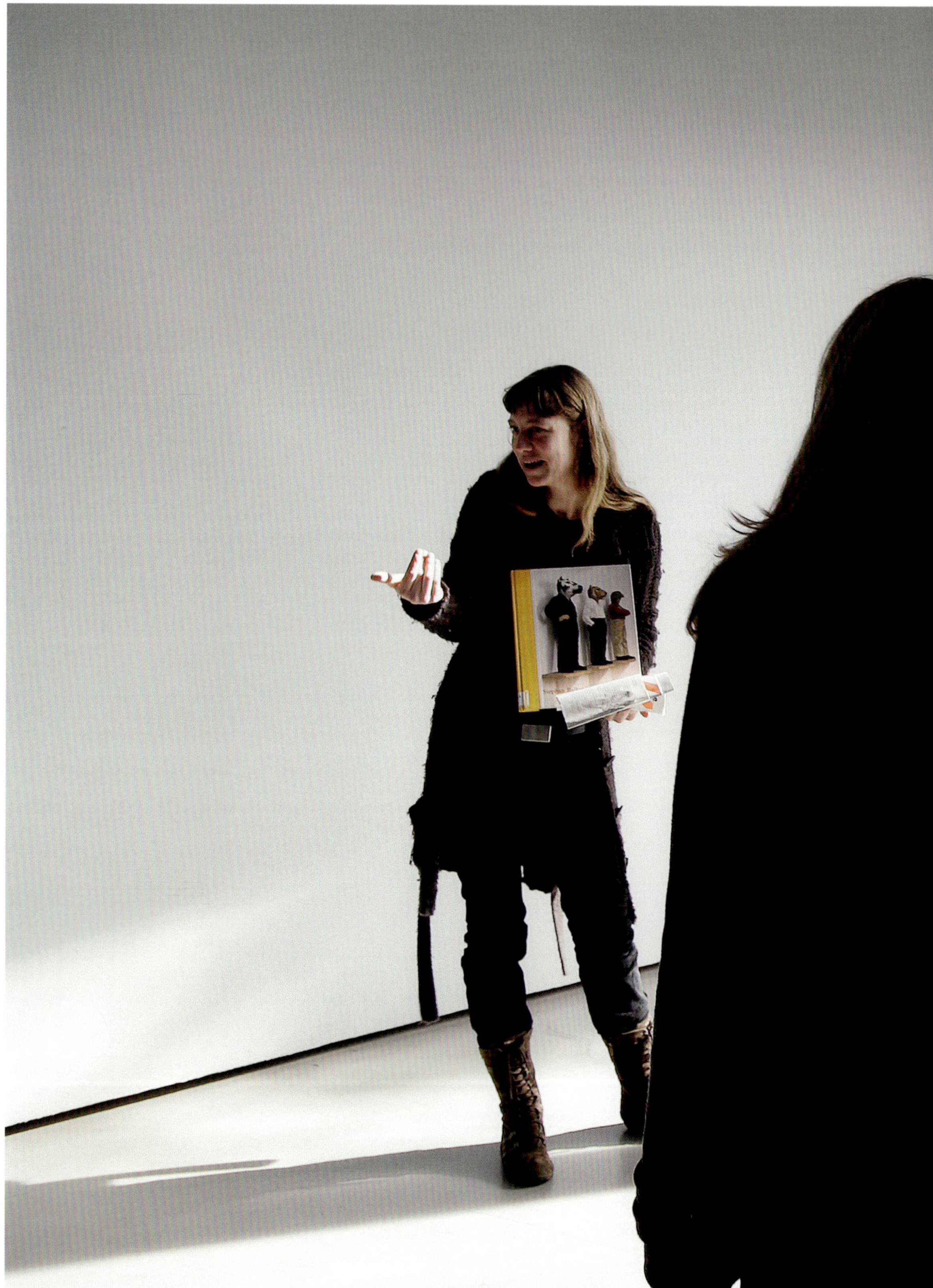

　　The Captured Museum　　Installation Views

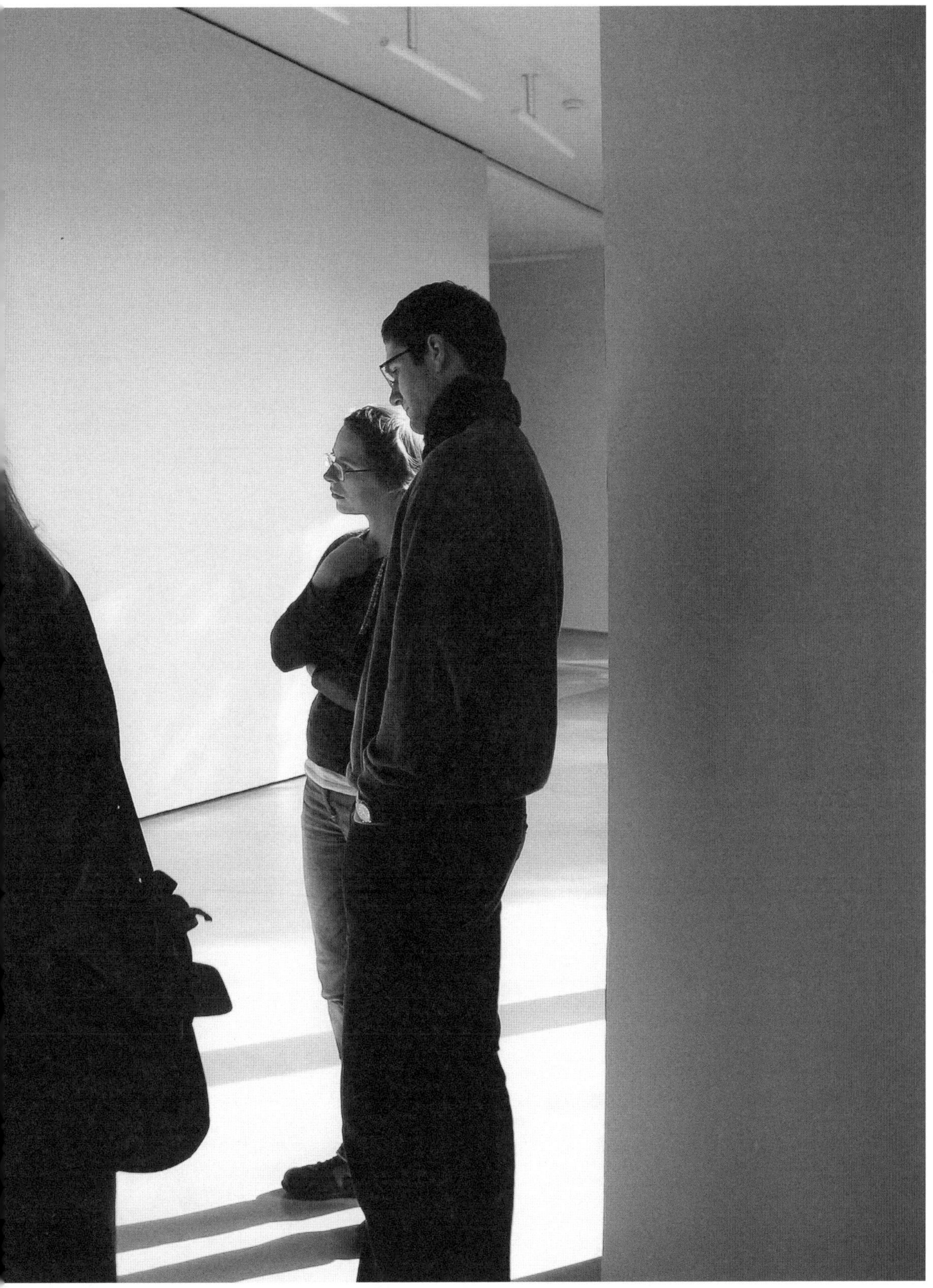

ALPHA 2000
MATTHIAS BRÜHL & DIETMAR SCHULZ

→ ALPHA 2000, founded by Matthias Brühl and Dietmar Schulz in 1990, is one of the leading IT-system companies in Central Germany today. The company operates from its three bases in Leipzig, Halle and Potsdam. In 2003, alpha 2000 introduced the 'Art Prize Future of Europe', which since then has been awarded on an annual basis, in close cooperation with the Museum of Contemporary Art in Leipzig. The enterprise also supports many social and cultural projects, encourages dialogue between countries and regions, and is involved in the area of education for children and young people. alpha 2000 has no intention of starting its own art collection.

→ MATTHIAS BRÜHL, born in Leisnig in 1969, studied Information Technology at the Open University of Hagen. Since 1990, he has been an Executive Shareholder of alpha 2000. He has also been a shareholder and member of the Board of Directors at DeskCenter Solutions AG since 2007, and since 2008 an Executive Shareholder of nutzwerk GmbH.

→ DIETMAR SCHULZ, born in Zeitz in 1964, also became an Executive Shareholder of alpha 2000 in 1991, following his training as an Information Technology Engineer. Since 2007, he has been the Chairman of the Board of DeskCenter Solutions AG and a member of the Board of the Industrieclub Mitteldeutschland zu Halle e.V. Dietmar Schulz has been an Executive Shareholder of nutzwerk GmbH since 2008.

The 'Art Prize Future of Europe', which was initially intended to run for a period of five years, is an award consisting of 5,000 euros in prize money. Until 2008, it was directed towards young artists from post-communist countries at the beginning of their careers, who were working under difficult economic conditions at the time of receiving the award. The prize was not linked with any form of service in return. A proposals jury, newly appointed each year, was responsible for putting forward proposals, whilst an awarding jury appointed for a five year period made the final choice of winners. Award-winners up to now have been: Kristina Leko/Zagreb, Rafał Bujnowski/Cracow, Jakup Ferri/Pristina, Iona Nemeş/Bucharest, and Kamen Stoyanov/Sofia. In 2009, alpha 2000 committed to awarding the art prize for a further period of five years. At the same time the prize was extended to include the whole of Europe, including countries outside the borders of the European Union. It is directed towards artists who are concerned with the questions and problems of a possible European identity. In addition to the prize money, the artist will also be given the opportunity for an individual exhibition at the GfZK. The 2010 prize-winner is Ahmet Öğüt/Istanbul.

In *Carte Blanche*, alpha 2000 decided to present the first five years of the 'Art Prize Future of Europe' and to show an exhibition featuring the works of the prize-winners.

LEIPZIGER VERLAGS- & DRUCKEREI-GESELLSCHAFT

BERND RADESTOCK

→ The LEIPZIGER VOLKSZEITUNG (LVZ, local daily newspaper), founded in 1894 with a circulation of 11,000, was one of the largest social democratic newspapers with an importance beyond the Leipzig region. Around 1914, the newspaper was the most important mouthpiece for the left wing of the SPD (German Social Democratic Party). In 1933, the newspaper was banned. After the war, the LVZ reopened in 1946 with a new printing works and editorial office. Until the collapse of the Communist system in 1989, it was used as an organ and mouthpiece of the SED's (German Socialist Unity Party) regional management. In 1991, the publishing houses Axel Springer and Madsack (Hanover) bought equal shares of the newspaper from the Treuhand Agency (set up in 1990 to privatise East German enterprises). Today Madsack is the sole shareholder, and the newspaper has nine regional editions reaching a circulation of about three quarters of a million readers in Leipzig and surrounding areas.

→ BERND RADESTOCK, born in Leipzig in 1942, was the Chairman of the Leipziger Verlags- und Druckereigesellschaft (Leipzig Publishing and Printing Society) until he retired in 2009. Radestock began his career at the newspaper in 1971. In 1976, he became the Manager of the Technology Department and made Director in 1987. After the collapse of the Communist system he became the Managing Director of the company.

The 'LVZ Art Prize' has been awarded every two years since 1994. It consists of a solo exhibition at the Museum of Fine Arts in Leipzig, a catalogue and 10,000 euros in prize money. Five experts are responsible for selecting the winning artist. Unlike the remaining members of the jury, who are newly appointed every two years, Hans-Werner Schmidt, the Director of the Museum of Fine Arts, is a permanent member of the jury. Bernd Radestock, the Director of the Leipziger Verlags- und Druckereigesellschaft, which publishes the LVZ in Leipzig, is also a permanent member of the jury, but without an entitlement to vote. Each member of the jury may put forward two proposals. The prize-winners to date have been: Via Lewandowsky in 1995, Neo Rauch in 1997, Jörg Herold in 1999, Tamara Grcic in 2001, Daniel Roth in 2003, Matthias Weischer in 2005, Claudia Angelmaier in 2007, Julius Popp in 2009. In 2005, a special prize was awarded in recognition of the work of Martin Kobe.

In *Carte Blanche*, all the winners of the 'LVZ Art Prize' up to 2007 were introduced in the Museum of Contemporary Art, and those of their works belonging to the collection of the Leipziger Verlags- und Druckereigesellschaft were exhibited. Other works from the collection were also shown.

BRIGITTE & AREND OETKER

→ BRIGITTE OETKER studied History, Literature, and History of Art in Aachen and Rome. From 1984 to 1990, she worked in Cologne as the Managing Director of the Cultural Committee of German Business within BDI and for the ARA, the Association for Cultural Affairs in Foreign Countries. Since 1989, Brigitte Oetker has published the *Yearbook of Modern Art* on behalf of the Cultural Committee. From 1993 to 1998, together with Mechthild von Dannenberg and Christiane Schneider, she was responsible for *Art at the Leipzig Trade Fair*, a project in which twenty-five international artists created permanent installations for the new exhibition centre. Since 2007, Brigitte Oetker has been a Professor of Creative Processes in Fine Arts at the Institute of Cultural and Media Management in Hamburg. She also works in a honorary capacity for the Villa Romana e.V. and the Institute of Art History (Max Planck Institute), both in Florence, and in Berlin for the exhibition space 'Büro Friedrich e.V.', the Humboldt University and the Charité Foundation.

→ AREND OETKER is an entrepreneur. He studied Business Management and Political Science in Hamburg, Berlin, and Cologne. Several cultural support associations have been founded on his initiative, for example, in Schleswig, Lübeck, Kiel, Hildesheim, Bielefeld and also the Friends of the Busch-Reisinger Museum in Harvard. He is a honorary member of many committees, boards of trustees, and institutions, for example as the President of the Donation Association for German Science, as the Chairman of the Committee of Fine Arts at the Cultural Committee of German Business within BDI e.V., and as the Chairman of the Board of the Berlin Philharmonic GmbH, both in Berlin. He is a member of the Committee of the Association of Friends of the National Gallery in Berlin, the Peter and Irene Ludwig Foundation in Aachen, and the German Foundation of Music in Hamburg. In 1990, Arend Oetker founded the Museum of Contemporary Art in Leipzig, in collaboration with Klaus Werner. Until 2002, he was one of the three shareholders of the Museum of Contemporary Art GmbH. Since the GfZK became a foundation, he has been the Chairman of the Foundation Board.

The commitment of Brigitte and Arend Oetker – as well as their passionate interest in art – is fired by the conviction that the promotion of art and culture is the responsibility of every social force, both public and private. Their own art collecting activities always result in generous donations and permanent loans of outstanding works of art.

In *Carte Blanche*, Brigitte and Arend Oetker decided to show a selection from their joint collection, put together over the last twenty-five years, including works they have donated to museums.

DOGENHAUS GALLERY

JOCHEN HEMPEL

→ The DOGENHAUS GALLERY was founded in Leipzig by Jochen Hempel in 1992. From 1993 to 1998, he also ran Dogenhaus Projects in Berlin. Today, as well as long-standing co-operations with East German artists such as Frank Berendt, Hartwig Ebersbach, Ulf Puder, Matthias Hoch, Kaeseberg and Peter Krauskopf, he also represents Stephan Balkenhol, Ina Bierstedt, Ruprecht Dreher, Leif Trenkler, Joe Amrhein, Reed Anderson, Graham Gillmore, Kent Iwemyr, Esko Männikkö, Ati Maier and Beat Streuli. The younger generation of Leipzig artists is present in the Dogenhaus Gallery with names such as Tilo Schulz, Julius Popp, Albrecht Tübke, Andreas Schulze and Rebecca Wilton.

→ JOCHEN HEMPEL, born in Rostock in 1965, was a founding member of the pop groups Stressco and Agentur Merkur in Leipzig between 1982 and 1988. In 1990, he opened the exhibition rooms 'Kunsthof Bocholt' in Bocholt (in cooperation with Michael Globisch). Before opening his own gallery, Hempel worked with artists from EIGEN+ART Gallery for several years, focusing on printed matter and graphic design (catalogues, editions, posters, invitations).

In *Carte Blanche* Jochen Hempel decided to show two positions: Julius Popp, an artist the gallery has represented since 2004, and the deceased American artist Mark Lombardi, with whom the gallery owner never worked.

LEON JANUCEK

→ **LEON JANUCEK, born in Berlin in 1953, worked in the film business for many years before taking over the family company in 1997. In 2005, he opened a company specialising in the design and manufacture of guitar amplifiers for professional musicians. He spends several months a year in India and is beginning to put together a collection of young Indian artists. Leon Janucek spends most of the year travelling.**

His art collection contains works from the 20th century and the present day, including Gabriele Münter, Carl Hofer, Max Pechstein and Muntean & Rosenblum, Julian Opie, Wilhelm Sasnal, Max Neumann, Dieter Finke, Maksim Mamsikov and Alexander Gnylytskyi. As he is from the Noack bronze founder family on his mother's side, his collection also contains a series of bronzes, including Käthe Kollwitz, Ernst Barlach, Georg Kolbe, August Gaul, Renée Sintenis and Anna Bogouchevskaia. Leon Janucek loans his works to museums.

In *Carte Blanche*, Leon Janucek did not show his own collection but initiated an exhibition and a catalogue for Dieter Finke. This was the first large retrospective and the first detailed catalogue of the œuvre of the seventy-year-old artist from Berlin.

VNG-VERBUNDNETZ GAS AG

GERHARDT WOLFF

→ VNG – VERBUNDNETZ GAS AG is a group of enterprises based in Leipzig, with activities all over Europe. Its core activity is the import and delivery of natural gas to major clients. The enterprises of the VNG group also provide extensive transport and storage solutions for natural gas and energy technology and energy services. The VNG AG group has its traditional roots in eastern Germany, but it also has trading activities, shares, and co-operations all over Germany as well as in central, eastern, and southern Europe.

→ GERHARDT WOLFF, born in 1944 in Obernigk/Silesia was trained as a bank clerk and worked in the Foreign Business Department of the Berliner Bank AG before studying Business Management at the Business Academy Berlin and the Free University of Berlin, where he did his PhD from 1972 to 1977. From 1977 to 1985, he was Head of the Board office, Company Secretary, and Department Director at the Grundkreditbank e.G. in Berlin. Following this, he was a member of the Board of Krone AG, Berlin until 1992. After a period working in real estate management, he was appointed to become a member of the Board of VNG – Verbundnetz Gas public limited company, representing business procedures and personnel in Leipzig. From 2007 until his retirement in October 2009, he was also Deputy Chairman of the Board of VNG AG. Additionally, Gerhardt Wolff has been teaching at the University of Leipzig as an Honorary Professor in International Management since 1997, and working as a freelance consultant since November 2009.

As well as a wide range of social commitments, including activities in cultural, sport and social areas, the VNG AG has built up two important art collections during the course of the years: One focusing mainly on photographic works, and the other on paintings and graphic art. The curators are Frank-Heinrich Müller (photography) and Christine Rink (painting and graphic art), who are responsible for the conception and upkeep of the collections. The painting and graphic arts collection consists mainly of works by artists from Saxony, particularly students or graduates of the Leipzig Academy of Visual Arts (HGB). The VNG AG photographic collection is regarded as one of the most important contemporary German collections of photographic art. All of the photographs were taken by former students of the HGB, commissioned by the VNG AG to document the social changes in East Germany between 1991 and 2001.

In *Carte Blanche*, works from both collections were presented together for the first time. In addition the VNG AG took the exhibition as an opportunity to start a new section of the photograph collection, under the title *EAST – for the record*, showing events from the years 1989 and 1990 in the form of a photographic synopsis.

GALLERY EIGEN+ART

GERD HARRY LYBKE

→ The GALLERY EIGEN+ART, based in Leipzig and Berlin, was opened in 1983 by Gerd Harry Lybke. The exhibition *Die neuen Unkonkreten* (The New Non-Concretists) marked the inception of the gallery EIGEN+ART. By the spring of 1990, Lybke had already participated in an art fair, the art frankfurt. Since then, Lybke has presented the works of his artists at all of the most important international art fairs. In the 1990s, the gallery was present at several temporary sites: Tokyo in 1990, Paris in 1991, Berlin in 1992, New York in 1993 and London in 1994. The second Gallery EIGEN+ART emerged from the temporary gallery in Berlin of 1992. The Gallery EIGEN+ART represents Ákos Birkás, Birgit Brenner, Martin Eder, Tim Eitel, Nina Fischer & Maroan el Sani, Stella Hamberg, Jörg Herold, Christine Hill, Uwe Kowski, Rémy Markowitsch, Maix Mayer, Carsten Nicolai, Olaf Nicolai, Neo Rauch, Ricarda Roggan, Yehudit Sasportas, David Schnell, Annelies Strba and Matthias Weischer.

→ GERD HARRY LYBKE was born in Meusdorf / Leipzig in 1960. After training and taking his school-leaving examination (Abitur), he worked as a nude model at the Leipzig Academy of Visual Arts from 1983 to 1987. On 10 April 1983 he opened the Gallery EIGEN+ART in his own apartment in Leipzig. Gerd Harry Lybke lives and works in Berlin and Leipzig.

The Gallery EIGEN+ART decided to place its various art fair activities at the centre of its participation in *Carte Blanche*, illustrating its attendance at five important contemporary art fairs Art Basel Miami Beach, Art Basel, Art Forum Berlin, Frieze in London and the Armory Show in New York City.

DORIS & KLAUS F.K. SCHMIDT

→ KLAUS F.K. SCHMIDT, born in Krefeld in 1942, founded the business and tax consultancy companies Deltax (1972) in Cologne and Rhe-el (1990) in Dresden. Since 1993, he has been the Chairman of the Board of Reiss AG Holding Company for around 400 tax consultancy practices nationwide. During his years of experience as a business and tax consultant, he has become a specialist advisor for artists, gallery owners and collectors. Many of his clients are some of the most important protagonists in the German and international art scene.

→ DORIS SCHMIDT, née Drenhaus, comes from Herne.

The collectors have been based in Dresden since 1990. Since 1994, Doris and Klaus F.K. Schmidt have been founding members of the Society of Modern Art in Dresden e.V., partly with the aim of drawing attention to the need for the private support of contemporary art and its institutions in Dresden. They donated two photographic works by Candida Höfer to the New Masters Gallery and many works on paper to the Kupferstichkabinett (collection of prints, drawings and photographs, part of the State Art Collections of Dresden). For more than thirty years, Klaus F.K. Schmidt has been sending editions of contemporary art to his clients to further their interest in art. Today, these are sought-after collectors' pieces. The promotion activities of Doris and Klaus F.K. Schmidt also include the founding of the Forum for Art in the Present in December 2001, together with Stefan Heinemann, Jens Zander, and Peter Herbstreuth. At the end of 2006, the couple placed part of their collection into the Schmidt-Drenhaus Foundation, of which they themselves were the founders. In its initial stages, around 1968, the Schmidt-Drenhaus collection placed its main emphasis on paintings. During the course of time, works on paper became increasingly important. Today, the collection comprises painting, photography, printed graphic works, drawings, collages, and objects. It always features several pieces of work by each author represented, whose artistic development is followed over a long period of time.
Doris and Klaus F.K. Schmidt 'collect to curate'. In their house in Dresden, new artistic directions are continually put to the test, just as in the early days in Cologne. Various exhibition projects, for example in Dresden (2006 and 2011) and Leipzig (2009) provide them with the opportunity to open up their collection for public viewing. In the spring of 2006, they showed a selection of works on paper and photographic works entitled *Heile Welt* (Safe World) for the first time in the Kupferstich-kabinett in Dresden. A second part featuring painting and objects will be shown in the exhibition hall at Brühl's Terrace in 2011.

In *Carte Blanche*, Doris and Klaus F.K. Schmidt showed part of their collection, along with examples of their civil commitment over several decades.

SACHSEN BANK

HARALD R. PFAB

The commitment of the Sachsen Bank/Landesbank Baden-Württemberg (formerly: Sachsen LB) towards promoting art and culture in Saxony and Central Germany has a long tradition. Its close and lively co-operation with the Museum of Contemporary Art goes back to the year 1998, when the GfZK opened in the Villa Herfurth. From this time onwards, the bank has supported a large number of solo projects, exhibitions, and project scholarships. Since 2008, the Sachsen Bank has continued its commitment by supporting the project series *Room 107*. In co-operation with the Museum of Fine Arts in Leipzig, the Sachsen Bank awards an art prize to artists at the beginning of their career. This prize was awarded for the first time in 2002, and since then every two years. The Sachsen Bank Art Prize consists of an exhibition for the prize-winner, an exhibition catalogue and the acquisition of a piece of work or a series of works for the Museum of Fine Arts Leipzig. The Sachsen Bank/Landesbank Baden-Württemberg Collection comprises around 350 works or series of works, with a special focus on contemporary art from Saxony. It contains works by artists such as Tim Eitel, Christine Hill, Neo Rauch, Evelyn Richter, Ricarda Roggan and Matthias Weischer.

→ HARALD R. PFAB, Chairman of the Board of Directors of the Sachsen Bank, born in Berchtesgaden in 1948, a 'passionate banker' since 1968, worked in the Business Customer Section of the Landesbank Baden-Württemberg for four decades. In September 2007, Harald R. Pfab became a member of the Board of the Sachsen LB, and since April 2008 he has been the Chairman of the Board of the Sachsen Bank. In addition to his banking activities, Harald R. Pfab works in the fields of culture and sports on a honorary basis. He is the Deputy President of the Association of German Cyclists e.V. (BDR), member of the Board of the Friends of Wolfegger Concerts e.V., and of the German Schiller Foundation. Since 2006, Harald R. Pfab has been Senator E.h. of the state of Baden-Württemberg.

The exhibition *Carte Blanche IX: Playing to a Home Crowd* gave an insight into the spectrum of art in the Sachsen Bank/Landesbank Baden-Württemberg Collection. Additionally, it drew a picture of a part of Leipzig's art history since the beginning of the 1990s. In several sections, the exhibition was complemented by works from the Collection Landesbank Baden-Württemberg. These included works by Martin Kippenberger, Christian Jankowski, Karin Sander, Thomas Locher, Michel Majerus, Andreas Slominski, and Wolfgang Tillmans.

HANS BROSCH
CIRCLE OF FRIENDS

ACHIM KÖNIG

→ The HANS BROSCH CIRCLE OF FRIENDS was initiated by Achim König (Deidesheim). Today, the society has twenty-four members, with Achim König as its spokesperson. Its aim is to promote and publicise the artistic work of Hans Brosch, born in East Berlin in 1943.

The members of the Circle of Friends are Anja and Jürgen Abendschein, Deidesheim; Karin and Sven Mario Alisch, Cologne; Susanna and Thomas Braun, Friedelsheim; Paul and Hanna Gräb, Bad Säckingen; Herbert Meyer-Ellinger, Cologne; Bettina and Erik Hamann, Würzburg; Josef Kloppenborg, Berlin; Anne-Katrin and Achim König, Deidesheim; Dorothea and Hans-Ulrich Kroll, Berlin; Volker Küster, Weeze; Virginie and Thaddée Mulliez, Marcq-en-Baroeul/France; Christian Schünemann, Berlin; Christoph Vohwinkel, Cologne; Caroline and Achim Wessel, Cologne; and Joachim Winter, Berlin.

→ ACHIM KÖNIG, born in Plettenberg (NRW) in 1965, completed his school leaving examination (Abitur) in Iserlohn (NRW). In 1986/1987 he studied Medicine in Verona, Italy and from 1987 to 1992 Dentistry in Cologne and Boston, USA. In 1995, he completed his PhD in Cologne. In 1997 he opened a dental practice with his wife Anne-Katrin König in Bad Dürkheim, on the German wine trail.

The Circle of Friends used their participation in the *Carte Blanche* project as an opportunity to show a retrospective of Hans Brosch and to produce a catalogue. Although the focus of the exhibition was put on recent works, some pieces from all stages of his artistic career were shown, including a series of paintings and drawings in large formats.

VIVIEN & HORST SCHMITTER

→ **VIVIEN SCHMITTER works as a freelance costume designer, formerly for the theatre and today mainly for television productions.**

→ **HORST SCHMITTER has worked in the media for over thirty years. In 1984 he founded the Schmitter Media Agency in Frankfurt am Main.**

Vivien and Horst Schmitter began collecting art in 1985. The main focus of their collection was on works by artists such as Ernst Wilhelm Nay, Bernard Schultze, Stefan Wewerka, Stephan Balkenhol and Donald Judd. In 1993, the Schmitters bought the 'Haus Rabe', a Bauhaus Villa in Zwenkau planned by Adolf Rading and Oskar Schlemmer.

One of the first ideas regarding their participation in *Carte Blanche* was to combine objects by the American artist Donald Judd with a collection of cowboy boots. Later an alternative concept was developed to show an exhibition curated by Jean-Christophe Ammann with works by Stephan Balkenhol.

On 26 February 2009, Vivien and Horst Schmitter unexpectedly withdrew from *Carte Blanche*. Consequently, the exhibition space remained empty for the scheduled period. Following their withdrawal from the project, Horst and Vivien Schmitter stopped all communication with the GfZK.

MUSEUM OF CONTEMPORARY ART LEIPZIG

→ The MUSEUM OF CONTEMPORARY ART LEIPZIG (GfZK) is an exhibition house for contemporary art and a museum of post-1945 art. It was founded in 1996 as a non-profit limited company and became a foundation in 2002; today it is one of the few models of a 'private-public-partnership' in the field of art: the running costs are shared between the Free State of Saxony, the City of Leipzig and the Friends Organisation of the museum. The Chairman of the Foundation is Arend Oetker. The museum's programme is funded mainly by the public sector, with the exception of the project *Carte Blanche*, which was financed privately.

The GfZK employs ten staff members and also works with freelance curators and students from various fields of study. Additionally, the house collaborates with a series of cultural and educational institutions at home and abroad.

The GfZK promotes and mediates international artistic positions in its own rooms and in public spaces. In 1998, the GfZK moved into the Villa Herfurth near Johanna Park, which was converted by the architect Peter Kulka from Dresden. In 2004 a second new exhibition building followed, designed by *as-if berlinwien*. In these rooms, eight to ten exhibitions are held each year, featuring mainly artists from the younger generation, but also important art historical perspectives of the past decades. Since 2007, the museum has been showing its collection in changing annual presentations and from various perspectives as regards contents. A library that is open to the public, research projects of several years' duration, scholarships awarded to young Saxon or international artists and a specific mediation programme for children, young people and adults, supplement and link in with the collection and exhibitions.

BARBARA STEINER

→ BARBARA STEINER, born in 1964 in Dörfles/Austria, studied History of Art and Political Science at the University of Vienna. She worked as a curator at the Art Association of Hamburg (1993–1994) and was Head of the Art Associations in Ludwigsburg (1997–1998) and Wolfsburg (1999–2000). In between, she also worked on a freelance basis in Vienna, Linz, Copenhagen, Lucerne, and Siena. Since 2001, Barbara Steiner has been curator and Director of the Museum of Contemporary Art Leipzig. She curates and writes with her main thematic emphasis on the politics of representation (institutional criticality, architecture, and display) and economic criticality.

In *Carte Blanche*, she curated *Carte Blanche V: Dieter Finke – Works* and was joint curator of *Carte Blanche II: LVZ Art Prize + Collection*.

ILINA KORALOVA

→ ILINA KORALOVA was born in 1974 in Sofia/Bulgaria, where she studied History of Art at the National Academy of Art. After this, she completed the Curatorial Programme at the De Appel Foundation in Amsterdam. In 2002, she received the scholarship for curators from Eastern Europe, jointly awarded by the Cultural Foundation of the Free State of Saxony and the GfZK. From 2003 to 2009, she worked as a curator at the GfZK. Since then, she has worked on a freelance basis. At the GfZK she curated the solo exhibitions of Muntean & Rosenblum, Monica Bonvicini, and Jeppe Hein, as well as group exhibitions such as *o.T. (City IV), Is there anything else you would like?* and *Introducing Sites.* In 2010, Ilina Koralova curated *Producing a Place* in Hellerau on behalf of the Art Association of Saxony and the solo exhibition of Ahmet Öğüt at the GfZK. Ilina Koralova also publishes in a number of exhibition catalogues and books. She edited *Againstwithin. On the consequences of modernism and the culture of critique, criticism and criticality in Europe – exemplarily examined in three selected cities*, 2006, and *Einen Ort herstellen* (Producing a Place), 2010.
In *Carte Blanche*, Ilina Koralova curated the exhibitions *Carte Blanche I: Art Prize Future of Europe*, alpha 2000, and she was involved in *Carte Blanche IV: Mark Lombardi, Julius Popp*, Dogenhaus Gallery, and *Carte Blanche VI: EAST – for the record*, VNG – Verbundnetz Gas AG.

JULIA SCHÄFER

→ JULIA SCHÄFER, born in 1972 in Rheinfelden, studied Creative Arts, Art Education, and German at the University of Osnabrück and the Academy of Fine Arts in Dresden. From 2000 to 2001, she was assistant to William Stover and Anne Barlow at the New Museum of Contemporary Art in New York, and from 1998 to 2001 she worked for the Art Museum in Wolfsburg on a freelance basis. Between 2001 and 2003, she was a trainee and since 2003 a Curator and Art Mediator at the GfZK. From 2006 to 2007, she was a lecturer in Curatorial Practice at the Burg Giebichenstein University of Art and Design in Halle/Saale, since 2006 she has been committed to the Kunstvermittlung AG (Art Mediation plc), Berlin, and since 2007 Head of the Art Mediation Team of the GfZK.
As a curator, Julia Schäfer investigates mediation strategies within the field of contemporary art. The mediation projects *Services*, 2001, *Sitzecke* (Corner Seating), 2003, *Schreibstation* (Writing Station), 2003, *Kiosk*, 2004, *Vermittlungscard* (Mediation Card), 2004, *Flurstücke* (Corridor as Display), and *Zwischenraum* (Interspace), 2007, were developed in connection with this. At the GfZK she has curated solo exhibitions with Artur Zmijewski, Antje Schiffers, Sofie Thorsen, Dorit Margreiter and Dora Garcia and group exhibitions such as *Home, Sweet Home, On Air, The Second Glance, Unsere Frau aus Minsk* (Our Woman in Minsk) and *What if?, Why show something that one can see?* Julia Schäfer was also involved in the following projects: *Deutschland sucht* (Germany searching), Cologne Art Association, 2004 and *Sexy Mythos* (Sexy Myth), NGBK Berlin 2006. In 2007, she curated the exhibition *As in Real Life*, P74 in Ljubljana and in 2008 *You are a mess honey* with students from the Academy of Fine Arts in Vienna.
In *Carte Blanche*, she curated the exhibitions *Carte Blanche VII: New York – Basel – Berlin – London – Miami* (Gallery EIGEN+ART) and *Carte Blanche I: Playing to a Home Crowd* (Sachsen Bank).

ANDREJA HRIBERNIK

→ ANDREJA HRIBERNIK was born in Slovenj Gradec/Slovenia in 1978. She studied Political Science at the University of Ljubljana. In 2006, she received the scholarship for curators from Eastern Europe, jointly awarded by the Cultural Foundation of the Free State of Saxony and the Museum of Contemporary Art. Since 2007, Andreja Hribernik has worked freelance for the GfZK and is involved in art mediation making use of new media and technology. In 2008/2009 she was jointly responsible for *Room 107: Arthur Zalewski* at the GfZK, an exhibition from a series featuring artists from Leipzig, supported by the Sachsen Bank. Andreja Hribernik is currently writing her dissertation at the Institute for Humanistic Studies in Ljubljana and working for the Moderna Galerija in Ljubljana. For *Carte Blanche*, she produced a series of video interviews with the participants and was joint curator of the project *Carte Blanche II: LVZ Art Prize + Collection*. She also created the GfZK homepage and drew up a project database for *Carte Blanche*.

HEIDI STECKER

→ HEIDI STECKER, born in Leipzig in 1964, studied Art Education, Aesthetics, and German in Dresden and at the University of Leipzig. In addition to her work in cultural and art mediation projects, Heidi Stecker became involved in the field of female research and higher education policy. Since 2000 she has been working at the Museum of Contemporary Art as the Head of the Press and Public Relations Departement and as a curator. She has been a lecturer at the Institute of Art History at the University of Leipzig since 2007. Heidi Stecker's research focuses mainly on art and cultural and educational policy in the 20th and 21st centuries, art in the GDR, female and gender research, and National Socialism and right-wing radicalism and their reflection in art and urbanism. At the GfZK, she was joint curator of *Publicly Private* in 2003, *Homezone. Via Lewandowsky, The Photographed City* and *Shrinking Cities 2 – Interventions* in 2005, the *Artworks Donation of the Cultural Committee of German Business within BDI* in 2006, the exhibitions from the GfZK collection *German Histories, KW – Hommage à Klaus Werner* and *Nichtorte, Orte* (Non-places, Places) in 2007, 2008 and 2009. In 2008, 2009, and 2010 she was responsible for *Cabinet – from the collection* and *Die Konservierungsmaschine. Sammlung und Restaurierung der GfZK* (The conservation machine. Collection and restoration at the GfZK). In 1994, Heidi Stecker was the co-editor of *EigenArtige Ost-frauen. Frauenempanzipation in der DDR und den neuen Bundesländern* (Unique East German Women. Female emancipation in the GDR and the former East German states) and *Veränderungen – Identitätsfindung im Prozeß. Frauenforschung im Jahre Sieben nach der Wende.* (Changes – the process of identity search. Female research in year seven after the fall of the Berlin Wall). In 2004, together with Anke Hagemann, she was responsible for the contribution *Wird Leipzig-Grünau zur national befreiten Zone?* (Is Leipzig-Grünau becoming a national liberated zone?) for *Shrinking Cities 1 – International Research* in Berlin. In 2006, work was begun on the collection catalogue of the GfZK, which since then has been published in several volumes with the title *Sammeln* (Collecting). For Carte Blanche, Heidi Stecker co-curated the exhibition of the Hans Brosch Circle of Friends, *Carte Blanche X: Hans Brosch*.

GUEST CURATORS

→ **ELKE HANNEMANN, born in Köthen in 1964, studied Cultural Studies and Literary History in Leipzig and has worked for the Gallery EIGEN+ART in Leipzig since 1992.**

→ **FRANK-HEINRICH MÜLLER, born in Haldensleben/Saxony-Anhalt in 1962, trained as a photographer before studying Photography at the Academy of Visual Arts in Leipzig. In 1994, he founded the 'Photographiedepot', a collection of photographic documentation in Leipzig, and gave lectures on architectural photography at the Hochschule für Architektur und Bauwesen (University of Architecture and Building) in Weimar. Since 2009, he has been teaching photography as a replacement professor at the Burg Giebichenstein University of Art and Design in Halle.**

→ **CARSTEN PROBST, born in 1966, studied History of Art, Philosophy, German and Slavonic studies in Tubingen, Munich and Hamburg. He lives in Berlin and is an author and art critic.**

→ **CHRISTINE RINK, née Mengering, was born in Leipzig in 1945. After completing her professional training as an antique dealer at the Staatlicher Kunsthandel der DDR (GDR State Art Dealers) in 1968, she studied History of Art/Aesthetics at the Karl Marx University in Leipzig. In 1979, she became the director of the gallery at the Hochschule für Grafik und Buchkunst (today the Academy of Visual Arts) in Leipzig, where she continued to work until 2009.**

→ **JOHANNES SCHMIDT, born in Dresden in 1969, studied History of Art, English and History at the TU Dresden, the University of Plymouth and the Università degli Studi di Bologna. After his studies, he completed a period of voluntary training at the State Art Collections of Dresden. From 2003 to 2006 he worked as a freelance curator and publicist, and since 2006 he has been the curator of the collection at the Dresden City Art Gallery.**

→ **CHRISTIANE SCHNEIDER, born in Karlsruhe in 1962, studied History of Art, German and Philosophy in Munich, Bonn and Cologne. She has worked as a curator since 1992. From 1994 to 1997 she was a co-curator of Art at the Leipzig Trade Fair; she has also worked at the Josef-Haubrich Kunsthalle in Cologne since May 1998. After a period of time working as an assistant at the Dia Center in New York, she became Exhibitions Director of the Haunch of Venison Gallery in London from 2002–2004, responsible for exhibitions by artists such as Rachel Whiteread, Diana Thater, Jorge Pardo, Richard Long, Thomas Nozkowski and Andy Warhol. Since 2005, she has been the director of westlondonprojects, a non-profit-making exhibition institution in London. Christiane Schneider has published contributions in art journals and exhibition catalogues. Since 2009, she has held a teaching post at the Institute of Cultural and Media Management at the Hamburg University of Music and Theatre.**

Synopsis of Interviews

With Matthias Brühl, Leon Janucek, Harald R. Pfab, Jochen Hempel, Doris and Klaus F. K. Schmidt, Bernd Radestock, Brigitte and Arend Oetker, Gerd Harry Lybke, Julia Schäfer, Ilina Koralova, Andreja Hribernik, Gerhardt Wolff, Achim König, Heidi Stecker, Dietmar Schulz, Frank-Heinrich Müller, Birgit Rebeck.

CONCEPTS OF THE ENEMY

Matthias Brühl: I've talked to a few people about the *Carte Blanche* project and in doing so I noticed that any negative reactions were mainly directed towards people who came in from the outside: the private person as a natural enemy.

Leon Janucek: It really reminds me of the film business. Everyone who works on a film thinks that the producer is their greatest enemy. Of course, that is just not true. In a similar way, in *Carte Blanche*, everyone also seems to have thought that the private collector or entrepreneur was an enemy of the museum. The mere fact that they could and should be mutually supporting one another seems to me to be the only way ahead, even if this does not correspond to the general public's awareness. I don't feel that I have been exploited, and neither do I feel as though I have exploited the museum.

Matthias Brühl: It turned out that businesses can support idealistic values; they can do good as well as being economically orientated. Even gallery owners! (laughs)

Barbara Steiner: Some of the groups involved in the art field seem to be particularly open to prejudice. Here I must say that banks and galleries are the perfect examples. In general, exhibitions held by banks do not attract a great deal of interest. People seem to think they know what to expect, right from the beginning. With gallery owners it is the other way round – there was an enormous amount of interest, but this was mainly directed towards business practices rather than what was on exhibit.

Harald R. Pfab: Of course I can understand anyone who takes this view of banks. There are various ways of looking at it. I also enjoy talking to journalists, and have done so several times in the past. Sometimes, during the course of the discussions, you can actually help someone towards gaining a new perspective.

Jochen Hempel: The prejudices towards gallery owners seem to have been built up over a period of time. In fact, not so many contemporary galleries earn huge amounts of money in a short space of time so that you might get the idea they must exploit everyone they come across just to make their fortune. Out of the twenty-four artists I work with today, I can only actually guarantee eight of them a living from my activity as a gallery owner. The important thing is that my gallery cooperates with other galleries, so that the load is shared out between us. In the end, a gallery can only do well if the artists it represents are doing well, and that is what we must work towards. It's just a myth that all we do is sit around and cash in our 50 per cent.

> **Klaus F. K. Schmidt:** The gallery owner has a vital function, not only within the marketplace, but also, and I must consciously stress this, as an art mediator. The gallery owner must be strengthened. He or she is a crucial factor for the continuing success of an artist.

> **Doris Schmidt:** … for the endurance of his or her success …

Jochen Hempel: Anyone who is seriously interested in art collections knows that they would often never have been started without the presence of the gallery owner as a mediator. And I am also convinced that people who are seriously concerned with art would never want to do away with the gallery owner.

MONEY

Matthias Brühl: The exhibitions were exceptionally high in quality and impact; this is perhaps owed to the fact that the parties involved had paid for them. This is why they showed such a high level of commitment towards their project and your institution.

> **Bernd Radestock:** Possibly this was also one of the reasons why the project was subjected to so much criticism, *because* we all paid money to exhibit. Maybe some people thought: he who pays, decides. But it would never occur to me to try to influence an exhibition in any way.

Harald R. Pfab: I would like to support what Mr Radestock just said. One may make careful suggestions, but one must never become dominant as an enterprise or as a person. A journalist once asked me: 'You are sponsoring this exhibition. So obviously you decided which pictures were to be exhibited?' But that would have been the very last decision I would have wished to make.

> **Brigitte Oetker:** There is a general lack of trust not only towards enterprises, but also towards private collectors. If a private collector holds an exhibition in a public gallery, the question always comes up: who benefits from it? If something is sold after the exhibition or even directly as a result of it – which has certainly happened in other cases – there is often bad blood.

Arend Oetker: The situation becomes difficult if someone wishes to resell works of art for speculative reasons.

Brigitte Oetker: If one is in a difficult situation, this is something that one can and ought to be able to do. What if you don't have any other choice? There is a moral side to the discussion what I find somewhat dubious: for example the assumption, without differentiation, that it is contemptible to resell a work of art. There are many reasons for selling something, and there may be the odd collector who at some point might say 'I would rather have something else.' This should also be regarded with respect.

Ilina Koralova: Jochen, what happens if someone brings a piece of art back to the gallery wanting to sell it again?

Jochen Hempel: I think it is better than the work being put up for auction. If it is resold through the gallery, the artist benefits a second time.

Gerd Harry Lybke: As soon as money's involved, most discussions start to get hypocritical. It's a fact that it's getting more and more difficult nowadays for a public gallery to fulfil its programme without money. And if a collaboration exists, for example with a private business, it should not be kept a secret. So in my opinion the transparency of a project like *Carte Blanche* is beneficial. What we are saying is this: This is not the situation we want, but it is the situation we are faced with at the present time. *Carte Blanche* shows this extremely clearly, because the project makes a statement right from the beginning: these are the conditions, these are the criteria, these are the coordinates the project runs under. So then it is possible to look at what comes out of it and decide if we find it worse or better than what went before. Of course, a project like this does not free the state from its responsibility; it challenges it to do more.

Barbara Steiner: The project is more than a reaction to an economic problem. It makes economic questions into questions of contents; they become an integral part of the institution's programme. It is an active approach, it meets the challenge of the new economic circumstances museums are faced with and picks them out as a central theme. And of course we have to consider where the strength of museums lies, in a climate where the large galleries are often in a better position regarding space, funds, and possibilities. Today, a museum can no longer afford to produce a certain kind of catalogue.

Gerd Harry Lybke: Unfortunately, museums are defenceless at present.

Barbara Steiner: I don't see it that way. We could also say: museums will possibly no longer have to publish a certain type of monograph in the future. We will leave the format of the coffee-table book and the star authors to you and get on with the discursive corrections … (laughs) Also, I don't see these developments as essentially negative, but they do make it necessary for museums to develop other strategies and tactics. For example we could concentrate more on tasks that are quickly forgotten, for example mediating art. I don't think that the power of definition has been transferred to the art market, if that's what you are trying to infer.

Gerd Harry Lybke: That is not what I wanted to say, no, that is nonsense. You still have the power of definition.

Barbara Steiner: No, that is something we no longer have, I am convinced of that. No single party in the field of art has the power of definition any more; it changes far more quickly, or it is being shared. This means that the relationships within the field of art are in constant motion, and they will form themselves in new constellations from one case to the next. Even the classical roles are disappearing. I see this as an extremely interesting development.

Julia Schäfer: Museums need support then. Let us talk about sponsoring. Sponsoring is clearly defined as a reciprocal form of business. But more often one can find hybrid forms of support, fluctuating between business and social commitment. Mr Pfab, do you offer pure sponsoring?

Harald R. Pfab: Sponsoring in our eyes is when we support an event run by the Chamber of Commerce. We give money to pay for a reception and in return we put our advertising material on display. That is classical sponsoring. We think very carefully before investing our money. How many people are likely to be at the event? How many potential customers might we be able to acquire? Then we work it all out – how much will it cost us to participate, and how many customers can we invite? Art sponsoring is different – we know in advance how much an exhibition will cost. Then we have to see how we can accommodate it within our general sponsoring budget. What are the minimum requirements accepted by the tax office? What service is expected in return? In this case it is enough if our advertising banners are hung outside the gallery and our name is printed in the catalogue. We are not concerned with demanding as much service in return as possible, but with finding a minimum solution. The important thing about art sponsorship is that the enterprise does not push itself forwards too much. This would only make a negative impression.

Julia Schäfer: What percentage of your marketing budget does that represent?

Harald R. Pfab: The board believes that it should be as high as possible.

COLLABORATION AND HIERARCHIES

Ilina Koralova: Up until now, our institution has only been involved with state-run organisations or foundations. In *Carte Blanche,* we had to communicate with people who had their own ideas. I learned that these two different models have to be approached in completely different ways. It is easier for a curator to deal with a foundation, as no one there tells you how to run the exhibition. As soon as they transfer the money to your account, you are given the freedom to make your own decisions. With private organisations there is a closer, more direct form of contact, and freedom becomes a question of personal trust. But once you have established your partner's confidence in a successful cooperation, you may suddenly find that you have even more scope than would be the case if you were working with a clearly regulated organisation.

Barbara Steiner: And it is interesting to observe that once you are successful here, money is no longer much of an object for a private organisation. I find this remarkable. If all the parties involved are pleased with the result, not so much as a final budget report is required. Of course we still gave one to them, for the sake of transparency, but no one actually asked us for it.

Ilina Koralova: Maybe it sounds ridiculous, but inviting artists, organising dinners, simply being generous, has become something that only private individuals can afford to do.

Julia Schäfer: In *Carte Blanche*, though, I did ask myself several times what possibilities remain open to me as a curator. In the end, I was at least able to develop a conceptual idea for both exhibitions. That was the scope of action available to me, and both partners went along with it. On principle, however, there was no room for new art to be produced, which I really missed. And I could not work directly with artists. I do find it interesting that none of the partners who were invited to take part gave the *Carte Blanche* back to us. Someone could have said 'I'll give you the money, you do what you want.'

Barbara Steiner: It would have been like saying 'My commitment to art consists of supporting the institution, because I trust it implicitly.' But it was primarily a case of the participants positioning themselves. And that did not necessarily have to do with the need for self-presentation. It was more about looking for a partner within the institution to exchange ideas about art and to see where one stands.

Julia Schäfer: I know, but it still could have been a more altruistic approach.

Ilina Koralova: What was the most interesting thing about *Carte Blanche* for you, Andreja?

Andreja Hribernik: It was the opportunity to gain an unusually deep insight into the way of thinking and approach of the individuals who took part. To see how far the invited guests were willing to get involved in the interests of an art institution, or to what extent they declared their intents but did not allow true involvement to take place in the end. I also found it highly interesting to observe that contact with the GfZK was of course most intense and lasting in those cases where people had a personal interest, which led them to become involved in an effective way.

Ilina Koralova: 'Did not allow true involvement to take place in the end' also means that they were not really interested in working together on an equal basis. I am convinced that the larger an organisation is, the greater its interest in exhibiting in the institution for the sake of its reputation rather than in entering into discussions with the institution and its representatives. I could sum it up by saying: in *Carte Blanche*, as an employee of the GfZK, I was simply expected to be of service. I knew there were certain people I needed to contact to deal with the various organisational procedures. Sometimes this was extremely difficult – invitation drafts and mail-outs had to be sent to the press department, who then sent them on to the management, who gave their approval or not as the case may be, until they were finally returned to me. So of course everything took much longer.

Julia Schäfer: Large organisations always find it important to control the framework within which their art is exhibited. Everything is regulated right down to the last detail, even press releases and other mail-outs have to be agreed upon word for word. I've had the same experience. But on the positive side, one has to say that they do not usually intervene as far as contents are concerned.

Ilina Koralova: Our ideas about how to approach a task were just very different. In large organisations there is a hierarchical view that conflicts with the way we do things at the GfZK. Our approach is very different here, for example we find it important to communicate with graphic artists as equal partners, they are always part of a team working on a certain project. In this kind of enterprise everyone has a hierarchical relationship to each another. So the curator employed by the enterprise takes all the decisions relating to the exhibition. He or she says what has to be done, and the graphic designers do it, it's as simple as that. But of course the curator also has someone above him or her, who he or she has to report back to. Julia, how did you go about dealing with the hierarchical structures and strict lines of communication?

Julia Schäfer: The choice of exhibits was left completely up to me. I had one contact person in the organisation. However, a great deal of additional effort was required to keep up with the high frequency of communication and reporting back that was expected. Especially as far as the logo and sending out texts was concerned – here I had to be extremely careful. If I changed so much as a small detail I had to send the whole text back to the bank. In some phases I really thought I would be pleased when I could make my own decisions again and not have to ask for permission all the time.

Ilina Koralova: Were any of your texts changed in any way?

Julia Schäfer: No. They simply wanted to see the texts. The procedure works according to a certain pattern, and I've got quite used to it by now as I've been working with the Sachsen Bank/LBBW for a number of years. But of course, it is nothing like our field of work, at least the way we work here at the GfZK. To some extent, I can understand that a bank that is active on this scale has to have certain strict regulations. People like us, who view the world in an extremely critical way, may sometimes find these formalities a little dubious. But many things are formal in a bank, right down to the dress code. When I go to the Sachsen Bank – which I have done hundreds of times – I always have to wait at reception for someone to come and pick me up. Whilst I'm waiting, I sit in one of the black leather armchairs and watch the employees. Actually they all wear a kind of uniform. But I must say that I have met a lot of people at the Sachsen Bank who find and use their own personal scope within these structures. So they are not 'prisoners' – otherwise this project, and many others in the past, would never have been possible.

BOUNDARIES

Barbara Steiner: In times of crisis, isn't there a grave danger of valuable pieces of work from private collections belonging to businesses being sold? The temptation must be there.

Bernd Radestock: If the worst comes to the worst, we shouldn't be under any illusions here. But I certainly hope it will never happen.

Barbara Steiner: This is the difference between a museum and an enterprise – we would never sell a work of art, not under any circumstances.

Bernd Radestock: We can only look at it in a practical way – the enterprise has bought the picture from the profits it has made – that is the difference between a private enterprise and a museum – it belongs to the enterprise, and if the enterprise at some point decides that it must part with the picture so as to carry on functioning, it simply must sell the picture, and no one is to blame for it.

Barbara Steiner: Of course, a collection belonging to an enterprise is far more at risk of being resold, at least at the moment ... but the danger for museum collections is on the increase too, and who knows how the situation will be in fifty years' time. Selling items from a collection is still a taboo for us. If a museum were to sell something from its collections, it would not receive any further donations. But you are right, who knows what might happen in the future.

B. Radestock: A museum has inhibition thresholds. These are not so high for an enterprise.

Gerhardt Wolff: The first priority of a privately-run enterprise is to make money. We cannot spend it until we have earned it. If we are successful in this, we have a little more leeway, but if not, things begin to get tighter. We have to think carefully about what we can afford to spend, over and over again. This is why we have to draw up budgets – for art as well as for everything else.

Ilina Koralova: Of course you are under obligation, especially towards your shareholders. I'm sure people ask what the VNG – Verbundnetz Gas AG spends its funds on?

Gerhardt Wolff: That depends on the current situation of the enterprise. Until the mid-1990s we were running a loss and the questions were especially probing: what do you do with all the money? What do you spend it on? As long as you are making a loss, you have to have very good reasons for making any additional commitments. If you are making a profit it becomes easier. But of course our shareholders on the board regularly ask us what we have spent money on.

Julia Schäfer: Mr Pfab, where do you set the boundaries for the enterprise you currently represent as far as art sponsorship is concerned?

Harald R. Pfab: On the one hand, there are clearly defined economic boundaries, and on the other hand, banks generally have a certain image, which is rather on the conservative side. So on the whole, they tend to be more hesitant as far as progressive art is concerned. But I believe that you sometimes have to find the courage to overstep boundaries. I was always aware of the point at which I was entering into a conflict, but I have never had real problems in dealing with this.

Julia Schäfer: In such cases it seems to me that the person who is dealing with the situation is vital. Someone else would probably have said 'That is too much for our bank' at a far earlier stage in the proceedings.

Harald R. Pfab: But when we are talking about economic questions, the personal context does not make much of a difference.

Julia Schäfer: But maybe it does? One person might say, 'Times are hard, we are stopping all sponsorship', whilst another would say, 'It is especially important that we continue to sponsor now. We cannot give as much, but we are not stopping altogether.'

Harald R. Pfab: Yes, that's true. It is possible to exert a little personal influence, but in difficult times it is limited. That is something we have to accept. But the baseline should be visible, in spite of economy measures.

Barbara Steiner: Doris Schmidt, how does a private collector view this? Where do your boundaries lie?

Doris Schmidt: I must say that we have always bought works of art that were way beyond our means, that were far more expensive than we could afford.

Barbara Steiner: How did you solve that problem?

Doris Schmidt: We paid in instalments. One of the first paintings we bought was a 'Scheibenbild' by Ernst Wilhelm Nay. Even at that time, it was almost impossible for us to finance, but thanks to Mrs Nay's generosity we were able to pay in instalments.

Barbara Steiner: How high are you prepared to go if you want to buy something?

Klaus F.K. Schmidt: We go up to our financial limits, but we would not borrow money to buy art in a big way. We wouldn't take out a loan, for example.

Doris Schmidt: But we did once sell a flat so that we could buy a painting.

Arend Oetker: At this point I must stress: Art never was and is not my first priority. My company and the people I employ are still far more important to me. Sprengel and Ludwig sold their companies and became collectors. I am an entrepreneur. I have other priorities, I also have financial boundaries. But my main reason for buying contemporary art is not because of the price, but because my wife and I enjoy looking out for new, real contemporary work – that is what is important to us.

PRIVATE COMMITMENT

Achim König: The Hans Brosch Circle of Friends is not made up of professional collectors. No museum has its mind set on our private collections, and conversely no private collector within the Circle of Friends is intent on using the museum to enhance the status or increase the value of his private collection by exhibiting it in public. The Circle of Friends consists of art enthusiasts who do not speculate on material profit. On the one hand, they are an example of private patronage beyond the large strategies of collecting; on the other hand, it is becoming evident that private commitment is able to fill in art-historical gaps to a certain degree.

Heidi Stecker: Where do you see the strengths of private commitment?

Achim König: The commitment of the Circle of Friends began at the point where public finances became limited. The Hans Brosch-exhibition at the GfZK couldn't have been done without our support. So I see us as supplying what public funds can no longer provide.

Barbara Steiner: Mr König, you are making an appeal for private individuals to support the public museum. In an interview you held, Brigitte, with Fischli and Weiss, it became obvious that these artists preferred private collections to public institutions. They said that public collections do not have the quality they expect …

Brigitte Oetker: Fischli & Weiss stress the importance of being in 'good company'. They find it important for their works to be shown in a context that interests them. Public purchases are frequently subject to compromise, as a decision to purchase a piece of art is made by a large committee, which means that a clear 'trademark' is often missing. What they most prefer is for a group of works to be put together and bought, as was the case at the Centre Pompidou, so that the pieces do not become isolated as is usually the case. In this way, they reach a larger public with a representative selection, and this is the most important thing for them.

Barbara Steiner: They wish for a visible signature in a collection. The artist Hanno Otten once made a similar critical remark to me concerning the anonymous conditions in public galleries. In contrast to the collector, a curator does not have to invest his own money for art, so he or she can go about collecting with far less risk.

Arend Oetker: My real motivation was to allow a collection like the one in Leipzig to develop publicly, but not as 'my' collection. I looked around for the gallery in Leipzig, but not for myself. The Cultural Committee of German Business laid the foundations with a donation of paintings. So we were able to retrieve works from a lot of museums in West Germany, where they were on permanent loan from the Cultural Committee, and brought them to the Leipzig gallery. It was a public transfer, so to speak. Some of the pre-1945 works we had sold in order to pay for a part of the building. The works of art that I had donated myself were then added to the main body of works brought to the Leipzig gallery by the Cultural Committee.

Barbara Steiner: You had originally bought these pieces for yourself.

Arend Oetker: They were works with which I identified. They were private pieces.

Barbara Steiner: Is it a programmatic requirement to say: on the one hand I support a public gallery in making acquisitions and on the other hand I collect art myself? I have one or two pieces I identify with. And at some point even those – perhaps not all of them, but a significant number – will go back into public ownership. Why is it so important for you to donate them? Many private collectors keep their works for themselves.

Brigitte Oetker: May I answer that? The decision to donate something to a collection also has something to do with your relationship with a certain place or certain individuals – Harvard, Leipzig, Hamburg, Cologne, Berlin, Peter Nisbet, Kasper König, Barbara Steiner. In Leipzig, Arend has also made donations to the Museum of Fine Arts, not only to the Museum of Contemporary Art. That is one thing. The other thing is that you buy works from artists you personally find very good, artists you assess only from your own point of view and wish to support. If you pass them on, your personal judgement has to stand up to public opinion. And by doing this, by buying these works and showing them, you are also strengthening these positions.

Leon Janucek: One thing I have learned from *Carte Blanche*, and also from my discussions with artists in general, is that my private art activities have not been particularly constructive up to now – because hardly anyone sees my collection. This means that the works of the artists – who of course have put a lot of creative energy and passion into them – disappear from the public eye. They are accessible only to myself, my friends, family, and acquaintances. Some time ago I was standing in front of the wall where my Hofers are on display. Karl Hofer's paintings are so wonderful! And I thought, this is not right, keeping these pictures to myself.

Barbara Steiner: A lot of these works of art are very significant from the point of view of art history. Let's take the painting *Die Steinwerferin*.

Leon Janucek: Since this moment, I have been thinking about how I can go about getting the pieces in my collection back on public display within the next ten years. Of course, that would also bring tax benefits, this I must admit. I have two daughters, and when I die they will have inheritance tax to pay. But if valuable works of art in my estate are made accessible to the public, there will be no estate tax to pay, or at least not so much. So to some extent my motivation has something to do with my daughters. But the artists are at least just as important to me. Their works must be shown to the public.

Barbara Steiner: Mr and Mrs Schmidt, you started up your own foundation some time ago, the Schmidt-Drenhaus Foundation. What led you to do this?

Doris Schmidt: The advantage of a foundation is that you can stipulate which paintings come into it, so you can place works of art together in permanent groups. However we did not put all of our works into the foundation. Our children need to have a certain amount of freedom. Our daughter will carry on taking care of the foundation, as she also collects art with her husband. Both of them are tax consultants, so they have a lot of contact with gallery owners and young artists through their work.

Julia Schäfer: Mr Pfab, as a banker, do you collect art on a private basis too?

Harald R. Pfab: Yes, on a modest level. The works of art one especially likes are often out of one's price range or they are already on display in museums – which I don't begrudge them of course! Still I have been successful in buying one or two small works from Classical Modernism for my home. Of course, private preferences and entrepreneurial commitment sometimes cause conflicts to arise, as on the one hand, one cannot and does not wish to deny one's personal taste, and on the other hand, on a professional level, one must sponsor exhibitions that are good for the enterprise but may not necessarily be to one's particular liking. I have certainly sometimes had to say to myself: my dear boy, this is not the kind of art you prefer, but we are still sponsoring it, because it is significant in some way. Apart from that, I am open to new things. I think that is something one must continue to be, in all walks of life.

Ilina Koralova: Mr Brühl, neither you nor alpha 2000 collects art.

Matthias Brühl: I have made a conscious decision not to buy paintings, as I do not wish to take part in an economic exchange in the sense of goods for money. The prize 'Future of Europe', which we have been awarding now for the last six years, is not based on any model of goods in return, as this would make me a market participant, which I am already on a day-to-day basis. My wish is to offer support, and that is my motivation. The most important thing for me is to give the artists the opportunity to carry on doing what is important to them. Of course, 5,000 euros help more in Pristina than in Leipzig, but more than anything it conveys a message to the artists: I and my work have been noticed.

Dietmar Schulz: In Germany we have an added advantage – as well as institutions being given state funding, private companies also play an active role in art sponsoring. The former East German states, that is to say, the former GDR, particularly benefit from an intact and helpful culture of support. In the countries in which we have awarded the prize, there is often no form of state or private support available. This is also why I consider the contribution of alpha 2000 towards art in the other post-communist countries to be extremely important.

PUBLIC COMMITMENT

Gerhardt Wolff: Our commitment is related to Leipzig: we are a business based in Leipzig and we also have a special situation here. So what could be more logical than making the most of the talents we have? We wanted and want to make sure that what happens in Leipzig is seen in other places. Our initiatives are not only linked with the field of art; we are also active in social areas and sports, but art has always been very special to us. On a political level we also give our support to the 'Verbundnetz für Toleranz', an alliance against extremism. Basically our commitment is geared towards creating positive awareness.

Ilina Koralova: Your commitment is directed not only outwards towards the public, but also inwards, towards the employees of the VNG.

Gerhardt Wolff: Both of these are important to us. We have noticed that the works of art that our company has purchased make quite an impression on our employees. They can choose which paintings or photographs are exhibited on the floor they work on. Certain members of staff within the building are responsible for this. They act as contacts, channel the requests, and make sure they are carried out. We do not want our collection to be static; we prefer it to be in continual motion. In this way, the pieces in the collection inspire lively discussions to take place.

Ilina Koralova: Would you say that your involvement with art is also a social commitment, and if so, to what extent?

Gerhardt Wolff: Of course we are committed to social issues. We do what other businesses also find beneficial – we try to be what is known as a 'corporate citizen', a good member of society. At the moment this is a highly controversial question, how far an enterprise can be or strive towards being such a thing, but we feel that it is necessary and we also think it is possible. I believe our past activities have been sufficient proof of this. Because of our shareholders and customers in the region we have a strong local character, so local references are of the utmost importance to us.

Ilina Koralova: So it would be damaging to your image if you were not socially committed?

Gerhard Wolff: Absolutely.

Harald R. Pfab: It could well be asked what motivates a bank to invest in and exhibit art. Of course in some way one has a duty towards public welfare, one must show commitment. On the one hand, of course, what we support first and foremost is clearly the bank, we want the bank to continue in its successful development, but on the other hand, we believe that it is our public duty to promote art. In my opinion, everyone who is in a position to do so should take part in supporting art. I say should, because unfortunately it happens less and less.

Julia Schäfer: That sounds like an appeal.

Harald R. Pfab: Yes, that is how it is meant. Everyone can or could make a contribution. But of course you have to like art, you can't pull people into line and say 'you will now devote yourself to art, because art is good for us, it improves the image of the bank.'

Barbara Steiner: Private individuals can engage in public commitment, but it is not their duty. Mr Schmidt, you and your wife choose to do so, with a passion.

Klaus F.K.Schmidt: It began in a modest way: for nearly forty years now, we have been sending editions to my clients on a regular basis, to encourage their interest in art.

Barbara Steiner: You also give your works of art away as donations. For example to the *Kupferstichkabinett* (Collection of prints, drawings and photographs, part of the State Art Collections in Dresden). What are your criteria for making donations like this?

Klaus F.K.Schmidt: The first large donation we made was to the State and University Library of Saxony, the SLUB. It is a new building designed by Ortner & Ortner, a wonderful piece of architecture! We had seen a painting by the artist Eberhard Göschel, entitled 'Aufgelöste Kartei' (Eliminated Index Card), an abstract painting. In this piece of work, the artist had reflected upon what he experienced when he gained access to his own Stasi file. When you look at the picture, you feel as though you are confronted with an enormous wall full of files and books. It is a wonderful picture, and we said to each other 'It has to hang at the entrance of the SLUB.' In the case of Candida Höfer it was obvious to us straight away: the photographic work by Candida Höfer belongs in the Albertinum, in the 'New Masters' gallery, because it portrays a tiny workroom that was photographed there. Contemporary art is underrepresented in Dresden. Through our actions we hope to inspire others to donate art to the Dresden State Art Collection. It's all about showing and encouraging civil commitment.

Doris Schmidt: We show our involvement publicly. That is to say, you have to make your commitment known to the public, otherwise it has no exemplary value. That is why we made reference to our commitment to art in the exhibition, so as to support the theme of *Carte Blanche*. How do art-lovers and collectors behave? How do they approach art? And in the end it is about more than collecting art.

Barbara Steiner: Also you probably have to proceed strategically if you want to achieve something for the sake of art. Mr Oetker, as an entrepreneur you carry a certain amount of weight, even more so as a successful entrepreneur. You use your position to make others listen to you, to motivate others, to remind them of their duty. It also works the other way around: you show commitment to art, and as a result it also gains in stature. It becomes important. It brings people together.

Arend Oetker: This is my intention and I use it consciously. For example, there would be no Leipzig Gallery without the Leipzig Trade Fair, to be more precise: If I had not been sitting in the Construction Committee of the Trade Fair at the same time as the leader of the Free State of Saxony, I would not have had such a perfect opportunity to plead my case. And in situations like this it is important to pursue medium- and long-term aims and to point out again and again the supreme importance of public responsibility for art and culture, particularly in other social environments and especially in those not related to art. So it is true that I have always used my economic position to further the cause of contemporary art.

THE PUBLIC MUSEUM

Gerhardt Wolff: I find the basic concept of *Carte Blanche* very attractive and interesting, to say that you will provide a public space where collectors are willing to show something, something that is sure to provoke an exchange of ideas. I think this is a good idea. It makes a big difference whether you see our collection in our company rooms or in an art institution.

Frank-Heinrich Müller: The walls of the GfZK are highly sought-after, there are a lot of people who would like to exhibit there. Whilst working on this project I certainly noticed people's reactions when you said 'we are presenting at the GfZK and there will be a book published by Steidl.'

Barbara Steiner: The museum enhances status. Compared with other non-art exhibition spaces it creates a specific environment for looking at art.

Birgit Rebeck (LVGD – Head of Marketing): This was especially true of our exhibition, because our paintings are usually displayed in the corridors, editorial offices, and conference rooms not really accessible to the public, at any rate not shown to their best advantage. It was really amazing for me and many of my colleagues to see how different our paintings looked in your gallery.

Bernd Radestock: The paintings were ideally presented in the gallery. It gave us the opportunity to see the paintings all together, and from another perspective entirely. Otherwise you go past them at a distance of less than two metres. In the gallery you could stand back and look at them from a distance.

Gerd Harry Lybke: The higher the standard of the museum is, the more profound an effect it has on the perception of art, and of course this makes it all the more important for my artists to exhibit in places such as this.

Barbara Steiner: (laughs) ... and all the more important for the gallery owner too, of course. So what you are saying is: if you are a gallery owner working in a museum, you are responsible for making sure that the museum stays a museum and is not turned into a gallery? It sounds as though the museum sets the standards.

Gerd Harry Lybke: Yes it does, independently of *Carte Blanche*. For example, let's take the current exhibition by Rémy Markowitsch. It could be shown in any museum, just as it is.

Barbara Steiner: And yet it is on display in a commercial gallery. Does the tendency towards presenting in a museum not also imply a concealment of the fact that a gallery is a place where things are sold?

Gerd Harry Lybke: I see the exhibition room in our gallery more like a space that is similar to a museum, where people can concentrate only on art and its relevance; perhaps somewhere far in the background there is the possibility of buying something. Because of the museum-like presentation, you can experience the artist and his work in an extremely intense way. If a single piece of work turns up later on its own, it is loaded with the first overall impression. And of course, at some point it is all about immortality. (laughs) But making artists immortal is unfortunately something that only succeeds from time to time.

Barbara Steiner: What determines the character of a museum? Imparting immortality?

Brigitte Oetker: I would say its collection, although: museums' collections are generally a conglomeration of different pieces of work chosen by various people and therefore somewhat lacking in coherency.

Barbara Steiner: I see this incoherence as an advantage, because it clearly shows how many different interests, at different times, are involved in influencing a collection. Collections reflect attitudes and concepts of value. In the best case, a public collection gives you a feeling for how inconstant quality is, and that it is not an objective quantity. You have to struggle for quality, you have to start from the beginning again and again, and these are processes that should be made visible by public museums. As a private individual, you don't have to do that (laughs).

Brigitte Oetker: As a public collector you have a particularly high level of responsibility, there are other criteria involved apart from quality. You have a wide area to cover, you have to provide information, and in my opinion it is also important to take local references into consideration. I think it is very important to respect the achievements being made in the area and to inform people about them. At the same time, it must also be possible to hold nationwide discussions. You have a great responsibility towards the people who visit the museum. You have to give them something they can hold on to, a mark of quality, because they trust you, the director of the museum, to make choices for them. So you have a duty there, too. A large number of different responsibilities merge together. And a private collector does not have any of these duties.

Achim König: Large private collections appear far more able to act in the art market than most public collections, whose budgets are often extremely limited.

Leon Janucek: It is true that the situation for museums has become difficult today. As long as museums could put on exhibitions, perhaps make acquisitions, carry out research, they did not need private individuals so much. Today they can no longer do all of these things, at least only under extremely tight constraints. Most museums no longer really have a budget for purchasing works of art or producing academic work. In a situation like this, new ways and means have to be found, and there is no point in being bigoted or afraid that a museum is starting to go down if private individuals get involved with it.

Matthias Brühl: I think that a museum needs input from the outside, from other people, exactly as it is supposed to be the case the other way round – that private individuals learn from museums.

Barbara Steiner: Mr König once told me that it was not so simple for the Hans Brosch Circle of Friends to get its foot in the door of a museum, there would always have to be a fortunate combination of circumstances and interests. So the input is not always welcome.

Achim König: As friends of Brosch, we were interested in finding out how to go one step further and help the painter Hans Brosch to gain recognition in museums. In my view, art critics and museums form a closed circle, they exist in a world of their own. Not all museums are open to outside concerns. But when things go well, it is a stroke of luck: The best case for me is when the enthusiasm of private art-lovers is combined with the professional expertise of a museum.

CONTEXT

Heidi Stecker: Whether or not an exhibition needs additional information is a very old discussion that comes up again and again, that is to what extent can art speak for itself. The question has a special pertinance as far as East German art is concerned, as the context within which it was created no longer exists. That is why it no longer means very much to people today. When we show Hans Brosch, we cannot assume that visitors will be able to recognise and classify its context, for example they do not know how explosive abstract art was in East Germany, or why it was such a sensation that Hans Brosch was invited to an important exhibition in Paris in 1975. I consider that it is my duty as a curator to provide this kind of information in the exhibition. It does not place constraints on the work of art, but it can be a great help towards understanding it.

Barbara Steiner: In most of the *Carte Blanche* exhibitions the contextualisation of the works of art was not an issue. Art was understood in the sense of a universal language and quality, more or less regardless of its context. Here I think one underestimates how much so-called neutral rooms and hanging principles have an impact on perception.

Heidi Stecker: It is not without reason that we often work with artists who give a lot of thought to such aspects, even seeing them as an integral part of their artistic work.

Barbara Steiner: Just as we do as curators of course. Julia, because you were given complete freedom as the curator of the exhibition by the Sachsen Bank/LBBW, you were able to make the transfer of the pictures from the bank to the exhibition room a theme.

Julia Schäfer: What interests me about this concept is that certain elements communicate a certain familiarity to the person looking at them, but because they are exposed in unfamiliar surroundings, they also become alien. You could say that familiarity is a lure for conveying something new: in order to look at an object more closely, it must be at the same time familiar and unfamiliar. Familiarity provides the starting point.

Heidi Stecker: In your exhibition design, you made frequent references to the bank – the furnishing, the surfaces, the writing, the colours ...

Julia Schäfer: I incorporated a piece of carpet, a piece of structured wallpaper, and office plants in the exhibition. I also made reference to the bank in the colour design and labelling. For example, on the labels you can read where each piece comes from, which room, who works there. For the walls, I only used colours that conform to the bank's regulations. However, it was important to me that I was not simply transferring the rooms of the bank to the exhibition on a 1:1 basis. They were just quotes. They did not only refer to objects, materials or surfaces, but also to the accessibility of the exhibition. Entry was forbidden to some of the rooms. This decision communicates the idea that not everyone is allowed access to these works of art, just as you cannot simply enter the bank building without an appointment. The positioning of our walls in the exhibition also makes allusions to this aspect: you keep walking into dead ends, or sometimes you have to go a long way round. The architecture of the new building is perfectly suited to this type of show. Transparency/lack of transparency is a common theme relating to this building and to the bank.

Heidi Stecker: That is exactly why I find it such a shame that a lot of highly interesting points of discussion were left out in the 'Hans Brosch' project, things that arise from his work and its context. Instead of integrating them in the exhibition, we had to practically find a place for them somewhere else, in the accompanying programme for example.

Ilina Koralova: I also found it rather a pity that the architecture played such a small part. Some people who took part in *Carte Blanche* did not take the architecture of the building into consideration at all. I had the impression they thought: the room is just there, now all I have to do is put the works of art into position. I on the other hand have always devoted a lot of attention to this architecture and its possibilities. I am interested in the interdependency between space and work as an important aspect of an exhibition.

Barbara Steiner: Some of the participants changed their assessment of the situation: in the beginning, the Schmidts couldn't really get to grips with the building, especially the colouring of the walls, I remember that quite clearly. In the preliminary stages I asked them how they wanted the walls, they said: 'The same as always.' For us that means grey. When they arrived to set up the exhibition, they were horrified by the colour, because for them 'The same as always' meant – white. Then we began to hold serious discussions about the architecture and the colouring of the exhibition walls. In the meantime they are thinking of painting their own rooms in Cologne the same shade of grey. So we have begun an interesting discourse on exhibition architecture.

IMAGE

Frank-Heinrich Müller: The artists who participate in a programme like this always name the art institutions in their biographies, and their gallery owners will always refer to them in their advertising material. It appears to me to be far more important to the artists where they exhibit than for the enterprises. It also strikes me that people are quick to bitch about entrepreneurial initiatives like this, but they don't mind using them for their own benefit.

Barbara Steiner: That confirms one of the main criticisms of *Carte Blanche*, namely that the GfZK automatically enhances the status of artistic positions. The interesting thing is that the artists evidently also immediately put it to use themselves, hand in hand with the enterprise so to speak.

Frank Heinrich Müller: But they would never admit it. And when people like this are writing their next CV, they will not hesitate to refer to the book published by Steidl, and then they will list their exhibitions in the GfZK and the Museum of Fine Arts. That is why the commitment of the enterprise must be seen in a much broader sense, instead of reducing it to image politics.

Harald R. Pfab: Why is image-building usually talked about in such a negative way anyway? When I started off in Ravensburg, my public relations work was strongly geared towards art sponsoring. After about two years, the bank went up to second place as far as public awareness was concerned. Although in fact, when it came to the real rating, our bank only actually came fifth. That means that our image was better than our actual economic position. When I left, we had reached second place in every respect. From this you have to conclude that the facts moved in the direction of the image.

Barbara Steiner: That would mean that economic development follows on and catches up with the image?

Harald R. Pfab: Yes, that can be the case. Again and again I have experienced a positive image having an extremely stimulating effect. Reality really can catch up with the image.

Heidi Stecker: ... and a negative image can be hard to get rid of. In *Carte Blanche* I found it highly counterproductive that it was blown up the proportions of a fictive scandal. It arose from hasty judgements being made before the project had even begun. I found it rather a shame that people did not focus on the matter at hand, because the questions asked by the actual project itself are explosive: what is the situation as regards the financing of cultural institutions, especially art institutions? Why are collectors who show their collections in museums praised so highly, whilst museums are despised for hosting them? Why do museums no longer receive the public funding to carry out the normal work of a museum? These are the things the project was actually about, things I find incredibly important, but they were scarcely mentioned in the end. In my opinion, *Carte Blanche* offered the perfect opportunity for public discussions, but nowhere near enough advantage was taken of it. I think for a start, it would have been beneficial if other museums and associations had taken part in our discussions, for example the Museums Association Saxony, for these issues are of urgent interest to them.

Barbara Steiner: Luckily, the end of the last *Carte Blanche* exhibition does not mean the end of public discussions. I am very optimistic that the debates will continue, as these issues really are of the utmost importance.

Index of Exhibitions and Installation Views

(Descriptions from left to right, from top to bottom)

Carte Blanche
GfZK: Friendly Enemies
26.1.–24.3.2008, GfZK-2
Curated by: Andreja Hribernik,
Ilina Koralova, Julia Schäfer,
Barbara Steiner
With works by: Hans Brosch,
Rafał Bujnowski, Martin
Eder, Jakup Ferri, Andreas
Gursky, Christine Hill,
Matthias Hoch, Donald Judd,
Oliver Kossack, Thilo Kühne,
Louise Lawler, Kristina Leko,
Muntean & Rosenblum,
Mark Lombardi, Olaf Nicolai,
Hanno Otten, Jorge Pardo,
Julius Popp, Neo Rauch,
Tobias Rehberger, Hans-
Christian Schink, Rosemarie
Trockel, Matthias Weischer
Exhibition design: Kay
Bachmann, Philipp Paulsen

→ 58/59
From the of Sachsen Bank /
Landesbank Baden-
Württemberg Collection:
Christine Hill, *Service
Slogans*, 2002, poster

→ 60/61
alpha 2000: Rafał Bujnowski,
Negative, 2007, painting; from
the Leon Janucek Collection:
Muntean & Rosenblum,
Untitled, 2005, drawing; from
the Sachsen Bank / Landes-
bank Baden-Württemberg
Collection: Christine Hill,
Service Slogans, 2002, poster;
from the VNG AG Collection:
Thilo Kühne, *Günthersdorf,
Saale Park*, 1996, photograph;
Hans-Christian Schink,
Seehausen bei Leipzig, 1996,
photograph; Matthias Hoch,
Leipzig-Mitte, Lange Straße,
1991, photograph; *Leipzig-
Mitte, Stephanstraße*, 1993,
photograph; *Leipzig-Thonberg,
Leninstraße*, 1991, photograph

→ 62/63
From the Brigitte and Arend
Oetker Collection (Berlin):
Hanno Otten, *Gedichte der
Fakten*, 1992, photograph;
alpha 2000: Rafał Bujnowski,
Negative, 2007, painting; from
the Sachsen Bank / Landes-
bank Baden-Württemberg
Collection: Oliver Kossack,

Chicken Run, 2003, painting;
Dogenhaus Gallery: Julius
Popp, *bit.string*, 2007, object

→ 64/65
Gallery EIGEN+ART: Olaf
Nicolai, *Jedem Ende wohnt ein
Anfang inne*, video; Neo Rauch,
Die Rolle, 1997, painting; from
the Sachsen Bank / Landes-
bank Baden-Württemberg
Collection: Christine Hill,
Service Slogans, 2002, poster;
Oliver Kossack, *Chicken Run*,
2003, painting

Carte Blanche I
alpha 2000: Art Prize
Future of Europe
5.4.–8.6.2008, GfZK-2
Curated by: Ilina Koralova
in collaboration with
Matthias Brühl
With works by: Rafał Bujnowski,
Jakup Ferri, Kristina Leko,
Ioana Nemeş, Kamen Stoyanov
Exhibition design: Kay
Bachmann, Philipp Paulsen

→ 66/67
Jakup Ferri, *Untitled*, 2008,
drawing, installation

→ 68/69
Rafał Bujnowski, *Untitled*,
2005, painting

→ 70/71
Kamen Stoyanov, *From one
place to another*, 2003–2005,
photographs; center: Kamen
Stoyanov, *The small Eiffel
tower meets the big one*, 2007,
video

Carte Blanche II
Leipziger Verlags- und
Druckereigesellschaft:
LVZ-Art Prize + Collection
21.6.–17.8.2008, GfZK-2
Curated by: Andreja Hribernik,
and Barbara Steiner in
collaboration with Bernd
Radestock and Birgit Rebeck
With works by: Claudia
Angelmaier, Wolfram
Ebersbach, Tamara Grcic,
Falk Haberkorn, Jörg Herold,
Via Lewandowsky, Rosa Loy,
Gerald Müller-Simon, Neo
Rauch, Daniel Roth, Yehudit
Sasportas, David Schnell,

Max Schwimmer, Sebastian
Stumpf, Andreas Wachter,
Matthias Weischer
Exhibition design: Kay
Bachmann, Philipp Paulsen

→ 72/73
Conference room in the
Leipziger Volkszeitung
company headquarters;
photo credit: Martin
Klindtworth

→ 74/75
Matthias Weischer, *Sitzgruppe*,
2005, painting; Jörg Herold,
Sachliche Lageplanung I, 1999,
painting, installation; Neo
Rauch, *Start*, 1997, painting;
Die Mauer, 1997, painting

→ 76/77
Tamara Grcic, *Lucy, Avon-
mouth*, 2001, DVD; *Kinder*,
2000, photograph; Via
Lewandowsky, *Schöner
Scheinen (Pumps)*, 1995,
photograph; *Schöner Scheinen
(Stiefel)*, 1995, photograph;
Toter Vogel from the series
Nullserie (Bad Nauheim), 1995,
photograph; *Über den toten
Punkt hinausgeschossen*, 1994,
object

Carte Blanche III
Brigitte and Arend Oetker:
Poems in View of the Facts –
Works from the Brigitte and
Arend Oetker Collection
30.8.–26.10.2008, GfZK-2
Curated by: Brigitte Oetker
and Christiane Schneider in
collaboration with Barbara
Steiner
With works by: Richard
Artschwager, John Baldessari,
Alighiero Boetti, William
Copley, Fischli / Weiss, Dan
Flavin, Ellen Gallagher,
Isa Genzken, Wade Guyton,
Josef Hoffmann, Mike Kelley,
Martin Kippenberger,
Manfred Kuttner, Sol LeWitt,
Vittorio Nobili, Hanno Otten,
Blinky Palermo, Jorge Pardo,
Andreas Schulze, Wolfgang
Tillmans, Rosemarie Trockel,
Franz West
Exhibition design: Brigitte
Oetker, Christiane Schneider

→ 78/79
Andreas Schulze, *Untitled*,
1987, painting; Jorge Pardo,
Untitled, 1995, objects; Mike
Kelley, *Dawning of Sexuality*,
1994, painting; Rosemarie
Trockel, *Plus Minus*, 1987,
object; Josef Hoffmann,
wardrobe cabinet, Wiener
Werkstätte, 1904

→ 80/81
Hanno Otten, *Königgrätz*,
2008, painting; Vittorio
Nobili, *Medea Stuhl*, 1955;
Rosemarie Trockel, *Made
in Western Germany*, 1987,
object; Fischli / Weiss,
Sichtbare Welt, 1997, films;
Richard Artschwager,
Pregunta III, 1994/1983,
object

→ 82/83
Fischli / Weiss, *Mauer*, 1987,
object; Rosemarie Trockel,
Twin 1, 2008, object; Franz
West, *Paßstück*, 1980, object;
Alighiero Boetti, *Udire tra le
Parole*, 1985, object; *Sciogliersi
come Neve al Sole*, 1986, object;
Richard Artschwager, *Untitled
(Book)*, 1985, object; Isa
Genzken, *Weltempfänger*, 1992,
object; Jorge Pardo, *Untitled*,
1996, object; William Copley,
Untitled, undated, object;
Franz West, *Paßstück*, 1980,
object; Alighiero Boetti,
Attirare l'Attenzione, 1985,
object; Martin Kippenberger,
Schreber, 1995, object; Ellen
Gallagher, *Odalisque*, 2005,
object; Franz West, *Paßstück*,
1980, object; *Untitled*, 1997,
object; Fischli / Weiss, *Napf*,
1987, object; Franz West,
Paßstück, 1980, object; Andreas
Schulze, *Untitled*, 1992,
painting

Carte Blanche IV
Dogenhaus Gallery: Mark
Lombardi / Julius Popp
8.11.2008–11.1.2009, GfZK-2
Curated by: Jochen Hempel in
collaboration with Ilina
Koralova and Joe Amrhein
With works by: Mark Lombardi,
Julius Popp
Exhibition design: Dogenhaus
Gallery

→ 84/85
Mark Lombardi, *Neil Bush, Silverado, MDC, Walters and Good*, 1996; *World Finance Corporation and Associates*, ca. 1970–1984; *Miami, Ajman, and Bogota-Caracas (Brigada 2506: Cuban Anti-Castro Bay of Pigs Veteran)*, 1999; *Narrative Structures*, 1990–2000; drawings

→ 86/87
Julius Popp, *micro.spheres*, undated, objects; background: Julius Popp, *micro.perpendiculars*, 2005–2008, objects

→ 88/89
Julius Popp, *bit.fall*, 2001–2005, object

Carte Blanche V
Leon Janucek:
Dieter Finke – Works
24.1.–22.3.2009, GfZK-2
Curated by: Barbara Steiner in collaboration with Leon Janucek and Dieter Finke
With works by: Dieter Finke
Exhibition design: Kay Bachmann, Philipp Paulsen

→ 90/91
Dieter Finke, *Untitled (Crow)*, undated, sculpture; background: *Untitled*, undated, sculptures

→ 92/93
Dieter Finke, *Untitled (Eagle)*, 2008, sculpture; *Falke*, 2007, sculpture; *Passage*, 1987, painting; *Untitled (Tiger's head)*, 2008, sculpture; *Untitled (Owl tree)*, 2008, sculpture

→ 94/95
Dieter Finke, *Strange Rain*, 1989/99, painting; *Untitled (Eagle)*, 1994, sculpture; *Untitled*, 2007, painting; *Fliegender Pelikan*, 2008, sculpture; *Black Lotus*, 2008, painting; *Untitled (Raven)*, 1999, sculpture; *Amazonas (Triptych)*, 2007, painting

Carte Blanche VI
VNG – Verbundnetz Gas AG:
EAST – for the record
The art collection of the VNG – Verbundnetz Gas AG
4.4.–7.6.2009, GfZK-2
Curated by: Frank-Heinrich Müller and Christine Rink in collaboration with Barbara Steiner and Ilina Koralova
Photographic collection: Ursula Arnold, Tina Bara, Max

Baumann, Sibylle Bergemann, Bernd Borchardt, Johannes Bruns, Karel Cudlin, Ursula Edelmann, Margit Emmrich, Arno Fischer, Gundula Friese, Gerhard Gäbler, Frank Gaudlitz, Sighard Gille, Konstanze Göbel, Willy Gursky, Ingrid Hartmetz, Matthias Hoch, Jürgen Hohmuth, Claudia Jeczawitz, Wolfgang Kil, André Kirchner, Harald Kirschner, Barbara Klemm, Thilo Kühne, Hansgert Lambers, Karl-Ludwig Lange, Dieter Leistner, Eva Leitolf, Werner Lieberknecht, Wiebke Loeper, Ute Mahler, Werner Mahler, Eva Mahn, Maix Mayer, Frank-Heinrich Müller, Günter Heinrich Müller, Peter Oehlmann, Dietrich Oltmanns, Helga Paris, Zayd Robert Paris, Manfred Paul, Ludwig Rauch, Timm Rautert, Joachim Richau, Evelyn Richter, Jens Rötzsch, Michael Ruetz, Michael Rutschky, Merit Schambach, Rudolf Schäfer, Michael Scheffer, Hans-Christian Schink, Regina Schmeken, Michael Schroedter, Erasmus Schröter, Ursula Schulz-Dornburg, Sigrid Schütze-Rodemann, Alfred Seiland, Kathrin Senf, Klaus Staeck, Günter Starke, Thomas Steinert, Helfried Strauss, Anett Stuth, Ines Thate-Keler, Peter Thieme, Camilo José Vergara, Wolf-Dieter Volkmann, Gerhard Weber, Wim Wenders, Marion Wenzel, Karin Wieckhorst, Thomas Wiegand, Thomas Wolf, Ulrich Wüst, Renate Zeun
Painting/drawing collection: Harald Alff, Gerhard Altenbourg, Nicolai Angelov, Christiane Baumgartner, Wolfgang E. Biedermann, Roland Borchers, Peter Busch, Jan Dörre, Ulrike Dornis, Hartwig Ebersbach, Wolfram Ebersbach, Tim Eitel, Jörg Ernert, Tom Fabritius, Peter Graf, Henriette Grahnert, Jens Hanke, Katrin Heichel, Madeleine Heublein, Hirschvogel, Friederike Jokisch, Petra Kasten, Oliver Kossack, Axel Krause, Michael Kunert, Tobias Lehner, Rosa Loy, Wilhelm Müller, Julia Müntz, Olaf Nicolai, Heide Nord, Akos Novaky, Petra Ottkowski, Gudrun Petersdorff, Jochen Plogsties, Ulf Puder, Neo Rauch, Arno Rink, Claudia Rössger, Sebastian Rug,

Thomas Scheibitz, David Schnell, Annette Schröter, Werner Tübke, Miriam Vlaming, Matthias Weischer
Exhibition design: Kay Bachmann, Markus Dreßen, Philipp Paulsen

→ 96/97
Maix Mayer, *Leipzig, Gabi hochschwanger im Wackerbad*, 1989; Margit Emmrich, *Bräuningshof bei Erlangen, Schülertreffen*, 1989; Frank-Heinrich Müller, *Magdeburg, auf der Pferderennbahn am Herrenkrug*, 1989; Margit Emmrich, *Bräuningshof bei Erlangen, Lachs-Essen*, 1989; background: Eva Leitolf, *München, Martin*, from the series *Tanzlokalportraits*, 1989; Eva Mahn, *Halle/Saale, Universitätsplatz*, 1989; Thomas Wolf, *Leipzig, Geburtstagsgäste*, 1989; Ludwig Rauch, *Berlin, Mauer am Brandenburger Tor, wenige Minuten vor der Maueröffnung*, 1989; Barbara Klemm, *Berlin, Die Mauer ist offen*, 1989; *Berlin, Mädchen auf der Mauer*, 1989; Peter Thieme, *Berlin, Stadtrundfahrt*, 1989; Helfried Strauß, *Leipzig, Eröffnung der Ausstellung „Zeitzeichen" im Museum der Bildenden Künste*, 1989; Regina Schmeken, *Berlin*, 1989; Gerhard Gäbler, *Berlin, Selbstportrait an der Mauer*, 1989; Max Baumann, *Werben (Elbe)*, 1989; Frank-Heinrich Müller, *Schwarzholz bei Stendal, Kappenfest, Freude herrscht*, 1989; Hansgert Lambers, *Berlin, Schönhauser Allee, Ecke Metzer Straße*, 1989; Eva Mahn, *Berlin, Wiedersehen*, 1989; Günter Heinrich Müller, *Ebendorf bei Magdeburg, BAB 2*, 1989; Max Baumann/Thomas Wolf, *Schwarzholz bei Stendal, Kappenfest*, 1989; Klaus Staeck, *Leipzig, Schmalzkuchenbäckerei*, 1989; Karl-Ludwig Lange, *Berlin, Potsdamer Platz*, 1989; Frank Gaudlitz, *Potsdam*, 1989; Regina Schmeken, *Berlin, Potsdamer Platz*, 1989; Renate Zeun, *Berlin, Die Leiter*, 1989; Manfred Paul, *Berlin, Eberswalder Straße/Oderberger Straße 15:00 Uhr*, 1989; Rudolf Schäfer, *Berlin, U-Bahn-Station Potsdamer Platz, Schwarzer Staub*, 1989; Timm Rautert, *Berlin, Das Loch in der Welt*, 1989; Michael Rutschky, *Berlin Alexanderplatz, Als käme tatsächlich ein neuer Tag*, 1989; Michael Rutschky, *Zwönitz,*

Dort schaut es aus wie in meiner Kindheit, 1989; Karin Wieckhorst, *Axel Krause und Neo Rauch im D-Zug nach Essen*, 1989; Eva Leitolf, *München, Petra*, aus der Serie *Tanzlokalportaits*, 1989; Michael Rutschky, *Erzgebirge, Hierher kommt die Geschichte nie*, 1989; Frank-Heinrich Müller, *Leipzig, auf der Pferderennbahn im Scheibenholz*, 1989; photographs

→ 98/99
Thomas Wolf, *Berlin, am Gleisdreieck*, 1990, photograph; Alfred Seiland, *Mödlareuth (Thüringen)*, 1990, photograph; Arno Fischer, *Berlin, Silvester am Brandenburger Tor*, 1989 photograph; Kathrin Senf, *Sassnitz, Fährhafen*, 1989, photograph; Peter Busch, *Im Park*, 2007, painting; Madeleine Heublein, *Bündel*, 1997, drawing; David Schnell, *Untitled*, 1999, painting; Thomas Scheibitz, *Untitled*, 1996, painting; Matthias Weischer, *Industrielandschaft*, 1999, painting; Christiane Baumgartner, *Schattentanz*, 1995, painting; Tim Eitel, *Fenster*, 1999, collage; *Ladung*, 1999, collage; *Ambiente*, 1999, collage; Hirschvogel, *Untitled*, 1998, drawing; Sebastian Rug, *Untitled*, 2005, drawing; Wolfram Ebersbach, *S-Bahnbrücke, Berlin*, 1988, painting; *Pont Royal, Paris*, 1990, painting; *Queensboro Bridge*, 1997, painting; Gerhard Altenbourg, *Ariadne*, 1973, objects; Julia Müntz, *Untitled*, 1999, drawing; *Voodoo II*, 1998, drawing; Jochen Plogsties, *Amore*, 2008, painting

→ 100/101
Ulrike Dornis, *Underground*, 1999, painting; *Gasometer*, 1999, from the series *Konstruktion*, painting; *Couple*, 1999, from the series *Konstruktion*, painting; Tobias Lehner, *Untitled*, 2005, painting; Wilhelm Müller, *Untitled*, 1992, drawing; *Untitled*, 1990, drawing; Petra Ottkowski, *Quadrate I*, 2001, painting; *Quadrate II*, 2001, painting; Akos Novaky, *Konstellation O*, 1998, drawing; Werner Lieberknecht, *Dresden, Portrait im Atelier: Manfred aus Amsterdam, Deborah aus London, Rob aus London, Eva aus Westberlin*, 1989 photographs;

Dietrich Oltmanns, *Leipzig, Eingang Staatsbank der DDR, Geldtauscher / Glücksritter*, 1989, photograph

**Carte Blanche VII
Gallery EIGEN+ART:
New York – Basel –
Berlin – London – Miami**
20.6.–16.8.2009, GfZK-2
Curated by: Julia Schäfer
in collaboration with the
EIGEN+ART team
With works by: Ákos Birkás,
Birgit Brenner, Carmen Brucic,
Martin Eder, Tim Eitel, Nina
Fischer & Maroan el Sani,
Stella Hamberg, Jörg Herold,
Christine Hill, Uwe Kowski,
Rémy Markowitsch, Maix
Mayer, Carsten Nicolai, Olaf
Nicolai, Neo Rauch, Ricarda
Roggan, Yehudit Sasportas,
David Schnell, Annelies Štrba,
Matthias Weischer
Exhibition design: Kristina
Brusa

→ **102 / 103**
Martin Eder, from the series
Les Nus, 2006–2008, photo-
graphs; Carmen Brucic, from
the series *Symmetrien des
Abschieds*, 2008, photographs

→ **104 / 105**
Jörg Herold, *Der Dokumentar-
archäologe im Land der beschleu-
nigten Folklore*, 2009, painting
(detail)

→ **106 / 107**
Fair booth *Miami*

**Carte Blanche VIII
Doris and Klaus F. K.
Schmidt: Listen to Your Eyes.
Works from the Schmidt-
Drenhaus Collection**
29.08.–25.10.2009, GfZK-2
Curated by: Doris and Klaus
F.K. Schmidt in collaboration
with Barbara Steiner and
Johannes Schmidt
With works by: Markus
Draper, Eckehard Fuchs,
Kerstin Gommlich, Beate
Gütschow, Eberhard
Havekost, Olaf Holzapfel,
Karl Horst Hödicke,
Benjamin Katz, Astrid Klein,
Bernd Koberling, Werner
Lieberknecht, Maurizio
Nannucci, Blinky Palermo,
Angelika Platen, Nina
Pohl, Thomas Ruff, Thomas
Scheibitz, Lutz Fritsch,
Thomas Schütte, Cindy
Sherman, Rosemarie Trockel
Exhibition design: Kay
Bachmann, Philipp Paulsen

→ **108 / 109**
Rosemarie Trockel, *Untitled
(The Face)*, 1998, object; *Out of
the Kitchen, into the Fire*, 1993,
video; *Zerstörte Küche*, undated,
photograph; *Ei*, 1993, object;
*Prototyp für ein Hühnerhaus
für 3–5 Hühner*, 1993/2009 ,
installation (reconstruction
based on the original design)

→ **110 / 111**
Thomas Scheibitz, *Schriftbild*,
2000, painting; *Buchstabe
(One)*, 2005, object; Blinky
Palermo, *Untitled*, 1968, litho-
graph; Markus Draper, *urban
halloween 2*, 1999, painting

→ **112 / 113**
Bernd Koberling, *Kaitum –
Kalixälv III (Schneefeld)*, 1969,
painting; *Steinbach*, 1972,
painting; Nina Pohl, *Untitled
(The longer the better)*, 2004;
Untitled, 2004; *Untitled (falling
water)*, 2004, photographs

**Carte Blanche IX
Sachsen Bank: Playing
to a Home Crowd.
Art in the Sachsen Bank /
Landesbank Baden-
Württemberg Collection**
7.11.2009–17.1.2010, GfZK-2
Curated by: Julia Schäfer
With works by: Tilo
Baumgärtel, Christiane
Baumgartner, Peter Busch,
Tim Eitel, Henriette
Grahnert, Christine Hill,
Christian Jankowski,
Matthias Kanter, Martin
Kippenberger, Uwe Kowski,
Susanne Kühn, Thomas
Locher, Michel Majerus,
Rémy Markowitsch, Olaf
Nicolai, Neo Rauch, Evelyn
Richter, Ricarda Roggan,
Christoph Ruckhäberle,
Andreas Slominski, Julia
Schmidt, David Schnell,
Annette Schröter, Wolfgang
Tillmans, Albrecht Tübke,
Matthias Weischer, Peter
Zimmermann
Exhibition design: Anna Lena
von Helldorff

→ **114 / 115**
Christian Jankowski, *Kunst-
markt TV*, 2008, DVD; Christine
Hill, *Service Slogans*, 2002,
poster; Christoph Ruckhäberle,
Die Rast, 2002, painting

→ **116 / 117**
Executive board meeting of
Sachsen Bank; Tim Eitel,
Sailor Moon / Chibi, 2000/2001,
painting

→ **118 / 119**
Neo Rauch, *Mittag*, 1997,
painting; Susanne Kühn,
Blick, 2002, painting; David
Schnell, *Kleine Hochbahn*,
2001, painting; *Mai*, 2001,
painting

**Carte Blanche X
The Hans Brosch Circle of
Friends: Hans Brosch**
23.1.–5.4.2010, GfZK-1
Curated by: Carsten Probst
and Heidi Stecker
With works by: Hans Brosch
Exhibition design: Kay
Bachmann, Philipp Paulsen

→ **120 / 121**
Entrance; Hans Brosch, *Aero-
plane IV* and *V*, 1978, drawing;
background: *Cheyenne*, 2005/
2006, painting

→ **122 / 123**
Hans Brosch, *Airport*,
1978/1979, painting; *Kleine
Barrikade*, 1983, painting;
Sonnensegel, 1974, painting;
Nina, 1996, painting;
Brandschatz, 1977, painting

→ **124 / 125**
Hans Brosch, *Sommerregen II*,
1987, painting; *Szene*, 1986,
painting; *Pique König*, 1986,
painting

**Carte Blanche XI
Vivien and Horst Schmitter:
'Cancelled'**
23.1.–21.3.2010, GfZK-2

→ **126 / 127**
Closed GfZK-2

→ **128 / 129**
Guided tour with Julia Kurz
(mediation team) through the
empty GfZK-2 building

Colophon

General Editor
Barbara Steiner

Text
Corruption, Corruptibility
and Complicity; *Carte
Blanche* – Preconditions –
Realisation – Responses –
Consequences and
Perspectives: Barbara Steiner
The interview with Matthias
Brühl, Dieter Finke, Jochen
Hempel, Andreja Hribernik,
Leon Janucek, Ilina Koralova,
Achim König, Gerd Harry
Lybke, Frank-Heinrich Müller,
Brigitte and Arend Oetker,
Harald R. Pfab, Bernd
Radestock, Birgit Rebeck,
Christine Rink, Julia Schäfer,
Dietmar Schulz, Doris and
Klaus F.K. Schmidt, Heidi
Stecker, Gerhardt Wolff is a
synopsis of interviews which
are printed in full in the
German edition of this
book, entitled 'Das eroberte
Museum', edited by Barbara
Steiner.

Press and picture editing
Heidi Stecker

Picture editing assistants
Paul Mellenthin, Ulrike Riebel

Translation
Corruption, Corruptibility
and Complicity; *Carte
Blanche* – Preconditions –
Realisation – Responses –
Consequences and
Perspectives: Oliver Kossack;
Interview and biographies
of the partners and curators
involved in the *Carte Blanche*
project: Louise Bromby

Proofreading
Inez Templeton

Design
Kay Bachmann, Markus
Dreßen, Philipp Paulsen

Image processing
Carsten Humme, Leipzig;
Scan Color Leipzig

Typeset in
Theinhart, Optimo;
Lexicon, TEFF

Paper
Munken Lynx Rough,
100 g/m²; BVS gloss, 135 g/m²

Overall production
DZA Druckerei zu Altenburg
GmbH

Photographers
GfZK: p. 36; Andreas Enrico
Grunert, Berlin: p. 39 above,
41 below, 42 below, 58–83,
90–5, 108–13, 120–7; Andreja
Hribernik, Ljubljana: p. 37
above, 41 above; Frank-
Heinrich Müller, Leipzig:
p. 39 below, 96–101; Edina
Nagy, Budapest: p. 31,
35 above, 37 below; Nino
Palavandishvili, Tiflis: p. 44,
128–9; Hendrik Pupat,
Leipzig: p. 35 below; Reinhard
Saczewski, Berlin: p. 42
above; Joanna Sokolowska,
Lódź: p. 38 above, 40 above,
40 below, 43, 106–7; Julia
Schäfer, Leipzig: pp. 114–19;
Wolfgang Thaler, Wien:
cover; Uwe Walter, Berlin:
pp. 84–9, 102–5; Gerald
Wesolowski, Berlin: p. 38
below

Picture and photo credits
Gerhard Altenbourg,
Claudia Angelmaier, Richard
Artschwager, Max Baumann,
Christiane Baumgartner,
Joseph Beuys, Ákos Birkás,
Alighiero Boetti, Roland
Borchers, Birgit Brenner,
Jan Dörre, Hartwig Ebersbach,
Wolfram Ebersbach, Martin
Eder, Tim Eitel, Arno Fischer,
Nina Fischer, Dan Flavin,
Lutz Fritsch, Sighard
Gille, Andreas Gursky, Beate
Gütschow, Jörg Herold,
Christine Hill, Matthias Hoch,
Donald Judd, Matthias
Kanter, Benjamin Katz, Uwe
Kowski, Axel Krause, Susanne
Kühn, Michael Kunert,
Eva Leitolf, Via Lewandowsky,
Thomas Locher, Rosa Loy,
Wilhelm Müller, Julia Müntz,
Carsten Nicolai, Olaf Nicolai,
Blinky Palermo, Gudrun
Petersdorff, Jochen Plogsties,
Ulf Puder, Neo Rauch, Ricarda
Roggan, Thomas Ruff,
Maroan el Sani, Thomas
Scheibitz, Julia Schmidt,
David Schnell, Annette
Schröter, Andreas Schulze,
Thomas Schütter, Max
Schwimmer, Klaus Staeck,
Rosemarie Trockel, Werner
Tübke, Matthias Weischer,
Peter Zimmermann VG
BILD-KUNST Bonn, 2010
pp. 84–9 all works courtesy
Dogenhaus Galerie Leipzig;
pp. 102–5 all works courtesy
Galerie EIGEN+ART
Leipzig/Berlin

© 2011 GfZK, authors

Supported by the Ministry for
Science and the Arts in Saxony
and by the Friends of the
Museum of Contemporary
Art Leipzig.

JOVIS Verlag GmbH
Kurfürstenstraße 15/16
10785 Berlin
jovis@jovis.de

ISBN: 978-3-86859-059-3